# PRAISE FOR THIS REMARKABLE BOOK!

"We were fortunate to work with Sam on a number of projects, from *the Elders* to the *B Team* and many more working with Richard Branson and a collection of leaders.  Sam is one of the best facilitators we've seen.  He is able to bring together a diverse group of characters and masterfully guide them on a journey to help them open themselves towards a common understanding and solid outcomes.  This book is a great insight into his unique skill set and wonderful leadership."

—Jean Oelwang, CEO Virgin Unite/Group Partner

"A wonderful book, and Sarah Fisk is an amazing facilitator.  As Board President I've learned so many skills for putting participatory values into practice.  I'm looking forward to our Board continuing to benefit from Sarah's consultation.  The *Facilitator's Guide* ought to be a resource to public service organizations everywhere."

—Deane Marchbein, President of the Board of Directors, Medecins Sans Frontieres (Doctors Without Borders)

"NCDD has long listed the *Facilitator's Guide* as one of the best-of-the-best resources for practitioners, and the field of public engagement has been deeply influenced by this seminal book.  The tools and concepts it presents are foundational for any group process facilitator, and I highly recommend adding the new edition to your bookshelf!"

—Sandy Heierbacher, Director and co-founder, National Coalition of Dialogue and Deliberation (NCDD)

"It was a revelation to find the *Facilitator's Guide* and realize someone had written down demonstrably the way our organization was already working organically.  Kaner and Fisk are masters of their craft.  Working with them and using this book has allowed us to put a translatable, trainable framework around what we do.  This has had a large impact and has helped us build our own capacity.  I highly recommend this book and working with Sam and Sarah."

—Harley K. Dubois, founder, Burning Man Project

i

"The *Facilitator's Guide* has been an incomparable resource for designing and leading more effective social architecture to get work done across diverse teams, functions and regions in my complex organization. The lessons and guidance I've taken from it have been nothing short of transformative for both my practice and my career."

—D. Wade Shows,
Director of Learning & Organizational Effectiveness,
Kaiser Permanente

"Sam Kaner is one of the world's leading experts on collaboration. His grasp of the challenges and dilemmas of collaboration is superb, as are his models and methods for facilitating complex processes. The second edition of this widely-used book reflects his accumulated wisdom and teachings. Clearly written and wonderfully illustrated, this book makes difficult issues understandable and provides sound, practical guidance."

—Sandy Schuman, editor, *Creating a Culture of Collaboration,* and founding editor, *Group Facilitation: A Research & Applications Journal*

"Our organization was founded to bring diverse partners together to work collaboratively to find solutions to difficult social problems. We know how immensely challenging it is to facilitate dialogue among multiple stakeholders. This amazing book is a comprehensive guide for meeting that challenge. I've worked with a myriad of consultants during the past 24 years, and Sam Kaner's approach is vastly superior for bringing about lasting system change."

—Kriss Deiglmeier, CEO, Tides Network

"In cross-functional environments, where diverse perspectives are intentionally brought together to produce high-quality thinking, a highly skilled facilitator can add great value – and Sam Kaner is one of the best. The *Facilitator's Guide* provides a full set of models and tools to enable an organization to reap the benefits of a well facilitated, participatory decision-making process. Having seen Sam's methods in action, I can attest to their power and effectiveness."

—Pierre Omidyar, founder and Chairman, eBay and Omidyar Network

*"Facilitator's Guide to Participatory Decision-Making* is an outstanding resource for tackling complex community and business challenges. We have used it both at the City of Denver and at the State of Colorado, for strategic planning in our nationally recognized child welfare programs and in our innovative programs to end homelessness. I keep a copy on my desk for easy reference."

—Roxane White, Chief of Staff for Governor John Hickenlooper, State Capitol, Denver Colorado

"At Stanford University I convene an annual conference attended by hundreds of non-profit leaders. Sam Kaner's keynote presentations, based on material from this book, are consistently top-rated and likely to inspire significant organizational change."

—Regina Starr Ridley, Publishing Director, *Stanford Social Innovation Review*

"Working with Sam Kaner has been one of the most useful and rewarding experiences of my years as a manager and leader. He brings precision, clarity, imagination, good humor and a humane touch to the challenges we who aspire to guide organizations face. Using the tools and skills he describes in this book, Sam shaped 40 independent-minded and strong-willed faculty into a thoughtful, engaged and strategically-oriented group. If you can't have Sam in person, I strongly recommend keeping a copy of *Facilitator's Guide* on hand."

—Edward Wasserman, Dean, Graduate School of Journalism, University of California, Berkeley

"As a leader of a firm involved with the governance and strategic oversight of multi-billion dollar organizations and portfolios, we find the principles and techniques in this book incredibly valuable in advancing the thinking of executive teams and boards. It has a direct effect on the impact our organizations have. Leaders and managers of any organization can benefit from the wisdom and pragmatic advice which this book delivers so effectively."

—Mike Mohr, founder and CEO, Comprehensive Financial Management LLC

"In my opinion, *Facilitator's Guide to Participatory Decision-Making* is the best book on collaboration ever written. I say this as someone who has been a CEO or executive director for more than 20 years. During that time I have worked with countless facilitators and organization development consultants. For depth of impact and overall effectiveness, Sam Kaner and his colleagues are top-of-the-line. This book is loaded with the tools and guiding principles that make Sam's work so compelling."

—Diane Flannery, founding CEO, Juma Ventures, and director, Global Center for Children and Families, UCLA, Semel Institute

"Sam Kaner and his team have helped me create a culture of collaboration in science. This is no easy task! Twenty-five years ago I started with nothing. Now my organization has the potential to make a large impact by discovering causes of the most devastating diseases that affect children. Sam's superb skills in strategic thinking and group facilitation, and his deep expertise in organization design and systems change have been essential for our success. In *Facilitator's Guide to Participatory Decision-Making*, Sam and his team translate their own learnings from many different kinds of work environments into concrete techniques that will benefit business, government and non-profits alike."

— John Harris, MD,
founder and CEO, California Birth Defects Monitoring Program, California Department of Health Services

"*Facilitator's Guide* gives readers tools and insights to enable effective participatory action and the potential to achieve strong principled results and positive social change."

—Michael Doyle, author, *How to Make Meetings Work*

"I am a longtime client and colleague of *Community At Work*. They are extraordinarily talented at facilitating effective teams and teaching others to do the same. Their consulting approach creates lasting solutions by promoting organizational health through collaborative working relationships. *Facilitator's Guide* reveals and explains many of their most compelling methods and practices."

—Ed Pierce, founder and CEO, Leadership Quality Inc.

"*Facilitator's Guide* takes the mystery and fear out of facilitating groups and provides useful tools for anyone working with groups. The materials are clear. The graphics are first rate. And complex issues are developed logically and with great care."

—Thomas Broitman, managing director,
Executive Education, PricewaterhouseCoopers, LLP


"This book is a must for anyone working with a team! It is loaded with new information, which will make your team facilitation and decision-making even better. It highlights key concepts underlying group process that are rarely defined in such a clear manner. And, at the same time, it provides easy-to-follow facilitation techniques to ensure group participation and convergence around decisions and ideas. This is a book that rarely stays on my shelf – I'm too busy using it as a reference. Truly a golden nugget in the vast pool of facilitation knowledge!"

—Tammy Adams, author, *Facilitating the Project Lifecycle*


"What a practical, sensible guide for helping groups work together in a realistic way! The graphics help you visualize how to manage many common – and puzzling – aspects of group behavior."

—Marvin Weisbord, consultant and author, *Productive Workplaces* and co-author, *Discovering Common Ground* and *Future Search*


"Marshall Medical Center is community based, and we have always valued a culture of participation. We frequently make inclusive decisions allowing buy-in to difficult actions we need to take as an organization. Using *Facilitator's Guide to Participatory Decision-Making* and working with Sarah Fisk has helped us to maintain and even increase participation while still making timely decisions. Rather than simply relying on Sarah, who is a true genius at facilitation, this book has allowed us to build our own capacity. We've learned how to convene multiple stakeholder teams, plan effectively, and make more sustainable decisions, thus maintaining our collaborative values as we grow to serve a wider community. I highly recommend this book."

—James Whipple, CEO,
Marshall Medical Center, El Dorado County, California

Dmitry Lazarev
President
*Facilitation Institute*
Moscow
**Russia**

Jackie Chang
Director 2009-2013
*Asia Region*
*International Association*
*of Facilitators*
Taipei
**Taiwan**

M. Bhakthar Vali Sab
Associate COO
*WASSAN*
*Watershed Support Services*
*and Activities Network*
Hyderabad
**India**

Robbie Alm
President
*Collaborative Leaders*
*Network*
Honolulu
**Hawaii**

Maureen Jenkins
Chair 2003 – 2006
*International Association*
*of Facilitators*
Chair 2008 – 2011
**IAF Netherlands**

Dr. Ed Rege
Process Leader
*PICOTEAM EA*
*Institute for People,*
*Innovation and Change*
*in Organisations*
Nairobi
**Kenya**

David Van Eyck
Training and
Capacity Building
*IWMI*
*International Water*
*Management Institute*
Colombo
**Sri Lanka**

"*This book
has had a profound impact
on the practice of facilitation
around the world.
I encourage my colleagues
to read it, study it,
and use it in their work.*"

Michael Walsh
Director 2014-2015
*Oceania Region*
*International Association*
*of Facilitators*
Melbourne
**Australia**

Xavier Estivill
Founder, Partner
and Senior Director
*MOMENTUM*
Barcelona
**Spain**

Beatrice Briggs
Director
*IIFAC*
*International Institute for*
*Facilitation and Change*
Cuernevaca
**Mexico**

Dale Hunter
Author
*The Art of Facilitation:*
*The essentials for*
*leading great meetings*
*and creating group synergy*
**New Zealand**

# Facilitator's Guide to Participatory Decision-Making

## Third Edition

**Sam Kaner**
*with*
**Lenny Lind, Catherine Toldi,
Sarah Fisk, and Duane Berger**

Foreword by Michael Doyle

**JB JOSSEY-BASS**™
A Wiley Brand

Cover design by Wiley

Cover illustration by Karen Kerney

Book design by Sam Kaner, Duane Berger, and Lenny Lind

Published by Jossey-Bass
A Wiley Brand
One Montgomery Street, Suite 1200, San Francisco, CA 94104-4594—www.josseybass.com

Jossey-Bass books and products are available through most bookstores. To contact Jossey-Bass directly call our Customer Care Department within the U.S. at 800-956-7739, outside the U.S. at 317-572-3986, or fax 317-572-4002.

Wiley publishes in a variety of print and electronic formats and by print-on-demand. Some material included with standard print versions of this book may not be included in e-books or in print-on-demand. If this book refers to media such as a CD or DVD that is not included in the version you purchased, you may download this material at **http://booksupport.wiley.com**. For more information about Wiley products, visit **www.wiley.com**.

**Library of Congress Cataloging-in-Publication data is on file.**

ISBN: 978-1-1184-0495-9

Printed in the United States of America

THIRD EDITION

*PB Printing*     10  9  8  7  6  5  4  3  2  1

# THE JOSSEY-BASS

# BUSINESS & MANAGEMENT SERIES

# DEDICATION

This book is dedicated to Michael Doyle and David Straus,

who found the language, the distinctions, and the methods
to bring inclusive, participatory values into the mainstream
of American management practices

and who, through their own continuing efforts and those of
their students and grandstudents and great-grandstudents,
may yet inspire humanity to use collaborative technology
for finding sustainable, nonviolent solutions to the world's
toughest problems.

# CONTENTS

# CONTENTS, page 2

I see group facilitation as a whole constellation of ingredients: a deep belief in the wisdom and creativity of people; a search for synergy and overlapping goals; the ability to listen openly and actively; a working knowledge of group dynamics; a deep belief in the inherent power of groups and teams; a respect for individuals and their points of view; patience and a high tolerance for ambiguity to let a decision evolve and gel; strong interpersonal and collaborative problem-solving skills; an understanding of thinking processes; and a flexible versus a lock-step approach to resolving issues and making decisions.

Facilitative behaviors and skills are essential for anyone who wants to work collaboratively in groups and organizations. Facilitative skills honor, enhance, and focus the wisdom and knowledge that lay dormant in most groups. These skills are essential to healthy organizations, esprit de corps, fair and lasting agreements, and to easily implement actions and plans.

Sam Kaner and the team from *Community At Work* have been developing and articulating these tools to further democratic action and to enable people from all walks of life to work together in more constructive and productive ways. The *Facilitator's Guide to Participatory Decision-Making* will give readers additional tools and insights to enable effective, participatory action and the potential to achieve strong, principled results and positive social change. Anyone wanting to increase their understanding of group dynamics and improve their skill at making groups work more effectively will benefit from this valuable book.

### The Purpose of Group Facilitation

Those who work with and lead organizations today have learned two lasting lessons in the last 25 years of concerted action research in this field of organization development and change. Lesson one: if people don't participate in and "own" the solution to the problems or agree to the decision, implementation will be half-hearted at best, probably misunderstood, and, more likely than not, will fail.

The second lesson is that the key differentiating factor in the success of an organization is not just the products and services, not just its technology or market share, but the organization's ability to elicit, harness, and focus the vast intellectual capital and goodwill resident in their members, employees, and stakeholders. When that intellectual capital and goodwill get energized and focused, the organization becomes a powerful force for positive change in today's business and societal environments. Applying these two lessons has become a key element of what we have begun to think of as *the learning organization.*

How do leaders and their organizations apply these two lessons? By creating psychologically safe and involving group environments where people can identify and solve problems, plan together, make collaborative decisions, resolve their own conflicts, trouble-shoot, and self-manage as responsible adults. Facilitation enables the organization's teams, groups and meetings to be much more productive. And the side benefits of facilitated or self-facilitated groups are terrific: a sense of empowerment, a deepening of personal commitment to decisions and plans, increased organizational loyalty, and the building of esprit de corps.

Nowhere are these two lessons put more into practice than in groups. The world meets a lot. The statistics are staggering. There are over 25 million meetings every day in the United States and over 85 million worldwide. Making both our work groups and civic groups work much more effectively is a lifelong challenge as rich as the personalities that people them. Thus, what I call "group literacy" – an awareness of and strong skills in group dynamics, meeting facilitation and consensus building tools like the ones in this book – is essential to increasing the effectiveness of group meetings. They enable groups to work smarter, harder, deeper, and faster. These tools help build healthier groups, organizations, and communities.

Facilitative mind-sets, behaviors, and tools are some of the essential ingredients of high-commitment/high-performance organizations. They are critical to making real what we've come to think of as *the learning organization.* These skills and behaviors are aligned with people's higher selves. People naturally want to learn them in order to increase their own personal effectiveness in groups and in their families as well as to increase the effectiveness of groups themselves.

## A Partial History of Group Facilitation

The concept of facilitation and facilitators is as old as the tribes. Alaskan natives report of this kind of role in ancient times. As a society we're starting to come full circle – from the circle of the tribe around the fire, to the pyramidal structures of the last 3,000 years, back to the ecology of the circle, flat pyramids, and networks of today's organizations. The philosophy, mind-set, and skills of facilitation have much in common with the approaches used by Quakers, Gandhi, Martin Luther King, Jr., and people in nonviolence movements over the centuries. More recently these include the civil rights movement, women's consciousness-raising groups, some parts of the environmental movement, and citizen involvement groups that started in the 1960s and 1970s.

Meeting facilitation started to appear as a formal process in the late 1960s and early 1970s and had become widespread by the late 1980s. Its proponents advocated it as a tool to assist people to become the architects of their own future. It evolved from the role of *learning facilitators* that emerged in the early 1960s. In learning or encounter groups, the facilitator's focus was on building awareness and enabling learning. These *learning/ awareness facilitators* played key roles in the nascent human potential movement and the women's consciousness-raising movement and continue to do so in today's version of lifelong learning situations where learning is seen as a dialogue rather than a rote process. Its pragmatic roots also include cognitive science, information processing theory, sociology, psychology, community organizing, arbitration and mediation principles, and experience.

Task-oriented group facilitation evolved out of the societal milieu of the last thirty years, especially in industrial and information-rich societies where time is a key factor. We needed to find methods for people to work together more effectively. Quality circle groups, cross-functional task forces, and civic groups were the early big users and advocates of this methodology. Facilitation was an informal, flexible alternative to the constricting format of parliamentary procedure and *Robert's Rules of Order*. Group facilitation was also an approach that was proactive, solving conflicts before they arose, as well as one that could handle multiple constituencies. It was a viable alternative to mediation-style approaches. Once participants in a learning group or consciousness-raising group raised their awareness, they wanted to take action. There was an expressed need to put their new insights and knowledge to work – to take actions, solve problems, plan, and make group decisions. Thus the role of the task-oriented facilitator evolved to serve these needs as well as the new approaches to organizational change and renewal that were developing in the early 1970s.

As two of the cofounders of meeting facilitation, David Straus and I were interested in giving people tools to architect their own more powerful futures. That meant giving them frameworks and tools to make the groups they worked and lived with much more effective, powerful, and productive. We saw group facilitation as both a social contract and a new, content neutral role – a more formalized third party role in groups. We articulated the difference and power between "content" and "process" neutrality. Content neutrality means not taking a position on the issues at hand; not having a position or a stake in the outcome. Process neutrality means not advocating for certain kinds of processes such as brainstorming. We found that the power in the role of the facilitator was in becoming content neutral and a process advocate – advocating for fair, inclusive, and open processes that would balance participation and improve productivity while establishing a safe psychological space in which all group members could fully participate.

The role of the facilitator was designed to help minimize wheel spinning and dysfunctional dynamics and to enable groups to work together much more effectively. Other key pioneers of facilitation in the 1970s were Geoff Ball and David Sibbet with their seminal work in graphic recording and graphic facilitation. The core concepts and tools of group facilitation seemed to grow out of the tight-knit organization development and training community in the San Francisco Bay Area in the 1970s and '80s. It is great to see Sam Kaner and his colleagues continuing this rich legacy of theory and skill building.

Researchers at the *Institute for the Future* postulate that it takes about 30 years for social inventions to become widespread. Group facilitation is one such social invention. Over these last 25 years, facilitation skills have spread widely in the United States and are being spread around the world. And now, organizations are coming full circle. Facilitators once again are being utilized in *learning organizations* to facilitate dialogue processes that surface deep assumptions and mental models about how we view our world. These existing mental models are often the underlying sources of conflict and dysfunction. By surfacing, examining, and changing them, we are able to work together in new ways to build new systems thinking models that assist groups in articulating their core values and beliefs. These new mental models serve as the foundation for organizations as they evolve, grow, and transform themselves to meet the challenges of the next century.

### Expanding Definitions of Facilitation

These skills have become so useful in organizations that they have spread beyond the role of facilitator: to facilitative leaders; to self-facilitative groups and teams; to facilitative individuals and even facilitative, user-friendly procedures. Facilitation has become part of our everyday language. The Latin root of *facilitate* means "to enable, to make easy." *Facilitation* has evolved to have a number of meanings today.

**A facilitative individual** is an individual who is easy to work with, a team player, a person aware of individual and group dynamics. He or she assists colleagues to work together more effectively. A facilitative individual is a person who is skilled and knowledgeable in the interpersonal skills of communication, collaborative problem solving and planning, consensus building, and conflict resolution.

**A facilitator** is an individual who enables groups and organizations to work more effectively; to collaborate and achieve synergy. She or he is a "content-neutral" party who by not taking sides or expressing or advocating a point of view during the meeting, can advocate for fair, open, and inclusive procedures to accomplish the group's work. A facilitator can also be a learning or a dialogue guide to assist a group in thinking deeply about its assumptions, beliefs, and values and about its systemic processes and context.

**A facilitative leader** is a leader who is aware of group and organizational dynamics; a leader who creates organization-wide involvement processes that enable members of the organization to more fully utilize their potential and gifts in order to help the organization articulate and achieve its vision and goals, while at the same time actualizing its spoken values. Facilitative leaders often understand the inherent dynamics between facilitating and leading and frequently utilize facilitators in their organizations.

**A facilitative group** (team, task force, committee, or board) is one in which facilitative mind-sets and behaviors are widely distributed among the members; a group that is minimally dysfunctional and works very well together; a group that is easy to join and works well with other groups and individuals.

I think you, the reader, will find this book very useful for your work in groups, whether you are a leader, a group member, or a facilitator. I especially recommend to you the insightful chapters on understanding group dynamics, facilitative listening, and the importance of values. Where this book also makes a real contribution is in the chapters on reaching closure and the gradients of an agreement. I enjoyed the learnings and insights I received from this book, and I am sure you will too.

Michael Doyle
San Francisco, California
March 1996

# INTRODUCTION TO THE FIRST EDITION

The benefits of group decision-making have been widely publicized: better thinking, better "buy-in," better decisions all around. Yet the promise often fails to materialize. Many decisions made in groups are neither thoughtful nor inclusive; they are unimaginative, watered-down mediocrities.

Why is this so?

To a large degree, the answer is deeply rooted in prevailing cultural values that make it difficult for people to actually think in groups. Without even realizing it, many people make value judgments that inhibit spontaneity and deter others from saying what is really on their minds. For example, ideas that are expressed in clumsy ways, or in tentative terms, are often treated as if they were decidedly inferior to ideas that are presented with eloquent rhetorical flourish. Efforts to explore complexities are discouraged, in favor of pithy judgments and firm-sounding conclusions. Making action plans – no matter how unrealistic they might be – is called "getting something done," while analyzing the underlying causes of a problem is called "going off on a tangent." Mixed messages abound: speak your mind but don't ask too many questions; be passionate but don't show your feelings; be productive but hurry up – and get it right the first time. All said, conventional values do not promote effective thinking in groups.

Yet, when it's done well, group decision-making remains the best hope for solving difficult problems. There is no substitute for the wisdom that results from a successful integration of divergent points of view. Successful group decision-making requires a group to take advantage of the full range of experience and skills that reside in its membership. This means encouraging people to speak up. It means *inviting* difference, not fearing it. It means struggling to understand one another, especially in the face of the pressures and contradictions that typically drive group members to shut down. In short, it means operating from *participatory* values.

| PARTICIPATORY GROUPS | CONVENTIONAL GROUPS |
|---|---|
| Everyone participates, not just the vocal few. | The fastest thinkers and most articulate speakers get more airtime. |
| People give each other room to think and get their thoughts all the way out. | People interrupt each other on a regular basis. |
| Opposing viewpoints are allowed to co-exist in the room. | Differences of opinion are treated as *conflict* that must either be stifled or "solved." |
| People draw each other out with supportive questions. "Is *this* what you mean?" | Questions are often perceived as challenges, as if the person being questioned has done something wrong. |
| Each member makes the effort to pay attention to the person speaking. | Unless the speaker *captivates* their attention, people space out, doodle or check the clock. |
| People are able to listen to each other's ideas because they know *their own ideas will also be heard*. | People have difficulty listening to each other's ideas because they're busy rehearsing what *they* want to say. |
| Each member speaks up on matters of controversy. Everyone knows where everyone stands. | Some members remain quiet on controversial matters. No one really knows where everyone stands. |
| Members can accurately represent each other's points of view – even when they don't agree with them. | People rarely give accurate representations of the opinions and reasoning of those whose opinions are at odds with their own. |
| People refrain from talking behind each other's backs. | Because they don't feel permission to be direct *during* the meeting, people talk behind each other's backs outside the meeting. |
| Even in the face of opposition from the person-in-charge, people are encouraged to stand up for their beliefs. | People with discordant, minority perspectives are commonly discouraged from speaking out. |
| A problem is not considered solved until everyone who will be affected by the solution understands the reasoning. | A problem is considered solved as soon as the fastest thinkers have reached an answer. Everyone else is then expected to "get on board" regardless of whether s/he understands the logic of the decision. |
| When people make an agreement, it is assumed that the decision still reflects a wide range of perspectives. | When people make an agreement, it is assumed that they are all thinking the exact same thing. |

Participatory and conventional approaches to group decision-making yield entirely different group norms.

Some of the differences are presented in the table on the page to the left. As the table implies, a shift from conventional values to participatory values is not a simple matter of saying, "Let's become a thinking team." It requires a change of mindset – a committed effort from a group to swim against the tide of prevailing values and assumptions.

When a group undertakes this challenge, its participants often benefit from the services a competent facilitator can provide for them. Left to their own devices, many groups would slip back into conventional habits. A facilitator, however, has the skills to help a group outgrow their old familiar patterns. Specifically, the facilitator encourages full participation, s/he promotes mutual understanding, s/he fosters inclusive solutions and s/he cultivates shared responsibility. These four functions (discussed in depth in chapter 3) are derived from the core values of participatory decision-making.

**Putting Participatory Values Into Practice**

The facilitator is the keeper of the flame, the carrier of the vision of what Michael Doyle described, in his foreword, as "a fair, inclusive and open process." This is why many facilitators help their groups to understand the dynamics and values of group decision-making. They recognize that it is empowering for participants to acquire common language and shared points of reference about their decision-making processes.

When a facilitator helps group members acquire process skills, s/he is acting in congruence with one of the core values of participatory decision-making: shared responsibility. This value played a prominent role in the design of *The Facilitator's Guide to Participatory Decision-Making*. It was written as a series of stand-alone pages that facilitators can photocopy and distribute to the members of their groups.

For example, newly forming groups often benefit from reading and discussing chapters 1 and 2. These pages take less than fifteen minutes to read; they are entertaining; and they provide the basis for meaningful conversations about the dynamics and values of participatory decision-making. Within the guidelines of the policy statement on photocopying (see page 373), feel free to reproduce any part of this book that will strengthen your group's capacity for reaching sustainable agreements.

### Facilitating Sustainable Agreements

The process of building a sustainable agreement has four stages: gathering diverse points of view; building a shared framework of understanding; developing inclusive solutions; and reaching closure. A competent facilitator knows how to move a group from start to finish through those stages. To do so, s/he needs a conceptual understanding of the dynamics and values of participatory decision-making (as provided in Part I of this book). S/he also needs a standard set of process management skills (as provided in Part II). And s/he needs a repertoire of sophisticated thinking tools, to propose and conduct stage-specific interventions (as provided in Part III and Part IV).

### Fulfilling The Promise of Group Decision-Making

Those who practice participatory methods often come to see that facilitating a meeting is more than merely an occasion for solving a problem or creating a plan. It is also an opportunity to support profound personal learning, and it is an opportunity to strengthen the capacity and effectiveness of the group as a whole. These opportunities are only realizable – the promise of group decision-making can only be fulfilled – through the struggle and the satisfaction of putting participatory values into practice.

# INTRODUCTION TO THE THIRD EDITION

### 1. The Power of Groups

When we began writing this book in 1990, the term *group facilitator* was still rather exotic. Most people said, "Facilitator? What's that?"

Things have shifted quite a bit in 25 years. From an obscure "neutral third party" role – narrowly focused on *helping groups do their best thinking* – now "facilitator" is a synonym for a wide collection of group leadership roles, from "trainer" to "chair" to "convenor" to "manager." Thus, at the time of this writing, in 2014, the word has come to mean anything and everything that is associated with healthy group functioning.

Yet in another sense, the essence of the role has remained constant: *facilitation,* first and most, *is about groups.* Whether the facilitator is teaching, or leading, or mediating, or simply managing a process, the purpose of the role is to strengthen the effectiveness of the group of people who are there to get the work done. The facilitator helps, serves, teaches, guides. Whereas it is the group that resolves, decides, produces, *acts.*

One of the great insights of the 20th century is this: sitting down to work in a small face-to-face group is, potentially, transformative. The opportunity is there, if you want it, to say what you're really thinking; and to receive feedback on what you've said and how it comes across; and to stretch and hear the thoughts and feelings of others whose worldviews diverge from yours; and to struggle and triumph as you learn how to think from those other points of view. Every time we sit down and roll up our sleeves to engage across the table of a small face-to-face group – of maybe five or ten or twenty people – every time we enter that context we enter the world of opportunities to change ourselves and grow.

And in the act of changing and growing, we shift the perceptions and the experiences of our group members too.

Which in turn makes the whole group stronger, and wiser, and more confident.  And often, more courageous.  As a group, we hold a key to changing the world.  Seldom do we use that key; seldom do we even try.  But the opportunity is there:  latent, waiting – if we want it.

We can call it participatory decision-making.  We can call it social innovation.  We can call it dialogue and deliberation.  We can call it cross-functional teams, or multi-stakeholder collaboration.  We can call it collective impact.  Whatever we call it, we are talking about unleashing the transformative power of face-to-face groups, first to raise awareness and evoke mutual compassion, and then – potentially – to embolden participants to align their aspirations and undertake new, jointly developed actions that aim, with hope and courage, to address, and even resolve, the world's toughest problems.

Such is the opportunity that awaits us when we engage in serious work in our face-to-face groups – and *this* is the context in which the role of facilitator matters most.  For those neutral, third party people who want to support face-to-face groups to do their best thinking, it is for you we wrote this book, and it is to you we tip our hat.  The work is challenging, the burden can be heavy, the temptations are endless, and at the end of the day the role is a journey on a profoundly lonely path.  To those readers who perceive this work as your calling, we salute you.

## 2. Participatory Culture

Notwithstanding the benefits of having a facilitator on hand, what is *the group's responsibility* in a participatory process?

In other words:  suppose a very talented facilitator were to help a group do a great job of wrestling with a tough problem.  The members participate fully.  They build mutual understanding.  They find a solution that works for everyone, and they move ahead with actions that bring the solution to life.  Everyone in the group states that the experience has been "life-changing" or words to that effect.  Now the facilitator's contract with the group ends, and she departs.

Where does that leave the group?

Based on our experiences of observing our own groups and many others, we think that even the best facilitation in the universe does not, in and of itself, adequately and sustainably address the fourth participatory value, *shared responsibility*. If group members want to sustain a transformation that has been inaugurated by a well-facilitated process of participatory decision-making, then it falls on them to install and preserve an authentically participatory culture – manifesting the four core values described in chapter 2 of this book:

- *Full participation*
- *Mutual understanding*
- *Inclusive solutions*
- *Shared responsibility*

This is a tough proposition for a group that has ended its relationship with its facilitator.

So long as a facilitator is engaged, s/he can capture the cooperation and enthusiasm of the group by, for example, using facilitative listening skills and for that matter the entire collection of tools described in this book. In effect, the facilitator guides the group members into a participatory mindset, and assists them to remain in that mindset, for the duration of the facilitated process.

To do that the facilitator works continuously to achieve three ongoing objectives:

- *Build and sustain a respectful, supportive atmosphere*
- *Stay out of the content and manage the process*
- *Teach the group new thinking skills as the process unfolds, in order to build their capacity for collaboration.*

These three practices are critical. They are the soil in which the four participatory core values take root. They are the facilitator's core competencies for building a participatory environment.

When a facilitator's contract with a group ends, the aftermath leaves the group in this quandary: they may have cultivated a participatory mindset sincerely – they may have truly seen the benefits of full participation and all the kindred participatory values – but who is now going to take responsibility for maintaining the respectful, supportive atmosphere? Who is going to manage the process of the group conversation? The only hope is that their facilitator, along the way, had a good strategy for *teaching the group how to do those things themselves*.

For facilitators who care about helping their groups to build durable participatory cultures, using good listening skills, for example, is just not enough! We have to teach people what we're doing. Hence, we have to encourage our groups to place on their agendas, every so often, a slot for *continuous learning*, for maybe 30-40 minutes and even sometimes an hour, when we can teach a new skill – a listening skill, an energy management skill, a categorizing skill, and so on. We need our meeting planners to understand what we're doing, so they will set aside adequate time for experiential activity that lets their group members learn like adults, with practice and feedback and a few minutes to debrief and integrate the learning. Then in subsequent meetings we need to help people find ways to *apply* their new skills.

In short, a facilitator can provide the group with the mindset, the models, the skills and the tools to:

- treat each other respectfully and supportively;

- step away from the content of their conversations so they can discuss and manage their own process; and

- engage in *continuous learning*, to build their capacity for collaboration.

In fact, when a facilitator is committed to transitioning a group from a temporary, facilitator-driven participatory environment to a durable, group member-driven participatory culture, s/he can begin transferring the models and tools right from the start of his or her time with the group, by focusing on building the group's communication and process-management capacity at every step of the way.

### 3. Using this Book to Build Participatory Culture

The third edition has more than 60 new pages of tools. That's a good thing in itself, and we are pleased to offer them to you. But much more important, from our perspective, is that we have re-organized the book, in subtle but hopefully very helpful ways, with the goal of making it easier for you to teach the tools to help *your groups* build *their own* participatory cultures.

For example, in chapter 21, we show you how to teach *The Diamond of Participatory Decision-Making* to your groups. In our actual consulting practice we find it invaluable to provide groups with shared points of reference, and shared language, so they can talk to one another about their own group dynamics. This is a quintessential discussion about the process, not the content, of a group's discussion. Also, we encourage you to use the tools in chapter 13, *Dealing with Difficult Dynamics,* the same way. For example, *Developing Supportive Group Norms* is a practice activity that goes to the very heart of helping a group share responsibility for building its own respectful, supportive atmosphere.

In fact, many of the tools of the entire book can be taught to your group, precisely in the same spirit as you are teaching them to yourself now. Pick out a page or two, pass them around or turn them into flipcharts or slides, let people discuss the ideas – whether in small groups or the whole group – and maybe create an opportunity for a bit of experiential learning.

### 4. Closing Thought

Facilitators can use humor and charm to finesse some of the trickiest moments in a participatory process. But when a facilitator transfers his or her expertise and knowledge, s/he commits to serving the development of group capacity. The facilitator's charisma becomes irrelevant. What endures is the clarity and effectiveness of the technical competence that the group has acquired. In your efforts to give that gift to your groups, we offer this book to support you.

Part One

# GROUNDING PRINCIPLES

# THE DYNAMICS OF GROUP DECISION-MAKING

## IDEALIZED AND REALISTIC MODELS OF COLLABORATION IN GROUPS

▶ **Misunderstandings About the Process of Group Decision-Making**

▶ **The Struggle to Integrate Diverse Perspectives**

▶ **The Diamond of Participatory Decision-Making**

# DYNAMICS OF GROUP DECISION-MAKING

INTRODUCTION

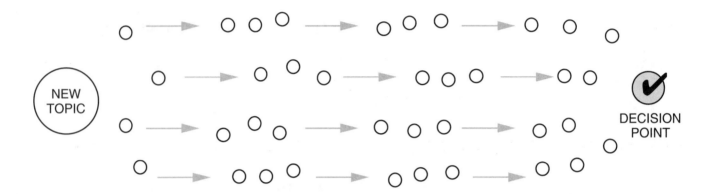

NEW
TOPIC

DECISION
POINT

This picture portrays a hypothetical problem-solving discussion.

Each circle – ○ – represents one idea. Each line of circles-and-arrows represents one person's line of thought as it develops during the discussion.

As diagrammed, everyone appears to be tracking each other's ideas, everyone goes at the same pace, and everyone stays on board every step of the way.

A depressingly large percentage of people who work in groups believe this stuff. They think this picture realistically portrays a healthy, flowing decision-making process. And when their actual experience doesn't match up with this model, *they think it's because their own group is defective.*

If people actually behaved as the diagram suggests, group decision-making would be much less frustrating. Unfortunately, real-life groups don't operate this way.

# DYNAMICS OF GROUP DECISION-MAKING

SAD BUT TRUE

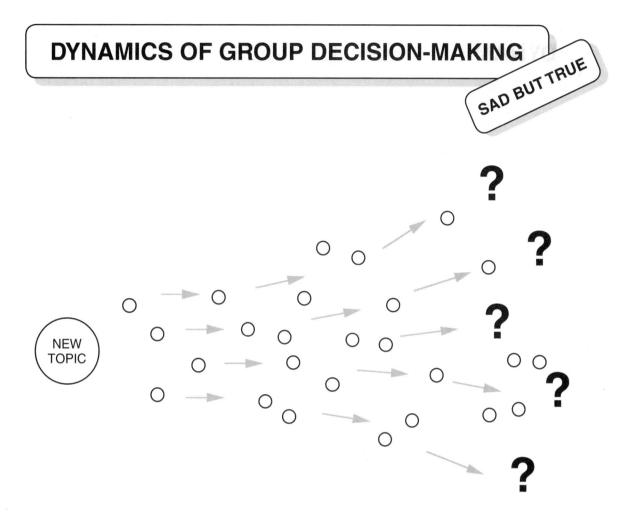

Group members are humans. We *do* go on tangents. We *do* lose track of the central themes of a discussion. We *do* get attached to our ideas. Even when we're all making our best effort to "keep focused" and "stay on track," *we can't change the fact that we are individuals with diverging points of view.*

When a discussion loses focus or becomes confusing, it can appear to many people that the process is heading out of control. Yet this is not necessarily what's really going on. Sometimes what appears to be chaos is actually a prelude to creativity.

But how can we tell which is which? How do we recognize the difference between a degenerative, spinning-our-wheels version of group confusion and the dynamic, diversity-stretches-our-imagination version of group confusion?

# DYNAMICS OF GROUP DECISION-MAKING

CLOSER TO REALITY

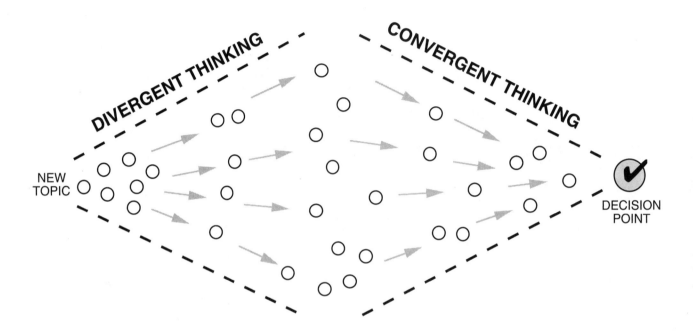

DIVERGENT THINKING

CONVERGENT THINKING

NEW TOPIC

DECISION POINT

At times the individual members of a group need to express their own points of view. At other times, the same people want to narrow their differences and aim the discussion toward closure. Throughout this book, these two types of "thinking processes" are referred to as *divergent thinking* and *convergent thinking*.

Here are four examples:

| DIVERGENT THINKING | | CONVERGENT THINKING |
|---|---|---|
| Generating alternatives | vs. | Evaluating alternatives |
| Free-flowing open discussion | vs. | Summarizing key points |
| Gathering diverse points of view | vs. | Sorting ideas into categories |
| Suspending judgment | vs. | Exercising judgment |

# DYNAMICS OF GROUP DECISION-MAKING

UNANSWERED
QUESTIONS

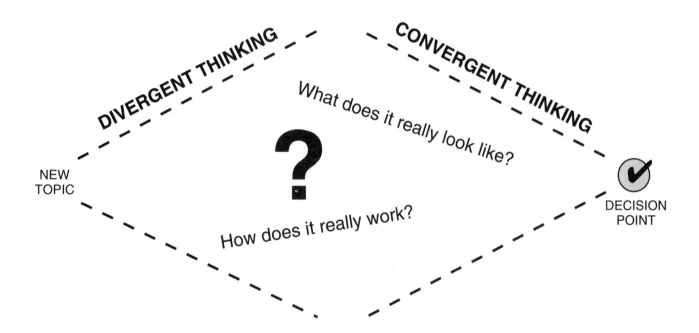

Some years ago, a large, well-known computer manufacturer developed a problem-solving model that was based on the principles of divergent thinking and convergent thinking.

This model was used by managers throughout the company. But it didn't always work so well. One project manager told us that it took their group *two years* to revise the reimbursement procedure for travel expenses.

Why would that happen? How does group decision-making *really* work?

To explore these questions in greater depth, the following pages present a series of stop-action snapshots of the process of group decision-making.

# DYNAMICS OF GROUP DECISION-MAKING

DISCUSSION BEGINS

DIVERGENT THINKING

DIVERSITY OF IDEAS

NEW
TOPIC

TIME

The early rounds of a discussion cover safe, familiar territory. People take positions that reflect conventional wisdom. They rehash well-worn disagreements, and they make proposals for obvious solutions.

This is the normal (and human) way for any problem-solving discussion to begin. *The first ideas we express are the ones that are easiest to think about.*

# DYNAMICS OF GROUP DECISION-MAKING

QUICK DECISIONS

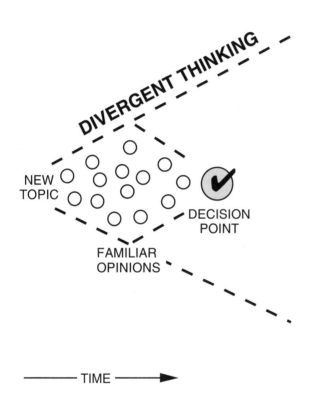

When a problem has an obvious solution, it makes sense to close the discussion quickly. Why waste time?

There's only one problem: most groups try to bring *every* discussion to closure this quickly.

# DYNAMICS OF GROUP DECISION-MAKING

NO OBVIOUS SOLUTION

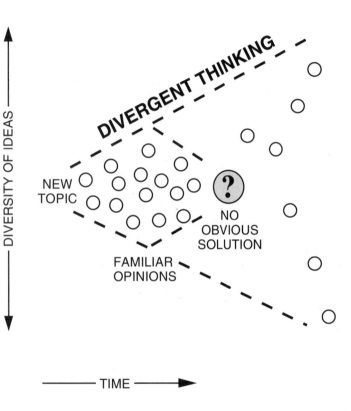

DIVERSITY OF IDEAS

DIVERGENT THINKING

NEW TOPIC

NO OBVIOUS SOLUTION

FAMILIAR OPINIONS

TIME

Some problems have *no* easy solutions. For example, how does an inner-city public school prevent campus violence? What steps should a business take to address the needs of an increasingly diverse workforce? Cases like these require a lot of thought; the issues are too complex to be solved with familiar opinions and conventional wisdom.

When a group of decision-makers has to wrestle with a difficult problem, they will not succeed in solving it until they *break out of the narrow band of familiar opinions* and explore a wider range of possibilities.

# DYNAMICS OF GROUP DECISION-MAKING

THE CLASSIC DEAD END

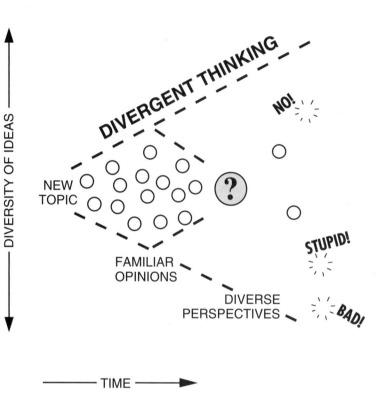

Unfortunately, most groups aren't very good at cultivating unfamiliar or unpopular opinions.

# DYNAMICS OF GROUP DECISION-MAKING

EXPLORING POSSIBILITIES

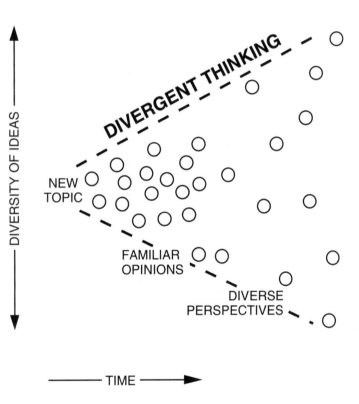

Now and then, when the stakes are sufficiently high and the stars are in proper alignment, a group can manage to overcome the tendency to criticize and inhibit its members. On such occasions, people tentatively begin to consider new perspectives. Some participants might take a risk and express controversial opinions. Others might offer ideas that aren't fully developed.

Since the goal is to find a new way of thinking about the problem, variety is obviously desirable . . . but the spread of opinions can become cumbersome and difficult to manage. Then what?

# DYNAMICS OF GROUP DECISION-MAKING

IDEALIZED PROCESS

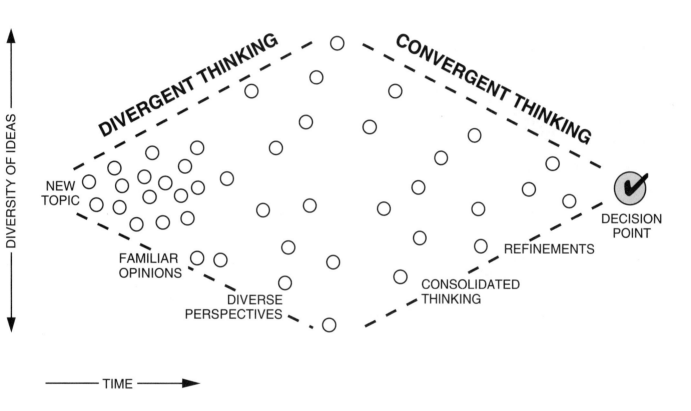

*In theory*, a group that has committed itself to thinking through a difficult problem would move forward in orderly, thoughtful steps. First, the group would generate and explore a diverse set of ideas. Next, they would consolidate the best thinking into a proposal. Then, they'd refine the proposal until they arrived at a final decision that nicely incorporated the breadth of their thinking.

Ah yes . . . if only *real life* worked that way.

# DYNAMICS OF GROUP DECISION-MAKING

TYPICAL PROCESS

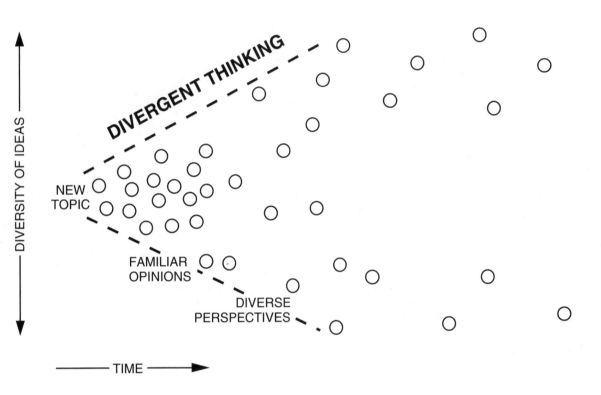

*In practice*, it can be hard for some people to stop expressing their own opinions and shift to listening to, and understanding the opinions of others.

And it can be particularly challenging to do so when a wide diversity of perspectives are in play. In such cases people can get overloaded, disoriented, annoyed, impatient – or all of the above. Some people feel misunderstood and keep repeating themselves. Other people push for closure . . .

Thus, even the most sincere attempts to solve difficult problems can – and often do – dissipate into confusion.

# DYNAMICS OF GROUP DECISION-MAKING

ATTEMPTED STEP-BACKS

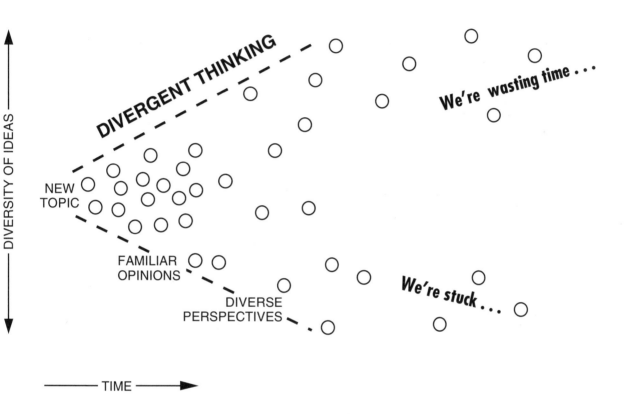

DIVERSITY OF IDEAS

DIVERGENT THINKING

We're wasting time . . .

NEW TOPIC

FAMILIAR OPINIONS

DIVERSE PERSPECTIVES

We're stuck . . .

TIME

Sometimes one or more participants will attempt to step back from the content of the discussion and talk about the process. They might say things like, "I thought we all agreed to stick to the topic," or "Does anyone understand what's going on here?"

Groups rarely respond intelligently to such comments, especially ones that sound like cranky rhetorical questions. More commonly, a process comment becomes merely one more voice in the cacophony: yet another poorly understood perspective to be absorbed into the general confusion.

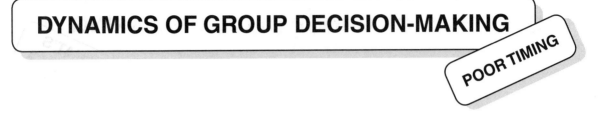

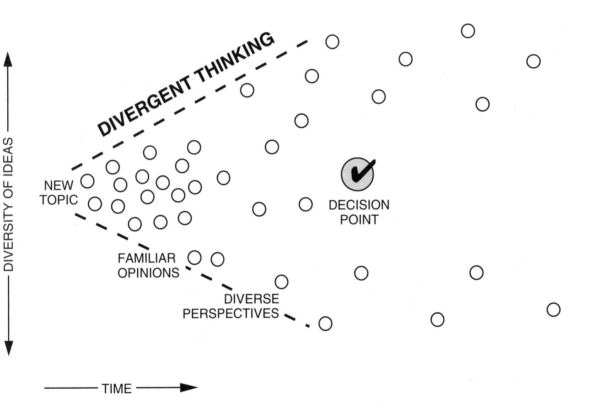

At this point in a process, the person in charge of a meeting can make the problem worse, if he or she attempts to alleviate frustration by announcing that s/he has made a decision. This is a common mistake.

The person-in-charge may believe that s/he has found a perfectly logical answer to the problem at hand, but this doesn't mean that everyone else will telepathically grasp the reasoning behind the decision. Some people may still be thinking along entirely different lines.

This is the exact case in which the person-in-charge *appears* to have made a decision before the meeting began. *"Why did s/he tell me I'd have a say in this matter, when s/he had already made the decision?"* Thus a good faith effort to streamline a rambling conversation can lead to distrust, and even cynicism.

# DYNAMICS OF GROUP DECISION-MAKING

WHAT'S MISSING?

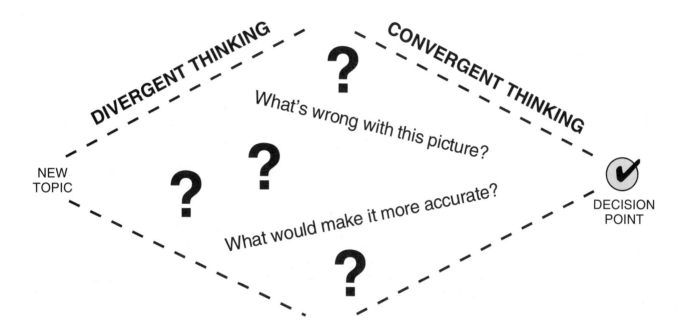

Obviously, there's something wrong with the idealized model. In real life, groups do not automatically shift into convergent thinking. Even after spending substantial time in divergent thinking activities, most groups who make it that far will run into obstacles like those noted on previous pages. In other words, they can easily get "stuck" in their divergence.

None of this is modeled in the diagram shown above. What's missing?

# DYNAMICS OF GROUP DECISION-MAKING

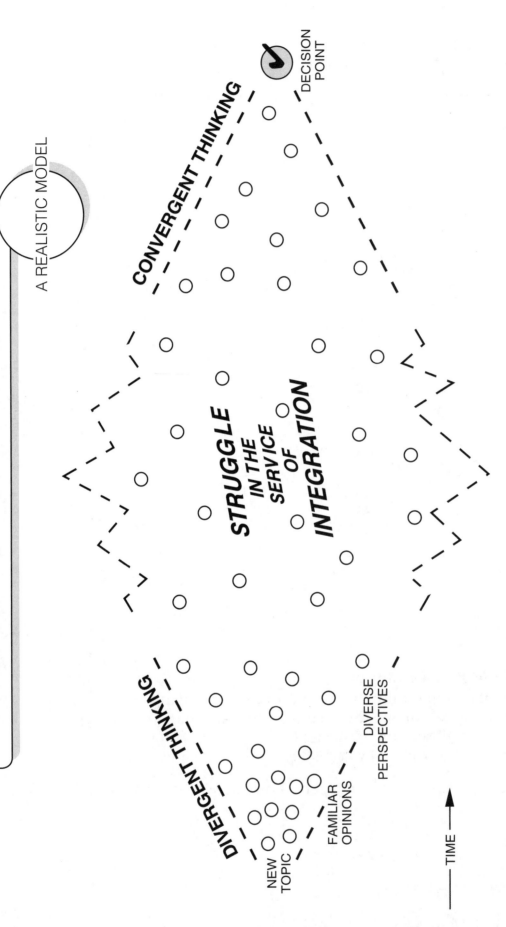

A REALISTIC MODEL

DIVERGENT THINKING

NEW TOPIC

FAMILIAR OPINIONS

DIVERSE PERSPECTIVES

STRUGGLE IN THE SERVICE OF INTEGRATION

CONVERGENT THINKING

DECISION POINT

TIME ⟶

A period of confusion and frustration is a natural part of group decision-making. Once a group crosses the line from airing familiar opinions to exploring diverse perspectives, *group members have to struggle in order to integrate new and different ways of thinking with their own.*

*Community At Work* ©2014

# DYNAMICS OF GROUP DECISION-MAKING

INTRODUCING
THE GROAN ZONE

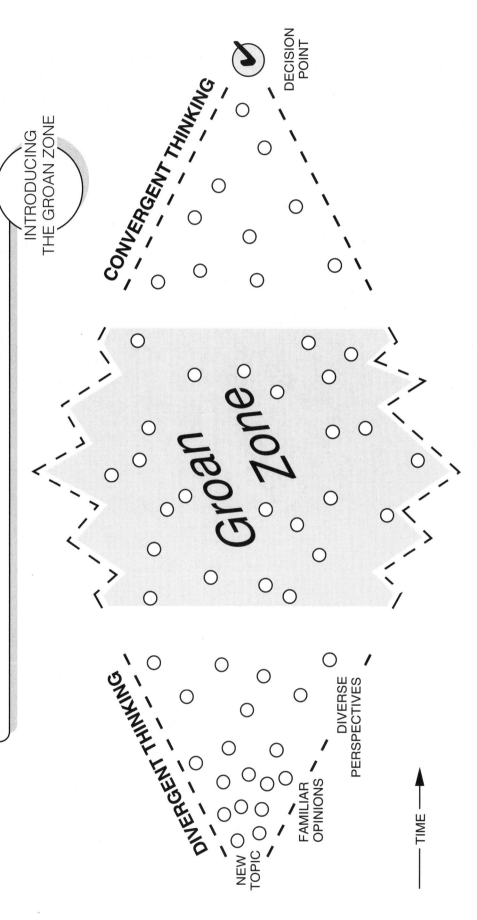

CONVERGENT THINKING

DECISION
POINT

*Groan Zone*

DIVERGENT THINKING

NEW
TOPIC

FAMILIAR
OPINIONS

DIVERSE
PERSPECTIVES

TIME →

Struggling to understand a wide range of foreign or opposing ideas is not a pleasant experience. Group members can be repetitious, insensitive, defensive, short-tempered – and more! At such times most people don't have the slightest notion of what's happening. Sometimes the mere act of acknowledging the existence of the *Groan Zone* can be a significant step for a group to take.

*Community At Work* ©2014

# DYNAMICS OF GROUP DECISION-MAKING

THE DIAMOND OF PARTICIPATORY DECISION-MAKING

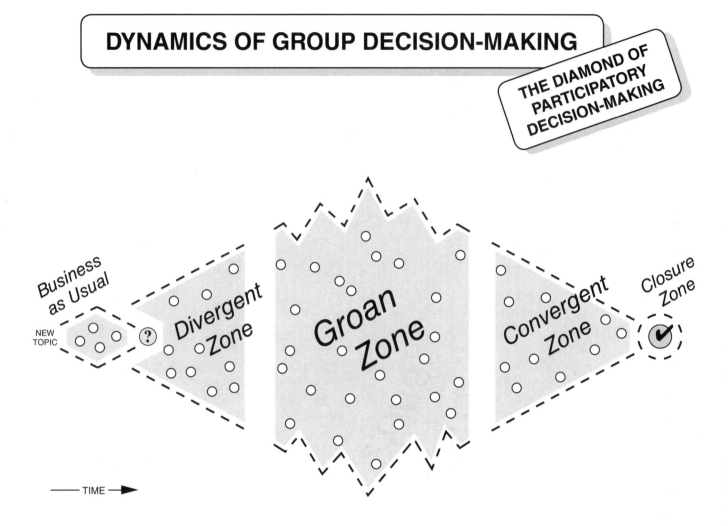

Business as Usual

NEW TOPIC

Divergent Zone

Groan Zone

Convergent Zone

Closure Zone

⟶ TIME ⟶

This is the *Diamond of Participatory Decision-Making.* It was developed by Sam Kaner with Lenny Lind, Catherine Toldi, Sarah Fisk and Duane Berger.

Facilitators can use *"The Diamond"* in many ways. It's a lens through which a facilitator can observe and react to the communication dynamics that occur in meetings. It can also be useful as a roadmap for designing agendas – especially to anticipate and plan for challenging conversations. And it can be used as a teaching tool, to provide group members with shared language and shared points of reference that enable them to be more adept at self-managing their meeting processes.

Fundamentally, though, this model was created to validate and legitimize the hidden aspects of everyday life in groups. Expressing difference is natural and beneficial; getting confused is to be expected; feeling frustrated is par for the course. *Building shared understanding is a struggle, not a platitude.*

# DYNAMICS OF GROUP DECISION-MAKING

**THE POWER OF A REALISTIC MODEL**

Business as Usual

NEW TOPIC

Divergent Zone

Groan Zone

Convergent Zone

Closure Zone

Understanding group dynamics is an indispensable core competency for anyone – whether facilitator, leader, or group member – who wants to help their group tap the enormous potential of participatory decision-making.

When people experience discomfort in the midst of a group decision-making process, they often take it as evidence that their group is dysfunctional. As their impatience increases, so does their disillusion with the process.

Many projects are abandoned prematurely for exactly this reason. In such cases, it's not that the goals were ill conceived; it's that the *Groan Zone* was perceived as an insurmountable impediment rather than as a normal part of the process.

This is truly a shame. Too many high-minded and well-funded efforts to resolve the world's toughest problems have foundered on the shoals of group dynamics.

So let's be clear-headed about this: misunderstanding and miscommunication are normal, natural aspects of participatory decision-making. The *Groan Zone* is a direct, inevitable consequence of the diversity that exists in any group.

Not only that, but the act of working through these misunderstandings is what builds the foundation for sustainable agreements. Without shared understanding, meaningful collaboration is impossible.

It is supremely important for people who work in groups to recognize this. Groups that can tolerate the stress of the *Groan Zone* are far more likely to find their way to common ground. And discovering common ground, in turn, is the precondition for insightful, innovative collaboration.

# 2

# PARTICIPATORY VALUES

HOW FULL PARTICIPATION STRENGTHENS
INDIVIDUALS, DEVELOPS GROUPS, AND
FOSTERS SUSTAINABLE AGREEMENTS

- ▶ The Four Participatory Values

- ▶ How Participatory Values Affect
  People and Their Work

- ▶ Full Participation

- ▶ Mutual Understanding

- ▶ Inclusive Solutions

- ▶ Shared Responsibility

- ▶ Benefits of Participatory Values

# PARTICIPATORY DECISION-MAKING CORE VALUES

In a participatory group, all members are encouraged to speak up and say what's on their minds. This strengthens a group in several ways. Members become more courageous in raising difficult issues. They learn how to share their "first-draft" ideas. And they become more adept at discovering and acknowledging the diversity of opinions and backgrounds inherent in any group.

For a group to reach a sustainable agreement, members have to understand and accept the legitimacy of one another's needs and goals. This basic recognition is what allows people to think from each other's point of view. And thinking from each other's point of view is the catalyst for innovative ideas that serve the interests of all parties.

Inclusive solutions are wise solutions. Their wisdom emerges from the integration of everybody's perspectives and needs. These are solutions whose range and vision are expanded to take advantage of the truth held not only by the quick, the articulate, the influential, and the powerful, but also the truth held by those who are disenfranchised or shy or who think at a slower pace. As veteran facilitator Caroline Estes puts it, "Everyone has a piece of the truth." *

In participatory groups, members recognize that they must be willing and able to implement the proposals they endorse, so they make every effort to give and receive input before final decisions are made. They also assume responsibility for designing and managing the thinking process that will result in a good decision. This contrasts sharply with the conventional assumption that everyone will be held accountable for the consequences of thinking done by a few key people.

\* Caroline Estes, *Everyone Has a Piece of the Truth.*
U.S. Cohousing Association, http://www.cohousing.org/cm/article/truth

# HOW PARTICIPATORY VALUES CAN AFFECT GROUP DECISION-MAKING

**FULL PARTICIPATION**

## QUANTITY AND QUALITY OF PARTICIPATION DURING A BUSINESS-AS-USUAL DISCUSSION

In a typical business-as-usual discussion, self-expression is highly constrained. People tend to keep risky opinions to themselves. The most highly regarded comments are those that seem the clearest, the smartest, the most well polished. In business-as-usual discussions, thinking out loud is treated with impatience; people get annoyed if the speaker's remarks are vague or poorly stated. This induces self-censorship, and reduces the quantity and quality of participation overall. A few people end up doing almost all the talking – and in many groups, those few people just keep repeating themselves and repeating themselves.

## FULL PARTICIPATION DURING A PARTICIPATORY DECISION-MAKING PROCESS

Participatory decision-making groups go through a business-as-usual phase too. If familiar opinions lead to a workable solution, then the group can reach a decision quickly. But when a business-as-usual discussion does *not* produce a workable solution, a participatory group will open up the process and encourage more divergent thinking. What does this look like in action? It looks like people permitting themselves to state half-formed thoughts that express unconventional – but perhaps valuable – perspectives. It looks like people taking risks to surface controversial issues. It looks like people making suggestions "from left field" that stimulate their peers to think new thoughts. And it also looks like a roomful of people *encouraging each other* to do all these things.

# HOW PARTICIPATORY VALUES CAN AFFECT GROUP DECISION-MAKING

MUTUAL UNDERSTANDING

**EXTENT OF MUTUAL UNDERSTANDING DURING A BUSINESS-AS-USUAL DISCUSSION**

In a business-as-usual discussion, persuasion is much more common than dialogue. The views of "the other side" are dissected point by point for the purpose of refuting them. Little effort, if any, is put into discovering the deeper reasons people believe what they do. Even when it appears unlikely that persuasion will change anyone's mind, participants continue to press home their points – making it appear as though the pleasures of rhetoric were the true purpose of continuing the discussion. Most participants tend to stop listening to each other, except to prepare for a rebuttal.

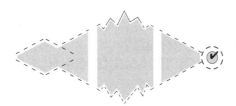

**EXTENT OF MUTUAL UNDERSTANDING DURING A PARTICIPATORY DECISION-MAKING PROCESS**

*Building a shared framework of understanding* means taking the time to understand everyone's perspective in order to find the best idea. To build that framework, participants spend time and effort questioning each other, getting to know one another – learning from each other. *Participants put themselves in each other's shoes.* The process is laced with intermittent discomfort: some periods are tense, some are stifling. But participants keep plugging away. Over time, many people gain insight into their own positions. They might discover that their own thinking is out-of-date or misinformed or driven by inaccurate stereotypes. And by struggling to acquire such insights, members might also discover something else about one another: that they all truly do care about achieving a mutual goal.

# HOW PARTICIPATORY VALUES CAN AFFECT GROUP DECISION-MAKING

INCLUSIVE SOLUTIONS

## SOLUTIONS RESULTING FROM A BUSINESS-AS-USUAL DISCUSSION

Business-as-usual discussions seldom result in inclusive solutions.  More commonly, people quickly form opinions and take sides.  Everyone expects that one side will get what they want and the other side won't.  Disputes, they assume, will be resolved by the person who has the most authority.  Some groups settle their differences by majority vote, but the effect is the same.  Expediency rather than innovation or sustainability is the driver of such solutions.  When the implementation is easy, or when the stakes are low, expedient solutions are perfectly good – but not when the stakes are high, or creativity is required, or broad-based commitment is needed.

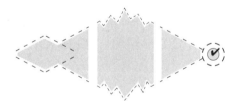

## SOLUTIONS RESULTING FROM A PARTICIPATORY DECISION-MAKING PROCESS

Inclusive solutions are not compromises; they work for everyone who holds a stake in the outcome.  Typically, an inclusive solution involves the discovery of an entirely new option.  For instance, an unexpected partnership might be forged between former competitors.  Or a group may invent a nontraditional alternative to a procedure that had previously "always been done that way."  Several real-life case examples of inclusive solutions are presented in Chapter 16.  Inclusive solutions are usually not obvious – they *emerge* in the course of the group's persistence.  As participants learn more about each other's perspectives, they become progressively more able to integrate their own goals and needs with those of the other participants.  This leads to innovative, original thinking.

# HOW PARTICIPATORY VALUES CAN AFFECT GROUP DECISION-MAKING

*SHARED RESPONSIBILITY*

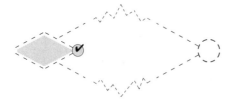

## THE ENACTMENT OF RESPONSIBILITY DURING A BUSINESS-AS-USUAL DISCUSSION

In business-as-usual discussions, groups rely on the authority of their leaders and their experts. The person-in-charge assumes responsibility for defining goals, setting priorities, defining problems, establishing success criteria, and arriving at conclusions. Participants with the most expertise are expected to distill relevant data, provide analysis, and make recommendations. Furthermore, the person-in-charge is expected to run the meeting, monitor the progress of each topic, enforce time boundaries, referee disputes, and generally take responsibility for all aspects of process management.

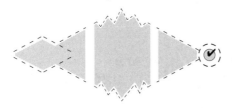

## SHARED RESPONSIBILITY DURING A PARTICIPATORY DECISION-MAKING PROCESS

In order for an agreement to be sustainable, it needs everyone's support. Understanding this principle leads everyone to take personal responsibility for making sure they are satisfied with the proposed course of action. Thus, people raise whatever issues they consider to be important. And everyone is expected to voice concerns if they have them, even when doing so could delay the group from reaching a decision. Furthermore, *shared responsibility* applies to the process of a meeting, not just to the content. Group members are willing to discuss and co-create the procedures they will follow; they share in designing their meeting agendas; they are ready to take on roles – facilitator, recorder, time-keeper, mediator, data-keeper, and so on. Overall, in a participatory process everyone is an owner of the outcome; participants acknowledge this as a core value and they act accordingly.

# THE BENEFITS OF PARTICIPATORY VALUES

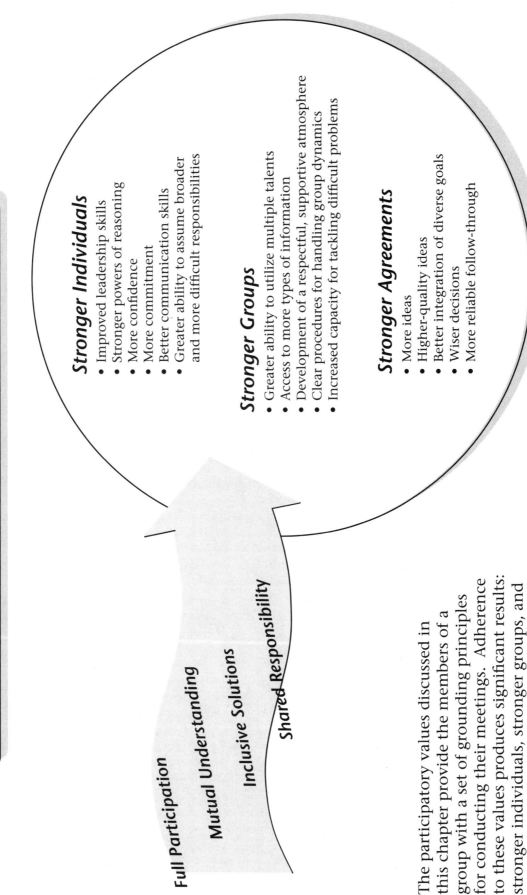

## Stronger Individuals
- Improved leadership skills
- Stronger powers of reasoning
- More confidence
- More commitment
- Better communication skills
- Greater ability to assume broader and more difficult responsibilities

## Stronger Groups
- Greater ability to utilize multiple talents
- Access to more types of information
- Development of a respectful, supportive atmosphere
- Clear procedures for handling group dynamics
- Increased capacity for tackling difficult problems

## Stronger Agreements
- More ideas
- Higher-quality ideas
- Better integration of diverse goals
- Wiser decisions
- More reliable follow-through

Full Participation

Mutual Understanding

Inclusive Solutions

Shared Responsibility

The participatory values discussed in this chapter provide the members of a group with a set of grounding principles for conducting their meetings. Adherence to these values produces significant results: stronger individuals, stronger groups, and stronger agreements.

*Community At Work* ©2014

# 3

# INTRODUCTION TO THE
# ROLE OF FACILITATOR

## THE EXPERTISE THAT SUPPORTS
## A GROUP TO DO ITS BEST THINKING

- ▶ **When Is a Facilitator Needed?**

- ▶ **First Function:**
  **Encourage Full Participation**

- ▶ **Second Function:**
  **Promote Mutual Understanding**

- ▶ **Third Function:**
  **Foster Inclusive Solutions**

- ▶ **Fourth Function:**
  **Cultivate Shared Responsibility**

## THE ROLE OF FACILITATOR

### WHAT IS A FACILITATOR, AND WHY HAVE ONE?

The facilitator's job is to *support everyone to do their best thinking.*  S/he encourages full participation; s/he promotes mutual understanding; s/he fosters inclusive solutions, and s/he cultivates shared responsibility.

How much value does this role have for a group?  The answer depends on the group's goals.

Consider the "status update" meetings that consist solely of announcements and reports.  Do the participants in those meetings need support to do their best thinking?  Not really.  And the same might be said of many *business-as-usual* monthly staff meetings, at which routine decisions are made about scheduling, task assignments and so on.  Such issues could be handled for years without any facilitation whatsoever.

But what about more difficult challenges?  For example, suppose a group's goal is to reduce violence on a high school campus.  The participants are parents, teachers, administrators and a police officer.  This group will quickly learn how difficult it is to make progress without facilitation.  Despite a common goal, their frames of reference are very different.  What seems to a parent like an obvious solution may seem simplistic to an administrator.  What seems reasonable to an administrator may seem cowardly to a teacher.  What seems responsible to a teacher may place too many demands on a parent.  For such groups, it takes plenty of support to do their best thinking!

Groups face difficult challenges all the time.  Long-term planning is hard to do well.  So is restructuring or reengineering.  This list goes on:  resolving high-stakes conflicts; introducing new technology into a workplace; defining the scope of a project that hasn't been done before.  In situations like these, a group is likely to make wiser, more lasting decisions if they enlist a facilitator who knows how to support them to do their best thinking.

Most individuals working in groups *do not know how* to solve tough problems on their own.  They do not know how to build a shared framework of understanding – they seldom even recognize its significance.  They dread conflict and discomfort, and they try hard to avoid it.  Yet by avoiding the struggle to integrate one another's perspectives, the members of such groups greatly diminish their own potential to be effective.  They *need* a facilitator.

# THE ROLE OF FACILITATOR

**FIRST FUNCTION**

## THE FACILITATOR ENCOURAGES FULL PARTICIPATION

### A Fundamental Problem: Self-Censorship

Inherent in group decision-making is a basic problem: *people don't say what they're really thinking.* It's hard to take risks, and particularly so when the response is likely to be hostile or dismissive. Consider these comments:

- "Haven't we already covered that point?"
- "Let's keep it simple, please."
- "Hurry up – we're running out of time."
- "What does *that* have to do with anything?"
- "Impossible. Won't work. No way."

Statements like these are oppressive. They discourage people from thinking out loud. The message is: if you want to speak, be simple. Be polished. Be able to say something smart or entertaining or keep your mouth shut.

We call these *"injunctions against thinking in public."* They run like an underground stream below the surface of a group's discussion, encouraging participants to edit their thinking before they speak. Who wants his or her ideas criticized before they are fully formed? Who wants to be told, "We've already answered that question"? Who wants to make an effort to express a complex thought while others in the room are doodling or whispering? This type of treatment leaves many people feeling embarrassed or inadequate.

*To protect themselves, people censor themselves.*

### The Facilitator's Contribution

Helping a group to overcome these subtle but powerful norms is a basic part of the facilitator's job. Effective facilitators have the temperament and the skills to draw people out and help everyone feel heard. They know how to make it safe for people to ask the "stupid question" without feeling stupid. They know how to make room for quiet members. In sum, facilitators know how to build a respectful, supportive atmosphere that encourages people to keep thinking instead of shutting down.

# THE ROLE OF FACILITATOR

*SECOND FUNCTION*

## THE FACILITATOR PROMOTES MUTUAL UNDERSTANDING

### A Fundamental Problem: Fixed Positions

A group cannot do its best thinking if the members don't understand one another. But most people find it difficult to detach from their fixed positions enough to actually listen to what others are saying. Instead, they get caught up in amplifying and defending their own perspectives.

Here's an example. A group of friends began exploring the possibility of forming a new business together. When the topic of money came up, biases emerged. One person wanted the profits divided equally. Another thought everyone should be paid on the basis of how much revenue they would generate. A third person believed the two visionaries should be paid more to make sure they would not leave. None of them were able to change their minds easily. Nor would it have been realistic to expect them to do so. Their opinions had been forming and developing for years.

And it gets worse! Each person's life experiences are so individual, so singular; everyone has remarkably different views of the world. What people expect, what they assume, how they use language, and how they behave – all these are likely sources of *mutual misunderstanding*. What's more, when people attempt to clear up a misunderstanding, they usually want their *own* ideas understood *first*. They may not say so directly, but their behavior indicates, "I can't really focus on what you are saying until I feel that you have understood *my* point of view." This easily becomes a vicious cycle. No wonder it's hard for people to let go of fixed positions!

### The Facilitator's Contribution

A facilitator helps the group realize that sustainable agreements are built on a foundation of mutual understanding. S/he helps members see that thinking from each other's points of view is invaluable.

Moreover, the facilitator accepts the *inevitability of misunderstanding.* S/he recognizes that misunderstandings are stressful for everyone involved. The facilitator knows that people in distress need support; they need to be treated respectfully. S/he knows it is essential to stay impartial, honor all points of view and keep listening, so that each and every group member has confidence that *someone* understands them.

# THE ROLE OF FACILITATOR

THIRD FUNCTION

## THE FACILITATOR FOSTERS INCLUSIVE SOLUTIONS

### A Fundamental Problem: The Win/Lose Mentality

It's hard for most people to imagine that stakeholders with apparently irreconcilable differences might actually reach an agreement that benefits all parties. Most people are entrenched in a conventional mind-set: "It's either my way or your way." As a result, problem-solving discussions often degenerate into critiques, rationalizations, and sales jobs, as participants stay attached to their fixed positions and work to defend their own interests.

### The Facilitator's Contribution

An experienced facilitator knows how to help a group search for innovative ideas that incorporate everyone's points of view. This can be a challenging task – the facilitator is often the only person in the room who has even considered the possibility that inclusive alternatives may exist.

To accomplish this goal, a facilitator draws from knowledge acquired by studying the theory and practice of collaborative problem solving. Thus s/he knows the steps it takes to build sustainable agreements:

- S/he knows how to help a group break free from restrictive business-as-usual discussions and engage in divergent thinking.

- S/he knows how to help a group survive the *Groan Zone* as its members struggle to build a shared framework of understanding.

- S/he knows how to help a group formulate creative, innovative ideas that reflect a weaving-together of several perspectives.

- S/he knows how to help a group complete its deliberations and arrive at a sound decision.

In short, the facilitator understands how to build sustainable agreements.

When a facilitator introduces a group to the values and methods that foster inclusive solutions, the impact is profound. Many people scoff at the very suggestion that a group can find meaningful solutions to difficult problems. As they discover the validity of this new way of thinking, they often become more hopeful about their group's potential effectiveness.

## THE ROLE OF FACILITATOR

FOURTH FUNCTION

## THE FACILITATOR CULTIVATES SHARED RESPONSIBILITY

### A Fundamental Problem: Reliance on Authority

In group settings, many people defer to the group's leaders and experts – often without giving their deferential behavior a second thought.

It's easy to understand why. Leaders wield power. They control resources. They have access to privileged information. They are networked with others who hold power. Likewise, experts have the training, the knowledge, the connections, and the familiarity with key issues.

Furthermore, remaining passive often seems to make such good sense! For one thing, speaking truth to power can have adverse consequences. For another thing, it may not be worth the bother if "nothing I can say would matter anyway." And finally, if the expert knows more than the others, why not accept that person's judgment and follow his or her advice?

Yet, terms like *empowerment, collaboration* and *self-managing teams* reflect a growing consensus that over-reliance on authority can be ineffectual. *"People support what they help to create,"* is how Marvin Weisbord put it.* But even when a leader *wants* to empower a group, many people find it hard to break the pattern. In turn, that passivity induces leaders to "get on with it" and do the work themselves — a self-perpetuating cycle of dependency on authority.

### The Facilitator's Contribution

Creating a culture of shared responsibility requires serious effort. The group's leader has to endorse the value of shared responsibility, and both the leader and the members have to develop the procedures and acquire the skills to make participatory decision-making work.

The existence of a facilitator often makes the crucial difference. S/he helps the group evolve from business-as-usual deference and dependency to assertiveness, collaboration, and shared responsibility. To help this happen, s/he is sometimes a coach, sometimes a teacher, sometimes a co-designer of systems and procedures, and sometimes a motivational speaker who inspires the group members to stand up and take risks. In this sense a facilitator is the steward of a profound culture change.

*M. Weisbord, *Productive Workplaces: Dignity, Meaning & Community in the 21st Century* (Pfeiffer, 2012).

## FACILITATOR SKILLS FOR PARTICIPATORY DECISION MAKING

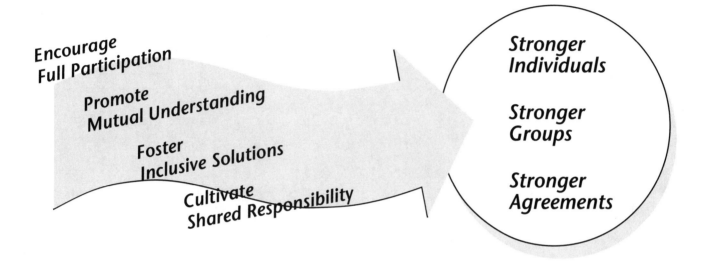

The facilitator's mission is to *support everyone to do their best thinking.*

This mission is enacted by the facilitator's four functions:

- *Encourage full participation*
- *Promote mutual understanding*
- *Foster inclusive solutions*
- *Cultivate shared responsibility*

When a facilitator effectively performs these functions, the results are impressive. S/he strengthens the skills, awareness, and confidence of the individuals who work in that group; s/he strengthens the structure and capacity of the group as a whole; and s/he vastly increases the likelihood that the group will arrive at sustainable agreements.

# Part Two

# FACILITATOR
# FUNDAMENTALS

# 4

# FACILITATIVE LISTENING SKILLS

## TECHNIQUES FOR HONORING ALL POINTS OF VIEW

- Respecting Diverse Communication Styles
- Paraphrasing
- Drawing People Out
- Mirroring
- Gathering Ideas
- Stacking
- Tracking
- Encouraging
- Balancing
- Helping People Listen to Each Other
- Making Space for a Quiet Person
- Acknowledging Feelings
- Validating
- Empathizing
- Intentional Silence
- Linking
- Listening for the Logic
- Legitimizing Differences
- Listening for Common Ground
- Listening with a Point of View
- Summarizing

## THE CALCULUS OF DIVERSITY

**THE LIMITS OF TOLERANCE**

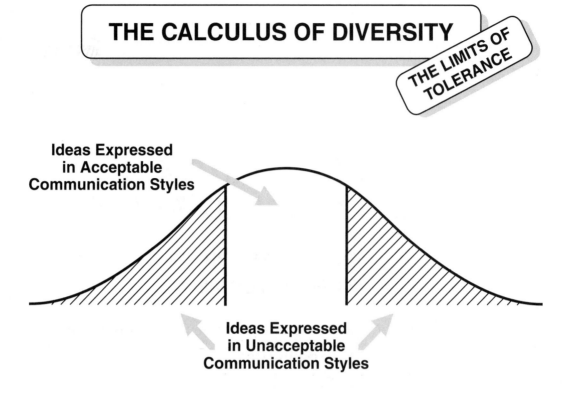

**Ideas Expressed in Acceptable Communication Styles**

**Ideas Expressed in Unacceptable Communication Styles**

An idea that is expressed in an acceptable communication style will be taken more seriously by more people. Conversely, ideas that are presented poorly or offensively are harder for people to hear. For example:

- Many people become antsy when a speaker is repetitious.

- Group members can be impatient with shy or nervous members who speak haltingly.

- Others may not want to listen to exaggerations, distortions, or unfounded pronouncements.

- Some people become overwhelmed when a speaker goes on a tangent and raises a point that seems unrelated to the subject.

- And some people are profoundly uncomfortable with anyone who shows too much emotion.

In an ideal world, useful insights and ideas would be valued regardless of how they were expressed. But in the real world, when a speaker has an unpleasant communication style people just stop listening to the substance of the ideas being expressed – no matter how valuable those ideas might be.

# THE CALCULUS OF DIVERSITY

**STRETCHING THE LIMITS**

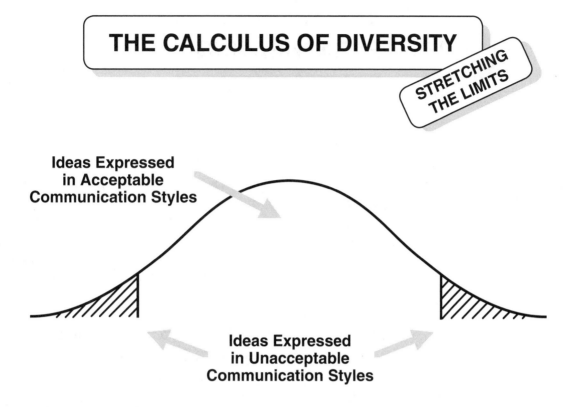

**Ideas Expressed in Acceptable Communication Styles**

**Ideas Expressed in Unacceptable Communication Styles**

Groups that tolerate diverse communication styles can utilize more of the ideas put forth by its members than groups who need those ideas to be expressed in an "acceptable fashion." By using good listening skills, a facilitator can be an excellent support to such groups. For example:

- When someone is being repetitious, a facilitator can use paraphrasing to help that person summarize his or her thinking.

- When someone is speaking haltingly, in awkward, broken sentences, a facilitator can help the speaker relax by drawing him or her out with open-ended, nondirective questions.

- When someone is exaggerating or distorting, a facilitator can validate the central point without quarreling over its accuracy.

- When someone goes off on a tangent, a facilitator can treat the speaker with full respect by asking the person to help everyone see how his or her point connects with the broader context.

- When someone expresses himself or herself with intense feeling, a facilitator can first acknowledge the emotion, then paraphrase the content of the thought to ensure that the speaker's point does not get lost amid the group's gut reactions to the feelings.

These situations demonstrate how important it is for a facilitator to listen skillfully and respectfully to *everyone*.

# PARAPHRASING

## WHY

- *Paraphrasing* is fundamental to active listening. It is the most straightforward way to demonstrate to a speaker that his or her thoughts were heard and understood.

- The power of *paraphrasing* is that it is nonjudgmental and, hence, validating. It enables people to feel that their ideas are respected and legitimate.

- *Paraphrasing* provides the speaker with a chance to hear how his or her ideas are being heard by others.

- *Paraphrasing* is especially useful on occasions when a speaker's statements are convoluted or confusing. At such times, it serves as a check for clarification, as in, "Is this what you mean?" followed by the paraphrase.

- In sum, *paraphrasing* is the tool of choice for supporting people to think out loud.

## HOW

- In your own words, say what you think the speaker said.

- If the speaker's statement contains one or two sentences, use roughly the same number of words when you paraphrase.

- If the speaker's statement contains many sentences, summarize it.

- To strengthen the group's trust in your objectivity, occasionally preface your paraphrase with a comment like one of these:

  - "It sounds like you're saying . . ."

  - "Let me see if I'm understanding you . . ."

  - "Is this what you mean?"

- When you have completed the paraphrase, look for the speaker's reaction. Say something like, "Did I get it?" Verbally or nonverbally, the speaker will indicate whether s/he feels understood. If not, *keep asking for clarification until you understand what s/he meant.*

## DRAWING PEOPLE OUT

## WHY

- *Drawing people out* is the skill that helps participants clarify, develop and refine their ideas without coaching or intrusion.

- It's common to ask a speaker directive questions, such as "What is your goal?" or, "How long will it take?" or, "How can you fix that problem?" Directive questions like these are often useful, but they work by pointing the speaker in the direction that the questioner thinks would be helpful. This interrupts the speaker's own train of thought, which can be problematic when the speaker is still formulating his/her own point of view.

- By contrast, open-ended, non-directive questions help the speaker – rather than the asker – do the thinking.

- *Drawing people out* sends this message: "I'm with you; I understand you so far. Now tell me more." This message supports people to think in more depth, and to say more of what they're thinking.

## HOW

- First paraphrase the speaker's statement, then ask open-ended, nondirective questions.

  Here are some examples:

  - "Can you say more about that?"

  - "What do you mean by . . . ?"

  - "What's coming up for you now?"

  - "How so?"

  - "What else can you tell me . . . ?"

  - "How is that working for you?"

  - "What matters to you about that?"

  - "Tell me more."

  - "Can you give me an example?"

  - "What's your thinking about that?"

- Here is a less common method that also works well. First, paraphrase the speaker's statement; then use *a connector* such as, "So . . ." or "And . . ." or "Because . . ." For example, "You're saying to wait six more weeks before we sign the contract, because . . . ?"

## MIRRORING

### WHY

- *Mirroring* is a highly structured, formal version of *paraphrasing,* in which the facilitator repeats the speaker's words verbatim. This lets the speaker hear exactly what s/he just said.

- Some people experience *paraphrasing* as veiled criticism. For them, *mirroring* is evidence of the facilitator's neutrality.

- Newly formed groups and groups unfamiliar with using a facilitator often benefit from the trust-building effects of *mirroring.*

- *Mirroring* speeds up the tempo of a slow-moving discussion. Thus, it is the *tool of choice* when facilitating a brainstorming process.

- In general, the more a facilitator feels the need to establish neutrality, the more frequently he or she should *mirror* rather than paraphrase.

### HOW

- If the speaker has said a single sentence, repeat it back verbatim – in the speaker's own words.

- If the speaker has said more than one sentence, repeat back key words or phrases.

- In either case, *use the speaker's words, not your words.*

- The one exception is when the speaker says, "I." Then, change the pronoun to "you."

- Mirroring the speaker's words and mirroring the speaker's tone of voice are *two different things.* You want your tone of voice to remain warm and accepting, regardless of what the speaker's voice sounds like.

- Be yourself with your gestures and tone of voice; don't be wooden or phony. Remember, a key purpose of *mirroring* is building trust.

## GATHERING IDEAS

| WHY | HOW |
|---|---|

**WHY**

- *Gathering* is the listening skill that helps participants build a list of ideas at a fast-moving pace.

- *Gathering* combines *mirroring* and *paraphrasing* – the reflective listening skills – with physical gestures. Taking a few steps to and fro, or making hand or arm motions, are physical gestures that serve as energy boosters. Such gestures help people stay engaged.

- When *gathering,* be sure to mirror more frequently than you paraphrase. This establishes a lively yet comfortable tempo that is easy for most participants to follow. Many people quickly move into a rhythm of expressing their ideas in short phrases – typically three to five words per idea. These phrases are much easier to record on flipcharts than long sentences.

**HOW**

- Effective *gathering* starts with a concise description of the task. For example, "For the next ten minutes please unpack this proposal by calling out all the areas that might warrant further discussion. I'd like to gather up all the ideas first, so we can see the full range of issues before we get specific."

- If it's the group's first time listing ideas, spend a little time teaching them *suspended judgment.* Example: "For this next activity, I'd like everyone to feel free to express their ideas, even the offbeat or unpopular ones. So please let this be a time for generating ideas, not judging them. The discussion can come as soon as you finish making the list."

- Now have the group begin. As members call out their items, mirror or paraphrase whatever is said.

- Honor all points of view. If someone says something that sounds off the wall, just mirror it and keep moving.

## STACKING

### WHY

- *Stacking* is a procedure for helping people take turns when several people want to speak at once.

- *Stacking* lets everyone know that they are, in fact, going to have their turn to speak. So instead of competing for airtime, people are free to listen without distraction.

- In contrast, when people don't know when or even whether their turn will come, they can't help but vie for position. This leads to various expressions of impatience and disrespect, especially interruptions.

- Facilitators who do not stack have to pay attention to the waving of hands and other nonverbal messages that say, "I'd like to speak, please." Inevitably, some members are skipped or ignored. With *stacking,* a facilitator creates a sequence that includes all those who want to speak.

### HOW

- *Stacking* is a four-step procedure. First, the facilitator asks those who want to speak to raise their hands. Second, s/he creates a speaking order by assigning a number to each person. Third, s/he calls on people when their turn to speak arrives. Fourth, after the final speaker, the facilitator asks if anyone else wants to speak. If so, the facilitator starts another stack. Here's a demonstration:

- Step 1. "Would all who want to speak, please raise your hands."

- Step 2. "James, you're first. Deb, you're second. Tyrone, you're third."

- Step 3. [*When James has finished*] "Who was second? Was it you, Deb? Okay, go ahead."

- Step 4. [*After the last person has spoken*] "Who'd like to speak now? Are there any more comments?" Then, start a new stack, and repeat Step 2 through Step 4.

## TRACKING

| WHY | HOW |
|-----|-----|

**WHY**

- *Tracking* means keeping track of the various lines of thought that are going on simultaneously within a single discussion.

- For example, suppose a group is discussing a plan to hire a new employee. Assume that two people are talking about roles and responsibilities. Two others are discussing financial implications. And two more are reviewing their experiences with the previous employee. In such cases, people need help keeping track of all that's going on, because they are focused primarily on clarifying their own ideas.

- People often act as though the particular issue that interests *them* is the one that *everyone* should focus on. *Tracking* makes it visible that several threads of the topic are being discussed. In so doing, it affirms that each thread is equally valid.

**HOW**

- *Tracking* is a four-step process. First, the facilitator indicates that s/he is going to step back and summarize the discussion so far. Second, s/he names the different conversations that have been in play. Third, s/he checks for accuracy with the group. Fourth, s/he now invites the group to resume discussion.

- Step 1. "It seems that there are three conversations going on right now. I want to make sure I'm tracking them."

- Step 2. "One conversation appears to be about roles and responsibilities. Another has to do with finances. And a third is about what you've learned by working with the last person who held this job."

- Step 3. "Am I getting it right?" Often someone will say, "No, you missed mine!" If so, don't argue or explain; just validate the comment and move on.

- Step 4. "Any more comments?" Now resume the discussion.

## ENCOURAGING

### WHY

- *Encouraging* is the art of creating an opening for people to participate, without putting any one individual on the spot.

- There are times in a meeting when some folks may appear to be "sitting back" or "letting others do all the work." Does this mean that they are lazy or irresponsible? Not necessarily. Perhaps they're just not feeling engaged by the topic at hand. Some people find that a bit of gentle encouragement helps them to relax and / or focus and / or connect with the topic on a meaningful level.

- *Encouraging* is especially helpful during the early part of a discussion. As people warm up to the subject, they are more likely to speak up without further assistance.

### HOW

- Here are some examples of the use of *encouraging* during a discussion:

  - "Who else has an idea?"

  - "Is there a student's perspective on this issue?"

  - "Does anyone have a war story you're willing to share?"

  - "What do others think?"

  - "Jim just offered us an idea that he called a 'general principle.' Can anyone give us an example of this principle in action?"

  - "Are there comments from anyone who hasn't spoken for a while?"

  - "What was said at table two?"

  - "Is this discussion raising questions for anyone?"

- At times it's useful to restate the objective of a discussion before posing the question. For example,

  - "We've been looking at the root causes of this problem. Who else has a comment?"

## BALANCING

### WHY

- The direction of a discussion often follows the lead set by the first few people who speak on that topic. Using *balancing*, a facilitator helps a group broaden its discussion to include other perspectives that may not yet have been expressed.

- *Balancing* undercuts the common myth that silence indicates agreement. It provides welcome support to individuals who don't feel safe to express views that they perceive as minority positions.

- In addition to the support it provides to individuals, *balancing* also has a positive effect on the norms of the group. It sends the message, "It is acceptable for people to speak their mind, no matter what opinions they hold."

- When a group appears to be polarized, a *balancing* question can elicit fresh new lines of inquiry.

### HOW

- Here are some examples of *balancing* in action:

  - "Are there other ways of looking at this issue?"

  - "Does everyone else agree with this perspective?"

  - "Okay, we have heard where many people stand on this matter. Does anyone else have a different position?"

  - "So, the group has raised various challenges to this proposal. Does anyone want to speak in its favor?"

  - "Can anyone play devil's advocate for a few minutes?"

  - "We've heard opinions from [stakeholder 'group A'] and [stakeholder 'group B']. How about some comments from [stakeholder 'group C']?" For example: "We've heard from the police; we've heard from the store owners. How about some comments from the youth in our neighborhoods?"

## HELPING PEOPLE LISTEN TO EACH OTHER

### WHY

- The questions on this page support people to interact with each other's ideas. Doing this work is a critical step towards building *mutual understanding.*

- The goal of good listening is to gain a window into the speaker's mind. But many group members feel that they are doing a good job of listening by simply paying attention to what's being said. They don't often take the step of questioning what they hear in order to gain a view of that person's context, assumptions, and values.

- This technique also plays an important role in group development and cohesion, as it helps everyone discover that they can question or challenge each other's ideas without upsetting people.

### HOW

- Here are some questions that *Help People Listen to Each Other.*

  - "What did you hear Jim say?"

  - "Does anyone have any questions for Joan?"

  - "Who else is resonating with what Kaneesha just said?"

  - "What part of Armando's idea doesn't work for you?"

  - "Who's got a response to William's comments?"

  - "Sue, how would Naomi's idea play out from where you sit?"

  - "Can you restate Ichiro's remarks in different words?"

  - "Do you feel that Alan understands what you said?"

  - "I wonder if we're getting your point, Ronnie. Can someone summarize?"

- After someone responds to one of these questions, follow by encouraging others to speak too. For example, "Does anyone have a similar view?" or "Did anyone else want to weigh in?"

## MAKING SPACE FOR A QUIET PERSON

### WHY

- *Making space* sends the quiet person this message: "If you don't wish to talk now, that's fine. But if you *would* like to speak, here's an opportunity."

- Every group has some members who are highly verbal and others who speak less frequently. When a group has a fast-paced discussion style, quiet members and slower thinkers may have trouble getting a word in edgewise.

- Some people habitually keep out of the limelight because they are afraid of being perceived as rude or competitive. Others might hold back when they're new to a group and unsure of what's acceptable and what's not. Still others keep their thoughts to themselves because they're convinced their ideas aren't "as good as" those of others. In all of these cases, people benefit from a facilitator who makes space for them to participate.

### HOW

- Keep an eye on the quiet members. Be on the lookout for body language or facial expressions that may indicate their desire to speak.

- Invite them to speak. For example, "Was there a thought you wanted to express?" or "Did you want to add anything?" or "You look as if you might be about to say something . . ."

- If they decline, be gracious and move on. No one likes being put on the spot, and everyone is entitled to choose whether and when to participate.

- If necessary, hold others off. For example, if a quiet member makes a move to speak but someone jumps in ahead, say, "Let's go one at a time. Terry, why don't you go first?"

- If participation is *very* uneven, consider suggesting a structured go-around to give each person a chance to speak.

# ACKNOWLEDGING FEELINGS

## WHY

- People communicate their feelings through their conduct, their language, their tones of voice, their facial expressions, and so on. These communications have a direct impact on anyone who receives them.

- That impact is much easier to manage when feelings are communicated directly rather than indirectly, and intentionally rather than unconsciously.

- Yet the fact remains that human beings are frequently unaware of what they're feeling. In other words, our communications are often driven or shaped by information that we aren't even aware of sending.

- By identifying a feeling and naming it, a facilitator raises everyone's awareness. By then *paraphrasing* and *drawing people out,* the facilitator assists the group to recognize and accept the feelings of its members.

## HOW

- *Acknowledging feelings* is a three-step process:

- First, when a group is engaging in a difficult conversation, pay attention to the emotional tone. Look for cues that might indicate the presence of feelings.

- Second, pose a question that names the feelings you see.

- Third, use facilitative listening to support people to respond to the feelings you named.

- Here are some examples of the second step in action. As the examples suggest, be sure to pose any observations as a question.

  - "You sound a bit worried. Is that accurate?"

  - "Looks like you're having a reaction to that. I'm guessing you're frustrated. Am I close?"

  - "From your tone of voice, you seem pleased. Is it true?"

  - "This discussion seems to be bringing up some feelings for you. Are you upset?"

  - "Is this what you're feeling . . . ?"

## VALIDATING

### WHY

- *Validating* is the skill that legitimizes and accepts a speaker's opinion or feeling, without agreeing that the opinion is "correct."

- Many facilitators wonder whether it is possible to support the expression of a controversial opinion without appearing to take sides. Can we acknowledge someone's feelings without implying we agree with the speaker's rationale for feeling that way?

- The answer is yes. *Validating* means *recognizing* a group's divergent opinions, not taking sides with any one of them.

- Just as you don't have to agree with an opinion to paraphrase it, you do not have to agree that a feeling is justified in order to accept and validate it.

- The basic message of *validating* is, "Yes, clearly that's one way to look at it. Others may see it differently; even so, your point of view is entirely legitimate."

### HOW

- *Validating* has three steps. First, paraphrase. Second, assess whether the speaker needs added support. Third, offer the support.

- Step 1. Paraphrase and draw out the person's opinion or feeling.

- Step 2. Ask yourself, "Does this person need extra support? Has he or she just said something that takes a risk?"

- Step 3. Offer that support by acknowledging the legitimacy of what the person just said. For example:
  - "I see what you're saying."
  - "I know just how that feels."
  - "I get why this matters to you."
  - "I can see how you got there."
  - "Now I see where you're coming from."

- Some people, when they feel validated, are prone to open up and say even more. When this happens, be respectful. You're not agreeing; you're supporting someone to speak his / her truth.

## EMPATHIZING

## WHY

- *Empathizing* is commonly defined as the ability to understand and share the feelings of another.

- This involves putting oneself in another person's shoes and looking out on the world through that person's eyes. The listener then imagines what the person might be feeling, and why – and forms this insight into a statement of acceptance and support.

- *Empathizing* and *validating* both serve to identify and legitimize feelings. *Empathizing* goes one step further: the listener attempts to *identify with and share the actual feeling.* For example, "If it were me I'd be worried!" "That must be really hard." "I'd be feeling very, very sad."

- Moreover, *empathizing* benefits the entire group, providing everyone with a fuller, compassionate understanding of a person's subjective reality.

## HOW

- *Empathizing* can be performed using different techniques.

- The most basic technique is to name what you think a person is experiencing. For example, "I imagine this news might be quite upsetting to you."

- Another technique is to mention the factors that led up to the person's experience: "After all the effort you made to keep this project alive, I imagine this news might be quite upsetting."

- A third technique is to speculate on future impacts. "I can see how this news could also play havoc with your other commitments. Has that brought up any feelings yet?"

- A fourth option is to identify concerns about communicating these feelings to others. "I can imagine it might be hard to talk about this topic in this group."

- Always ask for confirmation. If the speaker says, "That's not my experience," encourage him or her to correct your perception.

## INTENTIONAL SILENCE

### WHY

- *Intentional silence* is highly underrated. It consists of a pause, usually lasting no more than a few seconds, and it is done to give a speaker that brief extra "quiet time" to discover what s/he wants to say.

- Some people need brief silence in order to organize a complex thought and turn it into a coherent statement. Others need a bit of time to consider whether to take the risk to say something that might be controversial. Still others need the silence to digest what has already been said, so they can assess their own reactions and formulate their responses.

- *Intentional silence* can also be used to honor moments of exceptional poignancy. After a statement of passion or vulnerability, intentional silence allows the group to pause, reflect, and make sense of the experience.

### HOW

- Ten seconds of silence can seem a lot longer than it really is. The crucial element of this listening skill is the facilitator's ability to tolerate the awkwardness most people feel during even brief silences. If the facilitator can survive it, everyone else will too.

- With eye contact and body language, stay focused on the speaker.

- Say nothing, not even, "Hmm" or "Uh-huh." Do not even nod or shake your head. Just stay relaxed and pay attention.

- If necessary, hold up a hand to keep others from breaking the silence.

- Sometimes everyone in the group is confused or agitated or having trouble focusing. At such times, silence may be very helpful. Say, "Let's take a few moments of silence to think what this means to each of us."

## LINKING

| WHY | HOW |
|---|---|

### WHY

- *Linking* is a listening skill that invites a speaker to explain the relevance of a statement he or she just made.

- In conversations about complex subjects, it is hard for everyone to stay focused on the same thing at the same time. People often raise issues that seem tangential – in other words, irrelevant – to everyone else.

- When this occurs, it's not uncommon to hear a group member say something like, "Let's get back on track." Or, "Can we take this off-line?" Remarks like those are hard to take. Unless a facilitator intervenes, *the speaker is likely to simply stop talking.*

- Yet ideas that seem unrelated to the main topic can actually be connected with it, often in unexpected ways. *The thought that comes from left field is often the one that triggers the breakthrough.*

### HOW

- *Linking* is a four-step process. First, paraphrase the statement. Second, ask the speaker to link the idea with the main topic. Third, paraphrase and validate the speaker's explanation. Fourth, follow with an action from the list below.

- Step 1. *Paraphrase.* (Embarrassed by the group's complaints, some speakers will need the support.)

- Step 2. Ask for the linkage: "How does your idea link up with . . . [our topic]? Can you help us make the connection?"

- Step 3. Validate the explanation: "Are you saying . . . [paraphrase]?" Then say, "I see what you mean."

- Step 4. Follow with one of these:
  - *Draw out* the speaker's idea.
  - Use *balancing* or *encouraging* to pull for other reactions.
  - Return to *stacking*. ("Okay, we have Jim's idea. Whose turn is it to go next?")
  - If the idea is genuinely off-topic, record it on a *parking lot* flipchart.

## LISTENING FOR THE LOGIC

### WHY

- Solutions to challenging problems often emerge in phases. First, someone has an insight. Then other people see it and shape it into an idea that has good potential to be useful. Then comes the critical thinking that can refine the idea until it is worthy of implementation.

- But often when an idea hits that "good-but-still-rough" stage, some folks become impatient, preferring to delegate the critical thinking to one or two people to do the "detail work" elsewhere.

- In this climate an individual might try to give constructive criticism of the new idea, only to be dismissed by others who don't want to risk derailing the group's enthusiasm.

- *Listening for the logic* supports the person with the critique to express his / her thoughts fully. It also grounds the group. The message is, "If a facilitator can hear this line of reasoning, so can you."

### HOW

- From a standpoint of facilitator's technique, *Listening for the logic* is very similar to *paraphrasing* and *drawing people out.*

- What's different is what you are *listening for.* Rather than listen for signs of someone struggling to make a point, you're *listening for the logic of the speaker's reasoning,* and you are assessing whether the group appears to be digesting it or resisting it.

- A speaker is providing a logical analysis when, for example, s/he:
  - Challenges an assertion.
  - Identifies a bias.
  - Questions a requirement.
  - Seeks to clarify an ambiguity.
  - Makes explicit an assumption.
  - Points out a contradiction.

- When someone offers this type of reasoning and the group responds constructively, stay back and let everyone work.

- However, when you see a speaker's logic being pushed away, *paraphrase* it, *draw the speaker out,* and ask the group for their reactions.

## LEGITIMIZING DIFFERENCES

## WHY

- When someone feels strongly about a position s/he holds, it is often hard to see the merits of a competing point of view.

- When two or more parties hold different views, it's easy for them – and therefore, an entire group – to become mired in tiresome, repetitive advocacy and argumentation.

- *Legitimizing Differences* is a way for a facilitator to break this logjam. By recognizing that each party is making legitimate points, the facilitator demonstrates that everyone's views are being respected. This creates an opportunity for everyone to step back, take a breath, and acknowledge that their own perspective is not the only one with validity.

- It's surprising how often people are better able to understand one another's competing points of view when those differences are both legitimized by a neutral third party.

## HOW

- *Legitimizing Differences* is a three-step process.

- Step 1. Start with a sentence that demonstrates your good faith and neutrality; then tell people what you intend to do:

  "You're both making good points here. I want to now summarize them, so we can treat both views as legitimate."

- Step 2. Summarize their views:

  "Gina, if I'm getting you right, you're emphasizing the need for [doing XYZ] because not taking that step could lead to serious repercussions. Correct?"

  "Daniel, my impression is that you're pointing out that acting now, without data or a support system in place, will turn out even worse. Yes?"

- Step 3. Explicitly legitimize, and invite others to comment:

  "Your arguments both sound compelling – even though they lead to opposite conclusions! Does anyone have thoughts about this?"

# LISTENING FOR COMMON GROUND

## WHY

- *Listening for common ground* is a powerful intervention when group members are polarized. It validates the group's areas of disagreement and focuses the group on their areas of agreement.

- Many disputes contain elements of agreement. For example, advocacy groups often have heated internal debates over tactics, even while remaining agreed on key strategic goals. When members of a group take polarized positions, it can be tough for people to remember that they have *anything* in common. Such dichotomies can sometimes be transcended when a facilitator validates *both* the differences in the group *and* the areas of common ground.

- *Listening for common ground* is also a tool for instilling hope. People who believe they are opposed on every front may discover that they share a value, a belief, or a goal.

## HOW

- *Listening for common ground* is a four-step process. First, indicate that you are going to summarize the group's differences and similarities. Second, summarize differences. Third, note areas of common ground. Fourth, check for accuracy. Here's an example:

- Step 1. "Let me summarize what I'm hearing from each of you. I'm hearing a lot of differences but also some similarities."

- Step 2. "It sounds as if one group wants to leave work early during the holiday season, and the other group would prefer to take a few days of vacation."

- Step 3. "Even so, you all seem to agree that you want *some* time off before New Year's."

- Step 4. "Have I got it right?"

- Caution: To use this technique effectively, make sure that all parties are included. People whose views have not been at least partially integrated into a shared framework tend to stay focused on their own positions.

## LISTENING WITH A POINT OF VIEW

### WHY

- On occasion a group's facilitator is also the group's leader (or expert, or staff person) – in other words, a person who is not a neutral third party. This creates a dilemma: How does this person promote his or her own point of view effectively, while still making room for all other opinions to be voiced?

- The resolution – first and foremost – involves *the mind-set* of the person who is playing the dual role.

- On the one hand, s/he has to retain the mind-set of a leader, and *be responsible for clarifying his or her own thinking and communicating it effectively.*

- On the other hand, s/he has to adopt the mind-set of a facilitator, and *care about helping the group do its best thinking.* This requires a focus on supporting others to develop *their* lines of thought.

- *Listening with a point of view* supports this person to keep both roles in balance.

### HOW

- *Listening with a point of view* is a five-step process:

- Step 1. As the leader (or expert or staff person), raise the issue about which you have an opinion. State your position.

- Step 2. Ask for reactions.

- Step 3. Respond to participants' comments as a facilitator would, by *paraphrasing* and *drawing people out.* Err on the side of more drawing out rather than less. (Many people find it hard to challenge authority; they may need extra support to risk voicing a differing opinion.)

- Step 4. After *at least two* moves of facilitative listening, give yourself the floor to speak. Now make statements that reflect your own perspective. Answer questions, provide information, explain, advocate, and so forth.

- Step 5. Repeat Steps 2 through 4 as needed, remembering to balance expressing your own point of view with at least twice as much facilitative listening.

## SUMMARIZING

| WHY | HOW |
|---|---|

**WHY**

- Good facilitators know the value of encouraging participants to engage in vigorous discussion. But the most interesting conversations can also be the hardest ones to close.

- Making a deliberate effort to summarize a discussion helps participants consolidate their thinking. A restatement of key themes and main points helps people build categories and internalize them. These categories help improve one's understanding of what just transpired, and they also serve as memory aids to improve future recall.

- Ending a discussion abruptly can make a facilitator seem pushy. For example, suppose a facilitator said, "OK, time's up. Let's move to the next topic." This statement, while inoffensive, can be taken as an expression of impatience. Sometimes people respond with knee-jerk resistance. By comparison *summarizing* feels congenial and supportive.

**HOW**

- *Summarizing* is a 5-step process:

- Step 1. Restate the question that began the discussion: "We've been discussing the success of your program."

- Step 2. Indicate the number of key themes you heard: "I think people raised three themes."

- Step 3. Name the first theme, and mention one or two key points related to that theme: "The first theme was about your strategy. You explored its effectiveness and suggested some improvements."

- Step 4. Repeat this sequence for each theme: "Another theme was the validity of your main goal. You questioned whether it was feasible and realistic. Finally, you examined some personnel issues and you created a new staff role."

- Step 5. Pose a question to bridge to the next topic: "You have done some solid thinking about the effectiveness of the program. Anything else before you move to the next topic on the agenda?"

# 5

# CHARTWRITING TECHNIQUE

USING MARKERS AND FLIPCHARTS
TO SUPPORT FULL PARTICIPATION

▶ **The Power of a Group Memory**

▶ **The Role of ChartWriter**

▶ **Lettering**

▶ **Colors**

▶ **Symbols**

▶ **Formats**

▶ **Spacing**

▶ **Tips and Technique**

▶ **After the Meeting**

# THE POWER OF A GROUP MEMORY

In many groups, participation is not balanced. A few people do most of the talking, while others sit and listen. This pattern shifts dramatically when people's ideas are written on flipcharts that everyone can see.

Writing a group's ideas on flipcharts and displaying them on the wall provides participants with a *group memory.** This strengthens full participation in several ways.

First, *it validates.* Recording people's words sends the message, "This is a valuable idea." And when their *ideas* are valued, *people* feel valued. That's the central benefit of group memory.

Second, *having a group memory extends the limits of the human brain.* A vast amount of scientific research has shown that most people can retain roughly seven chunks of information in their short-term memory. Once someone's short-term memory is full, the person simply cannot absorb another idea without forgetting something. (For example, you can probably remember a new friend's seven-digit phone number by repeating it over and over. But try remembering two new phone numbers at once!)

In a meeting this can pose a real problem. Typically, people hang onto the ideas they care about, and let the rest float in one ear and out the other. The group memory solves this problem. Participants know that if they forget something, they can look at it on the chart. This frees the mind and supports people to keep thinking.**

It is important to recognize that the group memory is not merely a tool for keeping the record of a meeting. Primarily it is a vehicle for encouraging full participation. It equalizes and balances. It enlivens the discussion. It helps people work toward understanding and integrating each other's points of view. In summary, *group memory is one of the facilitator's most fundamental tools for supporting groups to do their best thinking.*

---

* The term "group memory" was coined by Geoff Ball, a California specialist in multi-party conflict resolution. He is the founder of RESOLVE, one of the nation's first consulting firms to promote collaborative problem-solving as an alternative to litigation.

** For a detailed discussion on the benefits of using a group memory, see "The Case for a Group Memory" by M. Doyle and D. Straus in *How to Make Meetings Work* (pp. 38–48). New York: Jove Press, 1982.

# THE ROLE OF CHARTWRITER

The chartwriter is the person who records the group's thinking on flipcharts. This role is also referred to as "the recorder" or "the scribe." The reason to have a chartwriter is to capture ideas and build a group memory.

Whenever possible, a chartwriter should record the speaker's exact words. People want to see their own ideas on the wall. And it is imperative that the chartwriter treat everyone's contributions equally. It's up to the group, not the chartwriter, to determine which ideas are valuable and which are not.

Sometimes, of course, a person's statement is too long or complex to be recorded verbatim. The facilitator would then probably assist by paraphrasing or summarizing the speaker's key themes. Once a speaker has confirmed the facilitator's paraphrase, the chartwriter can record the condensed version.

Many facilitators tend to perform the role of chartwriter themselves. Other facilitators bring a chartwriter along whenever a meeting is larger than five or six participants. In general the latter approach is superior to the former. To be optimally effective, facilitators should be facing forward, with their attention focused on group members – individually and collectively. In contrast, chartwriters stand with their backs to the group. Their attention is consumed by the requirement to keep pace with the flow of the discussion and capture ideas and meanings accurately.

Some groups might not want an outside chartwriter. In this case, a facilitator can ask the group to provide its own chartwriter – either by assigning someone in advance, or by calling for volunteers at key points in the meeting. (The facilitator can show the volunteer(s) a few pages from this chapter before the meeting or during a break. This is an excellent way to give a "quick course" in chartwriting.)

The purpose of having a group memory has already been discussed: it supports good thinking and strengthens participation. But in order for the group memory to fulfill that purpose it has to be *used* by the participants – and that's where the role of the chartwriter makes all the difference. Sloppy, crowded, illegible charts are not much better than no charts at all. By learning the simple techniques discussed in this chapter, a chartwriter can make the group memory inviting, helpful, and easy to read.

## LETTERING

### 1. PRINT IN CAPITAL LETTERS

*Readability is the goal.* Most group members have an easier time reading UNIFORM, CAPITAL LETTERS. Writing in cursive may be slightly faster, but taking a few extra seconds to print will probably make your text more legible.

### 2. MAKE THICK-LINED LETTERS

Use the *wide end* of the marker tip. Press firmly against the paper. Firm, thick-lined lettering is much easier to read from a distance than soft, thin-lined lettering.

### 3. WRITE STRAIGHT UP AND DOWN

Straight lettering is easier to read than *slanted* lettering.

### 4. CLOSE YOUR LETTERS

Don't leave gaps in letters like B and P. Letters without gaps are easier to read and less confusing. In contrast, letters with gaps require more concentration from the reader.

### 5. USE PLAIN, BLOCK LETTERS

Letters without curlycues are easier on the eyes. *Fancy script slows down reading time,* so it should be saved for occasional special effects.

### 6. PRACTICE MAKES PERFECT

If your printing isn't perfect, don't panic – practice!

A painless way to improve lettering is to practice whenever you might otherwise be doodling or taking notes, or writing grocery lists, memos, love letters – whatever. *Habits you develop with pen and paper will transfer to the flipchart.\**

---

\* Thanks to Jennifer Hammond-Landau, noted San Francisco graphic facilitator, who gave us this tip in 1982.

## COLORS

### 1. ALTERNATE COLORS

People read faster, retain more, and have a longer concentration span when the text is written in two or three colors rather than in mono-color. Therefore, alternate colors with each new speaker. It's not necessary to follow a pattern when you switch colors; the objective is simply to break the monotony in order to engage both sides of the brain.

### 2. USE *EARTH TONES* FOR TEXT

The earth tones are blue, brown, purple, black and green. They don't reflect as much light as hot colors, so they minimize eye-strain.

### 3. USE HOT COLORS FOR HIGHLIGHTING

The "hot colors" are orange, red, yellow, and pink. They are harder on the eyes and should be reserved for borders, shading and underlining, and for special symbols like arrows or stars. Note also that yellow is very difficult to see at a distance.

### 4. BEWARE OF COLOR CODING

Beginners often try to organize their work by color coding – one color for headings, a second color for key points, a third for sub-points, and so on. This usually turns into a mixed-up mess. A group's thinking process is generative and dynamic – the categories keep shifting as people build on each other's ideas. *"Rough-draft thinking" is not the time for color coding.* By contrast, color coding is very effective with documents like agendas that are created before the meeting begins or whenever the content of the document is known in advance.

### 5. USE THE *CHARTWRITER'S GRIP* TO HOLD FOUR MARKERS AT ONCE

The *chartwriter's grip* involves sticking a marker between each finger on the hand you don't write with. Keep the tops off and point the ink-tips outward. This grip makes it easy to alternate colors quickly and comfortably.

## SYMBOLS

### 1. BULLETS

Bullets are big dots that make items stand apart from one another. Use them often – especially when listing ideas.

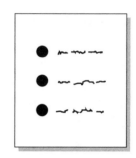

### 2. STARS

A star indicates that something is especially noteworthy.

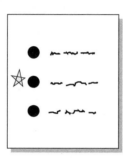

### 3. BORDERS

Borders have a pleasant visual impact. They can be used to frame a whole page or to highlight certain blocks of text or a title. Pink or orange borders work beautifully.

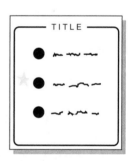

### 4. CIRCLES

Circles can do many things, such as:

- Lasso one idea and connect it with another.
- Highlight a decision that has been made.
- Emphasize the key issue(s) on a page.
- Create first-draft categories on the page.
- Break up the visual monotony of a page filled with text.

## SYMBOLS

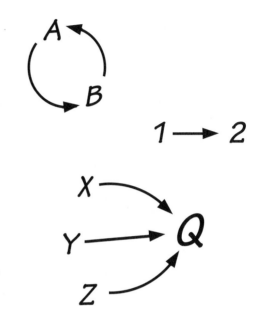

### 5. ARROWS

An arrow is a very powerful symbol. It makes vivid the connection between any two ideas. The nature of that connection might be causal, sequential, logical, or even cyclical. For example:

- Ideas A and B form a vicious cycle.
- Idea 1 comes first; Idea 2 comes second.
- Ideas X, Y and Z all belong to Topic Q.

Because an arrow is so powerful, the chartwriter must take extra care not to draw an arrow unless the connection has been explicitly suggested by a participant.

### 6. OTHER SYMBOLS

Many ideas can be expressed with simple drawings.

* The *Star-Person* was created by the great David Sibbet, renowned pioneer of *graphic facilitation*. For more on graphic facilitation, see Sibbet's series, *Visual Meetings* (2010), *Visual Teams* (2011) and *Visual Leaders* (2013), all published by John Wiley and Sons, Inc., San Francisco.

## FORMATS

### 1. THE LIST

The most commonly used format for recording a group's ideas is the list. It consists of a title (or heading), followed by a series of items, each demarked by an oversized dot known as a "bullet."

Some lists contain subdivisions of items organized into categories, as shown in the right-hand diagram. For lists of this type, the category titles are numbered or underlined. Bullets are used to demark the items within each category.

**TITLE**
- ITEM
- ITEM
- ITEM
- ITEM
- ITEM

**TITLE**
1. SUB-TITLE
   - ITEM
   - ITEM
2. SUB-TITLE
   - ITEM
   - ITEM

### 2. THE MATRIX

A matrix is a grid with headings placed both horizontally (across the top) and vertically (along the left side). A matrix can be used to help a group discuss relationships between two or more variables.

|        | PRO | CON |
|--------|-----|-----|
| IDEA 1 |     |     |
| IDEA 2 |     |     |
| IDEA 3 |     |     |

### 3. THE FLOWCHART

A flowchart can describe a logic pathway, or it can show a sequence of events.

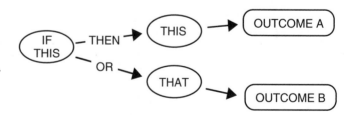

*Community At Work* © 2014

## MORE FORMATS

### 4. THE ORBIT DIAGRAM

An orbit diagram can highlight a key point and describe others in a less linear way.

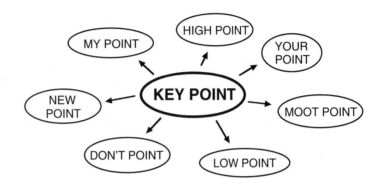

### 5. UNITY IN DIVERSITY

A gaggle of individual thoughts and feelings still add up to a community of shared experience.

When a group is using a go-around process, write a sentence after each person has spoken. Arrange the summary statements as shown to the right. When everyone has spoken draw a circle that connects all.

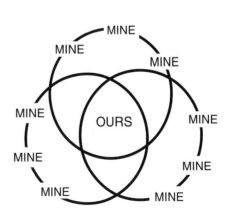

### 6. DIVERSE PERSPECTIVES AND COMMON GROUND

A simple Venn diagram can work like a picture that tells a thousand words, to show a group its points of commonality alongside its differences. Write what people seem to agree upon in the center of a page, and write all other comments on the periphery.

## FORMATS FOR OPEN DISCUSSION

### 7. BASIC PRINCIPLES

Open discussions are unstructured. During a period of open discussion, expect the group's ideas to flow in many different directions, at a tempo that is not always easy to predict. The chartwriter has to relate to this unpredictability by recording the discussion with a format that preserves maximum flexibility.

The general guideline is to leave plenty of empty space between ideas, especially during the early stage of the discussion. Later, as ideas weave together, you will have options for placing newly-integrated thoughts in helpful locations. Group members often catch on, and tell you where they want their ideas placed.

### FORMATS FOR OPEN DISCUSSION

Cover a wall with chart paper, and proceed as follows.

- Mentally divide the array of paper into five sections. Do not actually draw the sections on the paper. (The illustration below is meant only to show you, the reader, the arrangement of the sections.)

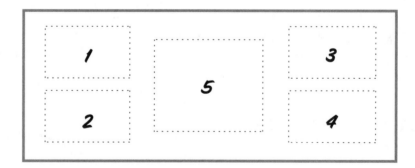

- As you record the discussion, put each completely new theme in a different section. Within each section, record using the list format. *Leave the center section blank.*

- As the discussion moves along, group members often discover that they can use the center space to list central themes of the discussion.

## SPACING

### 1. LETTER SIZE

One inch is normally a good height for letters. If you write smaller than that, many people won't be able to read the charts. But if your letters are larger than an inch, your charts will fill up too quickly, and you'll end up using extra sheets unnecessarily. (Which in turn means that you'd need more wall-space to keep everything displayed.)

One exception: When a group has more than, say, 30-40 participants, some people will be seated too far away to read one-inch letters. You must write large enough for everyone to be able to read your charts.

### 2. MARGINS

Wide margins – 2-3 inches on all four sides of a page – encourage members to edit or add to their previous ideas. This space is also useful for tallying votes – as, for example, when group members prioritize a long list of ideas. *White space is your friend.*

### 3. SPACE BETWEEN TWO LINES

Leave roughly one inch between lines of text, and leave up to one-and-a-half inches between lines when switching color.

### 4. INDENTATION

The less indenting you do, the better. Using indentation to demark sub-categories will create the same potential difficulty as color-coding: people's categories shift as their discussion unfolds.

### 5. UNDERLINING

Underline only titles and subtitles. Refrain from underlining for emphasis. (To note key ideas, use stars or circles, or yellow highlighter.)

### 6. DON'T CROWD THE BOTTOM OF THE PAGE

Participants often behave as if the task is finished once the page is full. If you start a new page, it's amazing how predictably a group will catch a second wind and start generating new material.

## TIPS AND TECHNIQUES

| WHAT TO LISTEN FOR | HOW TO WRITE IT |
|---|---|

### Suggestions

Example: "Let's check in with each other once a day until we actually hold the conference."

CHECK IN DAILY
TILL CONFERENCE

### Logical Connections

Example: "In this organization, it's clear to me that absences and low morale are related to one another."

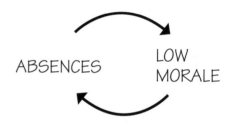

ABSENCES    LOW MORALE

### Summary Statements

Example: "I think we're saying that this program ought to target both teachers and parents."

TARGET GROUPS:
TEACHERS AND PARENTS

### Open Questions

Example: "I know this is off the subject, but I'm still confused about whether we're ever going to hire a new financial assistant."

HIRE FINANCIAL ASS'T?

 OPEN QUESTION

Don't worry about capturing every word a speaker says. Just be sure to preserve the meaning of what has been said.

## TIPS AND TECHNIQUES

### 1. SENTENCES ARE EASY TO READ, EASY TO REMEMBER

"Jim will phone Sue on Friday" is much easier to understand than "Jim Friday." Here's the guideline: *Will it be understandable in a week?*

### 2. DON'T BE SHY – WRITE "WE" AND "I"

Many novice chartwriters feel awkward writing a sentence like, "We want a meeting." They might write instead, "They want a meeting" or "You want a meeting." But since the charts are about the group's own goals, needs and commitments, the record should be in their own voice.

### 3. VERBS AND NOUNS ARE HIGH PRIORITY

Example: If you hear "I hope we remember to write a warm thank-you to that terrific caterer," capture the key verbs and nouns first: "Write thank-you to caterer."

### 4. ADJECTIVES AND ADVERBS ARE LOW PRIORITY

It's fine to write the adjectives and adverbs (like "warm" and "terrific" in the above example) but only if you have some extra moments.

### 5. USE ONLY STANDARD ABBREVIATIONS

Do not invent abbreviations so you can go faster. For example, don't write "defnt" for "definite" or "expl" for "explain." Here's a guideline: *Will it make sense to someone who didn't attend the meeting?*

### 6. TITLE EVERY PAGE

Every page needs a title so it can be identified a week later – even if you just write "[title of previous page], p.2."

### 7. ENCOURAGE PROOFREADING

Invite people to review your work. Accept corrections gladly – even ones that mess up your beautiful charts. Remember, that's how your charts become *their* charts.

## AFTER THE MEETING

### 1. CHECK TITLES AND PAGE NUMBERS

Make sure all pages are titled, numbered, and arranged in a way that will be understandable at a later date.

### 2. ROLL UP THE PAGES TOGETHER, AND LABEL THEM

Flipcharts are often brought back to the next meeting.  It is difficult to hang – or read – pages that have deep creases in them.  Roll, don't fold.

Label the outside of the rolled-up paper with three items of information:
- Name of the meeting
- Date of the meeting
- Topics

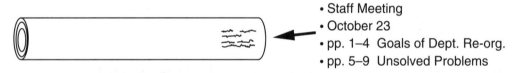

- Staff Meeting
- October 23
- pp. 1–4  Goals of Dept. Re-org.
- pp. 5–9  Unsolved Problems

### 3. SECURE THE PAGES WITH TWO RUBBER BANDS

Many people reach for tape to secure the pages once they're rolled.  Yikes!! Adhesive sticks so well that the pages will rip when you peel the tape later.

### 4. CLARIFY YOUR ROLE IN RELATION TO DOCUMENTATION

- If you are responsible for organizing the charts and making sure people get copies, consider making digital photos before you roll up the charts.  Digital documents are easier to copy, store, and distribute.

- If you are not responsible for documentation, offer to share these pointers with the person who is.

### 5. THESE STEPS DEMONSTRATE PROFESSIONALISM

These four steps demonstrate thoroughness and efficiency.  Group members will notice.  They may not acknowledge it in words, but they will recognize that they are working with someone who knows their craft.

# BRAINSTORMING

## THE THEORY AND TECHNIQUE OF SUSPENDED JUDGMENT

- ▶ **The Cost of Premature Criticism**

- ▶ **Suspended Judgment**

- ▶ **Ground Rules for Brainstorming**

- ▶ **Brainstorming Variations**

- ▶ **Facilitator Tips for Brainstorming**

# THE COST OF PREMATURE CRITICISM

Rough-draft thinking is just like rough-draft writing: it needs encouragement, not evaluation. Many people don't understand this. If they notice a flaw in someone's thinking, they point it out. They think they've been helpful. But rough-draft ideas need to be clarified, researched, and modified before being subjected to critical evaluation. The timing of critical evaluation can make the difference between the life and death of a new idea.

---

**CASE STUDY**

A small but growing law practice was looking for office space. The firm's administrator researched a range of possibilities, then offered a proposal: "I found 8,000 square feet on the north side of town that we can get for $10,000 per month for a one-year lease. And the owner will lower the rent to $8,000 if we sign a five-year lease. We could offset our rent by subletting to the current tenant. The north side isn't great at night, but it's close to public transportation and has plenty of parking. I think we should seriously consider this location."

This was a fully researched and developed proposal, ready to be critiqued. If it had any flaws, now was the time to find them.

However, several months earlier, the group had shot down the administrator's initial proposal. "Since larger spaces are cheaper," the administrator had said, "what if we rented a big office and sublet some of it?"

"Forget it," someone replied. "It will take far too much time and energy to find people to sublet."

Someone else said, "I don't want us to be responsible for too much space. After all, we will probably have to sign a five-year lease. We could really get stuck."

Note that these quick reactions were based on wrong assumptions. It did not require much effort to find a sublet, and there was no need to sign a five-year lease. Yet these judgments killed the idea before it had a chance to develop.

After the final discussion, the administrator stopped looking for places requiring sublets. He then discovered how difficult it was to find a smaller office in a good location at an affordable rent. Six months later, he returned to the notion of subletting and eventually developed the proposal mentioned above. Premature criticism cost the firm six months of wasted time.

---

Premature criticism is often inaccurate. And stifling. When ideas are criticized before they are fully formed, many people feel discouraged and stop trying. Furthermore, they may become unwilling to volunteer their rough-draft thinking at future meetings. They anticipate objections and keep quiet unless they can invent a counterargument. Thus, people learn to practice self-censorship. A group is then deprived of access to its most valuable natural resource: the creative thinking of its members.

## SUSPENDED JUDGMENT
### COMMON QUESTIONS AND ANSWERS

**1.** **How can I suspend my judgment if I truly do not agree with what someone else is saying?**

Suspended judgment does not imply agreement; it implies tolerance. You don't have to let go of *anything*. You're just making room for other people to express *their* ideas.

**2.** **What if I know that an idea won't work?**

Suspended judgment encourages people to use their imagination. This often produces impossible ideas. For example, "If we were all 20 feet tall, we could save lots of gasoline by walking more." Yet an idea like that can be the starting point for a new line of thought. You don't have to believe an idea is true; just let yourself try it on and see what your imagination produces. After all, "if humans could fly" was a crazy idea until the twentieth century.

**3.** **Isn't collecting silly ideas a waste of time? Wouldn't it be more efficient to focus on the realistic options?**

Suspended judgment comes into play when the so-called "realistic" options have all been evaluated and found lacking. Creative thinking, in other words, can be the best use of group time when nothing else works! What one person finds silly may be someone else's spark.

**4.** **Doesn't suspended judgment produce chaotic discussions that go off in a dozen directions?**

Only if the process is handled poorly. Clear ground rules and a firm, relatively brief time limit are the keys to effectiveness. As Edward de Bono says, informality in the content of a group's thinking requires formality in the structure of that group's approach to its thinking.*

**5.** **If I suspend judgment of an idea I think is wrong, how will I get a chance to critique that idea?**

Suspended judgment is *temporary*, not permanent. Most processes that call for suspended judgment are designed to last no more than thirty minutes. *Suspended* does not mean *abandoned*.

* Source: E. de Bono, *Lateral Thinking* (New York: Harper & Row, 1970), p. 151.

*— Community At Work —*

# GROUND RULES FOR BRAINSTORMING*

1. Every contribution is worthwhile.
   - Even weird, way-out ideas
   - Even confusing ideas
   - Especially silly ideas

2. Suspend judgment.
   - We won't evaluate each other's ideas.
   - We won't censor our own ideas.
   - We'll save these ideas for later discussion.

3. We can modify this process before it starts or after it ends, but not while it's underway.

*The inventor of brainstorming as a technique for stimulating creativity was Alex Osborn. His classic, *Applied Imagination* (New York: Charles Scribner & Sons, 1953), has spawned more than one hundred variations of brainstorming.

When introducing the technique of brainstorming to a group, briefly discuss the value of *suspended judgment*. Then ask each participant if s/he is willing to follow the ground rules shown above. If one or more members are not, ask the group to modify the ground rules to fit the needs of all members.

# OTHER EXPERTS' GROUND RULES FOR BRAINSTORMING

## Alex Osborn's Ground Rules for Brainstorming

1. Absolutely no evaluation.

2. Wildest possible ideas.

3. As many ideas as possible.

4. Build upon each other's ideas.

As described in James Adams', *Conceptual Blockbusting*, 1974, W.W. Norton & Co.

## Arthur B. VanGundy's Ground Rules for Brainstorming

1. Criticism is ruled out.

2. Freewheeling is welcomed.

3. Quantity is wanted.

4. Combination and improvement are sought.

Arthur B. VanGundy, *Techniques of Structured Problem-Solving*, 1988, Van Nostrand Reinhold & Co.

## Edward de Bono's Ground Rules for Brainstorming

1. Cross stimulation: one's mind must be stimulated by someone else's ideas. Relevance is not important.

2. Suspended judgment: no idea is too ridiculous to be put forward.

3. Formality of the setting: appoint a chairperson and a note-taker, and set a time limit.

Edward de Bono, *Lateral Thinking: Creativity Step by Step,* 1970, Harper & Row.

# BRAINSTORMING
# COMBINED WITH INDIVIDUAL WRITING

## BRAINWRITING

1. Seat members around a table.

2. Have someone state the problem to be solved.

3. Ask each person to silently write down four ideas for solving the problem on one sheet of paper.

4. Explain to group members that as soon as anyone has listed four ideas, s/he should exchange that page with someone else.

5. When someone has obtained a new sheet of paper, s/he should add one or two more ideas to it. Then trade this page for another.

6. Repeat for 15 minutes, or until most people run out of ideas.

7. Compare notes and discuss.

Source: H. Geschka, G.R. Schaude, and H. Schlicksupp, "Brainwriting Pool," *Chemical Engineering* (August 1973).

## THE TRIGGER METHOD

1. Have the group formulate a statement of the problem.

2. Have everyone silently write their questions and/or solutions on sheets of paper for 5 minutes.

3. Ask someone to read his or her ideas to the group.

4. Have the group discuss these ideas for a few minutes, with the goal of generating variations or totally new ideas. *Suspend judgment* for this 10-minute period.

5. Repeat Steps 3 and 4 for each member.

6. When everyone has had a turn, have the group select the most promising ideas for more analysis.

Source: A. B. VanGundy, Jr., *Techniques of Structured Problem Solving, 2nd ed.* (New York: John Wiley and Sons, 1998).

# CREATIVE EXTENSIONS OF BRAINSTORMING

## ROLESTORMING

1. Have everyone select a character. It can be a great leader, a fictional character, a typical customer – anyone who is not in the room.

2. Pose the question, and review the ground rules for brainstorming.

3. Instruct half the members to participate in the brainstorming from the perspective of their imaginary characters, while the other half give contributions from their own real-life perspectives.

4. After a few minutes, switch roles. Thus, the former roleplayers now leave their roles, and the others assume the roles chosen earlier.

5. Debrief. Discuss any insights obtained.

Source: R. E. Griggs, "A Storm of Ideas"
*Training*, 22 (1985) 56.

## REVERSE BRAINSTORMING

1. Have the group state its question in the form of a goal.

2. Reverse the goal, by posing questions that ask, in effect, "How could we achieve the opposite of our actual goal?" For example, "How could we design the worst possible website?" Have the group list those questions.

3. Now, ask participants to brainstorm solutions to the reverse questions. These will sound like, "A bad website would have no navigation bar."

4. To complete the brainstorm, have participants look over the solutions and explore any that might actually stimulate positive thinking about the original goal.

Source: J. G. Rawlinson,
*Creative Thinking and Brainstorming*,
(New York: John Wiley and Sons, 1981.)

# FACILITATOR TIPS FOR BRAINSTORMING

## DO

- Do a lot of *mirroring* to keep the pace brisk and lively.

- Do remind people to suspend judgment. No critiquing allowed.

- Do treat silly ideas the same as serious ideas.

- Do move around to hold people's attention and boost the group's energy.

- Do encourage full participation: "Let's hear from someone who hasn't spoken for a while."

- Do repeat the purpose often: "Who else can explain why our office systems are so inefficient?"

- Do start a new flipchart page before the previous one is full.

- Do give a warning that time is almost up.

- Do expect a second wind of creative ideas after the obvious ones are exhausted.

## DON'T

- Don't interrupt.

- Don't say, "We've already got that one."

- Don't say, "Ooh, good one!"

- Don't say, "Hey, you don't really want me to write that one, do you?"

- Don't favor the "best" thinkers.

- Don't use frowns, raised eyebrows, or other nonverbal gestures that signal disapproval.

- Don't give up the first time the group seems stuck.

- Don't simultaneously be the leader, the facilitator, and the chartwriter.

- Don't start the process without clearly setting a time limit.

- Don't rush or pressure the group. Silence usually means that people are thinking.

# 7

# TOOLS FOR MANAGING LONG LISTS

ORGANIZING DIVERGENT STRANDS
OF THOUGHT

- ▶ What to Do After Building a List

- ▶ Theory of Categorizing

- ▶ Creating Categories from Scratch

- ▶ Creating Categories Based on
  Predefined Criteria

- ▶ Categorizing with Sticky Notes

- ▶ Methods for Selecting High-Priority
  Items

- ▶ Formats for Selecting High-Priority
  Items

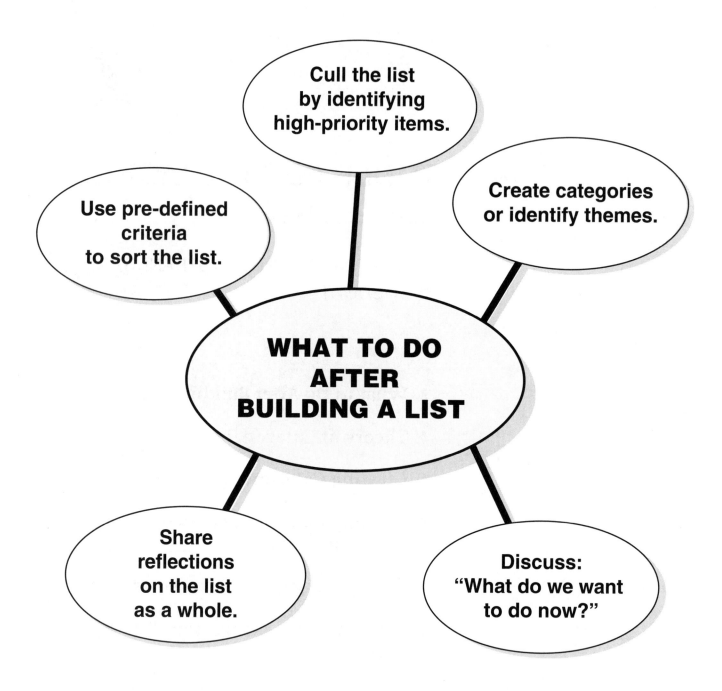

The volume of ideas generated by a divergent-thinking process can be overwhelming. Some groups respond to this dilemma by attempting to have everyone focus on a single idea chosen from the list. This strategy can easily plunge a group into the *Groan Zone*, because participants often differ in the issues they prefer to discuss. An alternative is to spend a few minutes organizing the raw material, using one of the techniques shown above.

# CATEGORIZING IN THE REAL WORLD

INTRODUCTION

When a group has finished a brainstorming process, they often want to categorize the resulting list of items. This is natural. Most people can't hold long lists in their head; they get overwhelmed. They need to organize the data. But categorizing involves two separate mental tasks – *creating categories* and *sorting items into categories* – and groups easily confuse these two tasks.

*Creating categories* is a relatively challenging task for a group, because people don't easily reach agreement on the meaning or the importance of a given category. Therefore, this task takes time. *Sorting*, on the other hand, is comparatively straightforward once the categories are well defined. The problem is that most groups want to *do* the task of creating categories, but they want it to *feel* as simple and easy as the task of sorting items into categories. This problem is illustrated by the following case study.

## CASE STUDY

A group of front-line supervisors brainstormed a list of "Ways to Get More Training." They decided to categorize the list. First they created four categories: *Workshops, Apprenticeships, Readings*, and *Finding Mentors*. Then they began to sort each item into the four categories.

Soon someone suggested that some of the items might better fit into a new category, *Going Back to School*. This elicited a debate on whether *Going Back to School* was the same as *Workshops*. The discussion ended with an agreement to add the new category. Then the group immediately got caught in a disagreement over where to place the item "take classes on computer skills." Should it be placed in *Workshops* or in *Going Back to School*? After a brief squabble, the members decided to put it in both places. But people were starting to get that feeling of, "Hey I don't care, let's just get on with it."

Then someone pointed out that many of their ideas for apprenticeships involved mentors. "Don't all apprenticeships," he asked, "require mentoring? I don't know if mentoring should even be a separate category." Several participants now got involved in a spirited discussion about the role of a mentor. They found this issue to be interesting on its own merits. Unfortunately, not everyone felt this way. A few members got very antsy. One person, irritation in her voice, asked, "What difference does it make? Come on, *please.*"

This led someone to say, "Let's get focused. What's our purpose here? What are we trying to accomplish by doing this categorizing?" And sure enough, the next three speakers had three different answers to that question.

At this point, forty minutes into what was expected to be a quick-and-easy sorting task, someone said, "Hey folks, we're making this way too hard. Let's just do it and get it over with." And many heads nodded, desperately. From that point on, everyone agreed to anything; the experience had gone sour, and people wanted just to be done with it. Five minutes later it was over.

And the finished product? It was typed up and promptly forgotten.

## CATEGORIZING IN THE REAL WORLD

INSIGHTS

### THE NATURE OF THE PROBLEM

Why is categorizing harder than people expect it to be? First of all, it's not uncommon to assume that crucial terms mean the same thing to everyone. ("Why are we wasting time over the meaning of *workshops?* Let's just use common sense.") But, in fact, people *don't* share common meanings for the terms they're using. This problem is inherent in the creation of categories by a group: some people prefer to slow down and clarify meanings, while others want to complete the task and move on. A tension between these two preferences lurks just below the surface in many categorizing sessions.

In addition, individuals vary greatly in the *number* of categories they use to organize their perceptions. Some people are detail-oriented. Their minds make a lot of distinctions between things; they tend to subdivide a list into many categories. Others are global thinkers. They make fewer distinctions because their minds operate at a more abstract level of analysis. Accordingly they tend to subdivide a list into fewer categories. Neither approach is right or wrong; they are simply different styles of processing information. But when people with diverse cognitive styles work together to create categories, they're destined to disagree on such issues as whether *workshops* is a separate category from *go back to school.* And since disagreements like these derive from individual cognitive styles, they can't be resolved by logical reasoning.

### USING PREDEFINED CRITERIA TO SORT A LIST

In the case study, it would have been much easier for the group if they had used predefined criteria to sort their list. For example, *cost* is a predefined criterion, as is *desirability.* If the group had employed categories like those, the sorting would have proceeded smoothly and produced useful results. After identifying some inexpensive training opportunities and some expensive ones, the group would have been able to discuss next steps.

Sorting the list into categories using predefined categories can usually be done by two or three people, who then bring their finished work back to the group for revision. Or the group could divide into teams that each sort the same list into different sets. For example, one team could sort by *Cost (Expensive, Inexpensive* or *No Cost)* while another sorted items by *Desirability (High, Medium* or *Low).*

# CATEGORIZING IN THE REAL WORLD

*OPTIONS*

## CREATING CATEGORIES FROM SCRATCH

*Creating categories as a group means having a philosophical discussion.* This is both the value and the cost of creating categories from scratch. A philosophical discussion puts a group into the *Groan Zone*, where they will have to struggle to integrate one another's beliefs and definitions. The process is uncomfortable and frustrating, and people will resist it. Sometimes the result is worth the struggle; often it is not.

When people present and define their own categories, they are essentially presenting their own worldview. Sometimes this is worth doing, such as when group members have not yet discussed their values or goals. Consider, for example, a community planning group made up of teachers, parents, and elected officials. The members of this type of group have diverse frames of reference. It may be well worth their time to use a discussion of categories as a way to develop mutual understanding. A similar example in a business setting would be a product-development group consisting of members from marketing, manufacturing, and research and development. In cases like these, the opportunity to define categories can prove very useful.

## SUMMARY

Because the opportunity to categorize a list arises so frequently in meetings, facilitators must understand the differences between *creating categories* and *sorting*. Those who do, can make a real contribution to the development of a group's thinking skills.

*Creating categories* is a difficult task. It takes a lot of time and can produce a lot of frustration. It should be done when people want to gain a deeper understanding of one another's values and goals.

*Sorting items into predefined categories* is a fairly simple task. It should be done whenever the primary reason for categorizing a list is to reduce the list to a mentally manageable number of items. A list of thirty or forty items can be sorted in roughly 10 minutes by two or three people. The results can then be reviewed by the whole group and revised as needed.

# TWO METHODS OF CATEGORIZING

## CREATING CATEGORIES FROM SCRATCH

1. Each person in turn proposes his or her own set of categories. It is acceptable to propose one category or many on each turn.

2. Everyone takes as many turns as they want. Combinations and variations are encouraged.

3. After all sets of categories have been listed, discuss them.

4. Sometimes the group's thinking converges easily into one set of categories. If so, the task is done. If not, be prepared for a lengthy discussion.

## CREATING CATEGORIES BASED ON PREDEFINED CRITERIA

1. As a group, select one or more predefined criteria to use as categories (e.g., "How urgent is each item: high, medium or low?" See page 93.)

2. Recruit two or three people to sort the list into the selected categories.

3. The sorters review the list item by item, making sure to place every item in a category.

4. Clarify that it is perfectly fine to place one item in more than one category, especially if there is disagreement about which category is "right."

5. When the list is sorted, reconvene the large group, and revise as needed.

# CREATING CATEGORIES BASED ON PREDEFINED CRITERIA

## CRITERIA ——————— CATEGORIES ———————

| IMPORTANCE | Very high | High | Important to some; not to all | Moderate to low |
|---|---|---|---|---|
| TIME NEEDED | A lot | Some | Not much | Unknown |
| COST | Expensive | Mid-range | Cheap | Unknown |
| FEASIBILITY | Probably will work | Fifty-fifty chance | Probably won't work | Uncertain |
| DESIRABILITY | Highly desirable | Worth a try | Undesirable | Unknown |
| URGENCY | High | Medium | Low | Unknown |
| NEXT STEPS | Collect more info | Talk to boss | Meet with someone | Analyze further |

There is nothing sacred about these categories; they are simply useful in many situations. Some situations may require categories not listed on this page. For example, it might be useful to sort for "degree of controversy" or "how much fun could this be?" Use whatever fits the circumstances.

# CATEGORIZING WITH STICKY NOTES

## DESCRIPTION

- Participants write their ideas on stickies, then post them on a wall.

- Once all ideas have been posted, participants approach the wall and move the sticky notes around, grouping related ideas into themes.

- The entire process is done silently.

- Anyone may relocate a sticky note from one cluster to another. Thus, ideas move back and forth until everyone accepts the categorization. The titles of the themes emerge from the group as well.

- In this way, participants develop a common understanding of the themes as they are built.

## INSTRUCTIONS

1. Hand out large sticky notes, and have people write their ideas, one per sticky.

2. Ask everyone to post their completed sticky notes on the front wall.

3. Next, have everyone go to the wall and cluster the sticky notes into common themes. No talking is permitted.

4. Each time a new cluster is created, a participant should title that cluster with a different colored sticky note.

5. Over the next several minutes, expect the clusters to change as new participants rethink the groupings.

6. The process ends when everyone sits, indicating acceptance of the categories.

# CATEGORIZING QUESTIONS AT A LAUNCH MEETING

## DESCRIPTION

- New initiatives are often launched at special meetings attended by a large cross-section of planners, implementers, and other stakeholders. These meetings typically begin with a presentation by the sponsor, followed by an extended session of *questions & answers*. The remainder of the day's agenda is usually spent organizing the group, in prep for the upcoming stages of work.

- The questions raised during the *Q&A* can cover a wide range: mission and goals, decision-making authority, roles and responsibilities, resources, timelines, and so on. But attempting to answer them extemporaneously, as they arise, *is not effective*. Most group members become overwhelmed and many stop listening. Instead a facilitator can record everyone's questions on a flipchart, call for a break, and work with the presenter to sort the questions into categories and prepare answers that are clear and succinct.

- A set of categories that groups find particularly helpful is provided on the right-hand side of this page.

## INSTRUCTIONS

1. When the sponsor's presentation ends, invite the group to call out questions. Record them all on flipcharts, then call for a break.

2. On the break, facilitate the sponsor to sort the list into three categories:

   - "Questions I will answer right now."

   - "Those I can answer later today, as we discuss the planning process in more detail."

   - "Those for which the answers must be figured out – by the people in this group – at various stages of the work going forward."

3. After the break, post the now-sorted version of the list on a wall.

4. Have the sponsor name the three sets of questions and explain when they will be answered. Then move into "Questions I will answer right now."

# SELECTING HIGH-PRIORITY ITEMS FROM A LONG LIST

## STRAW VOTE

1. Each member gets three, four, or five straw votes to distribute however s/he wants.

2. It is permissible to cast all votes for a single item.

3. Half-votes are permitted, but not encouraged.

4. The top few items become the group's high-priority list.

   Advantages:
   • Fast and dirty.
   • Obvious items are clear.

## DIVIDE THE LIST BY THREE

1. Divide the number of items on the brainstormed list by three.

2. Each person receives that number of choices.

3. Everyone may distribute his or her choices any way s/he wants.

4. The top third of the list – the items chosen most often – becomes the high-priority list.

Advantages:
• Preserves creative ideas.
• Protects minority voice.

## ALL YOU GENUINELY LIKE

1. Each person casts one vote for every item s/he wants the group to treat as a high priority.

2. Only one vote per item per person.

3. All items that receive unanimous or nearly unanimous support become the group's high-priority list. (Note: Most groups accept "near unanimity" – i.e, unanimity minus one or minus two.)

Advantages:
• Reflects what people actually feel.
• Identifies unanimous preferences.

# SELECTING HIGH-PRIORITY ITEMS FROM A LONG LIST

FORMATS

| METHOD | HOW TO DO IT | MAJOR ADVANTAGE | MAJOR DRAWBACK |
|---|---|---|---|
| ITEM BY ITEM | The facilitator reads down the list one item at a time, totalling the hands raised for each item. For example: "How many people like *item 3*? How many like *item 4*?" | The procedure is intuitive to participants and needs no explanation.<br><br>Reduces awareness of the preferences of influential members. | With lengthy lists of options, this is usually a tedious, draining experience. |
| PERSON BY PERSON | Each person takes a turn to state his or her preferences. Often a go-around is the simplest way to get this done. | Builds shared understanding of everyone's reasoning.<br><br>Supports people in attempting to influence the group, regardless of the status of their role. | Those who go last have an unfair advantage: they can revise their preferences based on what others have said. |
| EVERYONE AT THE WALL | Everyone stands up, takes a colored marker, and puts dots beside his or her preferences. | People get out of their chair and move around. This is energizing. | With short lists, this method is often overkill. |
| SECRET BALLOT | All items on the list are numbered. Members indicate preferences by writing their chosen numbers privately on paper. Results are tabulated by two or more people. | Useful in highly controversial situations, especially when someone might make a different choice if his or her vote were going to be made public. | Reinforces the perception that it is not safe for people to reveal their preferences openly. |

## TEN COMMON TACTICS
### FOR MISHANDLING A LENGTHY LIST

☐ **1.** Roll up the flipcharts and put them under your desk.

☐ **2.** Take a break, and never come back.

☐ **3.** Say, "Let's categorize these quickly, then move on."
And then, two hours later. . .

☐ **4.** Publish the list in the next newsletter, to show everyone that your group is making progress.

☐ **5.** Vaguely recall a similar list that was generated at a meeting last year; then postpone further consideration of the current list until the old one can be found. "After all, we don't want to do the same work all over again."

☐ **6.** Have someone go away and sort the list. Then at the next meeting, forget to put that person on the agenda.

☐ **7.** Give the flipcharts to the administrative assistant with no further instructions.

☐ **8.** Assume that every item is now taking care of itself. Later, complain bitterly about the problems that still exist: "I thought we decided . . . "

☐ **9.** Try to shorten the list by combining items. Then argue over the meaning of each new item.

☐ **10.** Congratulate yourself on a very productive meeting.

# 8

# FACILITATING OPEN DISCUSSION

TECHNIQUES FOR SUPPORTING A
FREE-FLOWING EXCHANGE OF IDEAS

- Introduction

- Organizing the Flow of a Discussion

- Techniques for Broadening Participation

- Helping Individuals Make Their Points

- Managing Divergent Perspectives

- Starting and Ending Open Discussion

## FACILITATING OPEN DISCUSSION

## INTRODUCTION

*Open discussion* is the unstructured, conversational, familiar way of talking in groups. People speak up when they want to, and talk for as long as they choose. It is *absolutely essential* to know how to facilitate an open discussion; it is by far the most common approach to thinking in groups.

*Open discussion* serves many purposes. If someone raises an important issue, the entire group can discuss it. And if the issue does *not* engage the group, someone else can switch topics simply by voicing a new line of thought. Points of dispute can be clarified. Analyses can be deepened. Proposals can be sharpened. Stakeholders can express diverse perspectives.

At its best, *open discussion* can be very effective. But many such discussions are hard to sit through. Sometimes the conversation meanders or drifts. Sometimes a few individuals dominate. Or people talk past one another without even attempting to link their comments to each other's ideas. Too often, the term *"open discussion"* becomes just a synonym for *"Groan Zone."*

## FACILITATING OPEN DISCUSSION

*The facilitator's job is to support everyone to do their best thinking.* In general, this means encouraging full participation and promoting mutual understanding. Nowhere more than during *open discussion* is this role so plainly needed. An open discussion, by its very nature and design, should in theory foster high levels of participation and mutual understanding, yet in practice, that standard is rarely attained.

Hence, two fundamental questions guide the facilitation of *open discussion*:

1. How can the flow of discussion be organized for optimal participation?

2. When broad participation produces a range of diverse perspectives, how can the communication of those perspectives be managed so that group members understand and are understood by each other.

Facilitators who address these questions productively enable *open discussion* to reach its potential as a mainstay of participatory decision-making.

# FACILITATING OPEN DISCUSSION

## ORGANIZING THE FLOW OF A DISCUSSION

**A BASIC PROBLEM**   During an open discussion, many groups have trouble establishing whose turn it is to speak next.  Usually the decision is left to each person via the unspoken rule, "Speak up when you have something to say." This principle may seem reasonable, but in practice it can create confusion and inequity.  Those who think it polite to wait for a lull before speaking will wait much longer than those who jump in whenever a current speaker takes a breath.  Also, the way one enters a discussion can create a lasting impression: those who are more assertive can be seen by some as rude or domineering; those who are more tentative might be perceived as having less to contribute.

**STACKING**   This technique is an effective and easy-to-master method for directing traffic.  To stack, follow these steps:

1) Tell the group: "Please raise your hand if you'd like to speak."

2) Before anyone actually begins speaking, assign a number to each person. "You'll be first . . . You're second . . . You'll go third . . ." and so on.

3) Invite the first person to begin.

4) When that person finishes, call on the person next in line: "Who was second?  Was it you, Maria?  Okay, your turn – go ahead."

5) After the stack is complete, begin the next stack by asking, "Does anyone else want to speak?  If so, please raise your hand now."

**INTERRUPTING THE STACK**   The problem with stacking is that it impedes spontaneity.  No matter how provocative someone's remarks might be, anyone who wants to react must wait until the end of the current stack in order to raise one's hand and respond.  Many minutes could elapse, during which time the discussion could move in a new direction.  To handle this problem, the facilitator can adopt a technique called *interrupting the stack*.  If s/he sees a flurry of hand-waving after a controversial statement, s/he can say:

> "I'm going to take a few responses to this last comment.  For those of you who are already in line to speak, don't worry.  I won't forget about you. I will definitely return to the designated speaking order soon."

*Interrupting the stack* can create the impression that the facilitator is playing favorites.  To prevent this, a facilitator should mention at the outset that s/he might temporarily interrupt a stack if there is a sudden burst of energy.

## FACILITATING OPEN DISCUSSION

**ADVANTAGES AND LIMITATIONS OF STACKING**   Facilitators who rely too much on *stacking* often receive comments like these:  "I felt you were being very fair and even-handed with us, but it raised too many topics at once.  I couldn't follow the discussion."  Or, "I wanted us to go deeper into the heart of the controversy, but I felt you were too intent on having everyone participate.  I would have preferred more debate from those most familiar with the issues."  As the examples illustrate, *stacking* alone is not sufficient.

Nonetheless it is a very important intervention.  Often it is *stacking* that enables a group to break habitual patterns of deference.  For example, *stacking* is sometimes the simplest way to help a rigidly hierarchical group make room for participation from low-status members.  Similarly, it can manage the flow of an argument that might otherwise have spun out of control.  In the final analysis, *stacking* is the simplest and most accessible technique for organizing the flow of an open discussion.

## TECHNIQUES FOR BROADENING PARTICIPATION

**THE PROBLEM**   Not all groups can benefit from *stacking*.  For example, some groups engage in a fast-paced, almost competitive style.  For them, *stacking* would seem artificial and forced.  Likewise, *stacking* is too controlled for small groups consisting of, say, three or four members.

Yet even in those groups, some folks might still not know when they can speak up.  The problem is exacerbated when a discussion falls under the influence of a few highly active participants, whose sheer volume of verbiage can discourage others from remaining engaged.  When *stacking* won't work, facilitators need other ways to make room for less frequent contributors.

**ENCOURAGING**   Some people need a warm, gentle nudge to speak up, even when they have something they know they want to say.  *Encouraging* provides that extra bit of permission.  The technique is to ask questions like:

- "Who else wants to say something?"

- "May we hear from someone who hasn't talked for awhile?"

The whole group benefits from *encouraging* questions.  Frequent participators are freed to speak without fear that their contributions will overpower others, and infrequent participators are freed to speak without seeming rude.

## FACILITATING OPEN DISCUSSION

**BALANCING**   This technique is used when the facilitator has a suspicion that people are holding back in order avoid an argument.  In a neutral, friendly tone, a facilitator can ask:

- "Are there other ways of looking at this?"

- "Does anyone have a different point of view?"

- "Would someone like to play devil's advocate for a moment?"

These questions lend a modicum of support to anyone who is privately assessing whether to express a view that differs from what has been said so far.  Of course, if alternate perspectives do not surface right away, it's probably not wise to keep pushing further at that moment.  Often, people in a group come around, and are more ready to speak up, as the trust-and-safety levels gradually rise in response to good facilitation.

**FINDING LIKE MINDS**   This technique is a mirror image of *balancing*.  Instead of using divergent perspectives as the principle for broadening participation, *finding like minds* seeks the same outcome by inviting members to give voice to convergent perspectives.  For example, a facilitator may say things like:

- "Who else feels similarly?"

- "Has anyone else had a comparable experience?"

Note that the purpose of asking a question like this is *assuredly not* to move a group in the direction of closure.  Just the opposite, in fact.  Its goal is to increase the number of people who are participating.  In order to protect against premature closure, a facilitator might follow up with a balancing question like, "Who feels differently?" This will stimulate more thinking.

**USING THE CLOCK**   This technique involves statements like:

- "We have five minutes left.  I want to make sure we've heard from everyone who wants to speak, particularly those who haven't had a chance yet.  Who wants to speak?"

- "We have time for only one or two more comments – perhaps we should hear from someone who hasn't spoken for a while."

While these statements are delivered to the entire group, the quiet members hear the deeper message:  "The stakes have just been raised a bit:  if you want to speak, now is your chance."

## FACILITATING OPEN DISCUSSION

**MAKING SPACE**  The technique of *making space* involves a supportive question that is aimed at a specific individual.  For example, a facilitator may say things like:

- "Leticia, were you just about to say something a couple of minutes ago?"

- "Steve, you look as if you might want to speak.  True?"

- "Jackson, is something coming up for you?"

This move is particularly helpful when a participant makes a gesture that appears to mean, "May I talk?" or "I have an opinion too."  For example, some people lift their index finger without raising their hand.  Others raise their chin in a sort of reverse nod.  Someone else might look directly at a facilitator and crinkle his nose or purse her lips, as if to say, "No, I don't agree with what was just said."  These are nonverbal cues that give a facilitator permission to invite a quiet member to speak.

Of course, it's not always wise to call on someone by name.  Many people do not want to be singled out.  So good judgment is needed.  In a comfortable setting when people already know one another well, and especially when the facilitator has already built good relationships with everyone, the technique tends to works fine.  In other circumstances a facilitator might prefer to rely on *encouraging* and *balancing* – less direct but still effective ways to support quiet members without putting them in the spotlight.

**TOLERATING SILENCES**  A typical silence during an open discussion lasts about three to five seconds.  A painfully long silence lasts ten or fifteen seconds.  Those silences mean that *people are thinking*.  For example, people may need a few seconds to form an analysis of a complex problem.  Or in a tense meeting, participants might become quiet while they search for tactful ways to express difficult feelings.  Silence is not dysfunctional; it occurs when participants turn inward.  Yet some facilitators find it exceedingly hard to tolerate silences of those lengths.  This has little to do with the needs of the group.  Rather, it reflects the facilitator's *own* discomfort with silence.

To discern *your* level of discomfort, ask a friend to help with this experiment.  During a conversation, say, "Okay, let's be quiet now."  Let five seconds go by.  Now discuss how that felt.  Repeat the experiment with a lapse time of fifteen seconds.  *Tolerating silence* is like any other skill – it is acquired through practice.  Let *someone else* break the silences in your conversation.

## FACILITATING OPEN DISCUSSION

### HELPING INDIVIDUALS MAKE THEIR POINTS

**PARAPHRASING AND MIRRORING**  Reflective listening techniques like those on pages 44 and 46 are deceptively simple.  They keep the focus of attention on the individual who was just speaking, and they don't push for any response in particular.  The speaker can decide for himself or herself whether to continue talking or stop.  This is an empowering intervention.

When a facilitator engages in *paraphrasing* and *mirroring*, it is important to do it for as many participants as possible.  Otherwise, some people will wonder why the facilitator seems to be playing favorites.

At the same time, constant reflective listening can become tedious and annoying.  It slows down the pace and impedes spontaneity.  Therefore, many facilitators reserve the use of *paraphrasing* and *mirroring* primarily for times when the need for support is obvious – for example, when a speaker is having difficulty being clear, or when two people are talking past one another.  If reflective listening is done mainly during moments of obvious need, the intervention is rarely perceived as preferential treatment.

**DRAWING PEOPLE OUT**  This fundamental listening skill helps a speaker develop a line of thought.

- "Tell me more . . ."
- "What would be an example?"

(See page 45 for a good collection of questions like these.)

When a facilitator decides to draw someone out, s/he is in effect making the judgment that there is value in hearing more from the person who has been speaking.  In this way, the facilitator has a subtle but real influence on who gets how much airtime – and whose ideas will become better articulated, better organized, and ultimately more accessible to other members.

Therefore, it is imperative that facilitators resist the temptation to focus mainly on the people whose ideas sound the most promising.  *This would violate the cardinal rule of impartiality.*  (Soon enough, group members would suspect that the facilitator had a hidden agenda.)  Instead, use paraphrasing with those whose statements are difficult for others to understand.

## FACILITATING OPEN DISCUSSION

### MANAGING DIVERGENT PERSPECTIVES

---

**CASE STUDY**

The owner of several large parking garages decided to install automated ticket payment machines at each location. A month before the change took effect, he met with his nine managers to discuss his plans for implementing the change.

Partway through the meeting, the owner raised the problem of customers who lose their tickets. He asked for suggestions.

Someone quickly responded with an idea for a penalty.

Someone else thought that idea might not be wise. "We might upset our long-time customers."

A third person predicted that the cashiers wouldn't cooperate. "Those are the most vulnerable jobs. Many cashiers will be out of work in a few months."

Another person agreed, then wondered, "Is this really worth doing? Morale is going to be terrible. Could we just slow down and maybe reconsider?"

A fourth person said he did not favor abandoning the project, but he did have concerns about the reliability of the equipment. He asked, "Should we test for glitches at our small locations first?"

At this point, the owner became impatient, scolding everyone for failing to "stay on topic."

In response, the room went quiet. The managers were not sure what would be acceptable to say, so they just stopped trying.

---

This is a common situation. The owner felt the managers were wasting time on side issues. Yet in reality, no one was misbehaving. *In fact, the opposite was true.* The managers were doing their best to formulate their ideas. The owner had invited them to discuss a problem; the employees were trying to help.

For example, the person who took the cashiers' perspective realized, in the course of thinking out loud, that a layoff was imminent – with all its unpleasant consequences. Likewise, the person who suggested testing the equipment was remembering his last job, where a new I.T. system, installed without adequate testing, had created many problems.

This is precisely how divergent perspectives can produce frustration and misunderstanding. The managers were making sincere efforts to problem-solve. It's just that they were each working from their personal frames of reference. They were drawing on their own experiences to spot issues that, if handled poorly, could hurt the firm. The owner's impatient exhortation to stay on topic did not sit well; they felt they *were* on topic.

# FACILITATING OPEN DISCUSSION

**THE FACILITATOR'S CHALLENGE**   The parking garage discussion is an example of a common challenge that many facilitators do not handle well. It's tempting to say something like, "It seems as if we're getting off track," or "I think we should return to the topic of lost tickets." These interventions sound good, but they are usually ineffective. They tell participants, in effect, "Your own frame of reference is not valid.  It's getting in the way."

The reality is that everyone approaches a discussion from his or her own individual frame of reference.  The meaning, the significance, and the priority of any given point of view are all matters of interpretation.  And each participant arrives with different instincts about such matters.  *It's essential for a facilitator to recognize that this is not unhealthy.*

The *goal* of a good discussion is to produce more harmony among individually different perspectives – to reconcile the diversity through a process of mutual understanding.

But many people seem to think that participants should *start out* with that harmony.  When they hear statements they consider to be tangential, they seek to solve the problem of divergent perspectives through a process of persuasion or control.  "That's a side issue." "Let's get back to the point." "Would everyone please get focused?"  These statements may get someone to stop talking, but they do nothing to make him or her feel understood.

The point is that people of goodwill can and do differ on such matters as what's important and what's not; what's on track and what's off track; what's useful and what's useless.  When these differences occur, discomfort arises.  This is normal and healthy.  It means people are participating.  But the discomfort can deepen – even to the point of ruining a group's ability to think together – when participants don't realize that their individual perspectives are biasing their assessment of the value of one another's contributions.  At such times, people become impatient with one another: they say things they regret, they stop listening, or they act childishly.

What can a facilitator do to prevent this deterioration?  In other words, how does one facilitate an open discussion that has entered the *Groan Zone*?  The remaining pages of this chapter describe many useful tools, along with advice on avoiding some common technical missteps, during periods when a discussion has branched out to multiple lines of thought.

# FACILITATING OPEN DISCUSSION

**SEQUENCING IN ACTION**   A group of teachers were meeting to discuss the curriculum.  Carter, a second-year teacher, made a controversial statement.  Toni, the librarian, had a private reaction: "Uh-oh, Carter's on his bandwagon again," thought Toni.  "This is wasting our time."  But the next speaker responded to Carter's points in earnest.  Soon, Toni said, "Folks, let's get this discussion back on track."  Someone else then said, "Thanks, Toni.  I agree – we're drifting."  Carter, feeling insulted, then gestured with irritation.  Toni, already impatient, now felt even more annoyed.

If a facilitator had been present, a simple *sequencing* intervention might have produced an entirely different result.  The facilitator could have intervened after Toni's remark and said, "We appear to have two conversations going on simultaneously.  Some of you want to respond to Carter's statement.  At the same time, others of you would prefer to return to the previous topic.  So here's what I'm going to do.  I'll take two or three more comments on Carter's statements; then I'll ask Toni to reintroduce the other topic.  We'll spend at least a few minutes on *that* line of thought.  Then, if necessary, we can take stock to decide what's most important to focus on at that point."

This example demonstrates how to sequence a discussion:

1) Validate both perspectives.

2) Focus the group on one line of thought for a few minutes.

3) Shift to a *different* line of thought for the next few minutes.

4) If necessary, ask the group to decide what to focus on next.

**ADVANTAGES AND LIMITATIONS OF SEQUENCING**   When a facilitator sequences two conversations that are underway simultaneously, s/he is keeping a discussion focused without taking sides.  This intervention usually earns a group's appreciation.  By identifying and labeling two separate lines of thought, the facilitator helps participants keep track of what's going on.  And validating both perspectives creates more safety for everyone.

However, *sequencing* is not effective for managing more than two topic-areas.  It just doesn't work to make participants sit through three or four topics that many of them aren't interested in discussing.  So be advised not to even try this maneuver — the group won't let you live it down!

## FACILITATING OPEN DISCUSSION

**CALLING FOR RESPONSES** *Calling for responses* is a method for preserving the focus of a discussion while encouraging participation from new speakers. Examples of the technique are:

- "Does anyone have a reaction to what Erin just said?"

- "Does anyone have questions for the people who just spoke?"

Questions like these guide whoever speaks next to remain on the same track as the person who has just spoken.

As always, the ideas that receive a facilitator's support are likely to be more fully discussed. Yet since the facilitator is asking for broader participation, this move is rarely opposed or even distrusted. Participants tend to view *calling for responses* as a neutral effort to keep the discussion moving. This tends to be true even when it is apparent that the facilitator has made a choice between two or more topics. So long as a facilitator makes the choice in good faith – not for the sake of favoring certain ideas but rather to keep the discussion balanced – most group members will give the facilitator the benefit of the doubt.

**DELIBERATE REFOCUSING** A facilitator can deliberately refocus a discussion by saying things like:

- "For the past ten minutes, you have been talking about topic ABC. But some of you indicated that you wanted the group to discuss topic DEF, too. Is now a good time to switch?"

- "A while ago Robin raised an issue, but no one responded. Before we lose that thought altogether, I just want to check: Does *anyone* have a comment for Robin?"

*Deliberate refocusing* is directive, and it is often felt as such – as a non-neutral choice by the facilitator to cut off discussion before the group has completed a train of thought. Therefore, it's best to frame the intervention as a question rather than as an instruction. That way, participants can choose whether to make the shift or remain with the topic at hand.

After all, it not only calls on people to move their attention from one topic to another, but in doing so it shifts their focus away from one set of speakers, and points their attention at a different set of speakers. Hence, it can come across as a non-neutral intervention.

## FACILITATING OPEN DISCUSSION

**TRACKING**  As illustrated by the case of the parking garage managers, open discussions often branch into several distinct subconversations. *Tracking* means keeping track of those various lines of thought.  A facilitator *tracks* by following these steps:

1) Say to the group: "I think you are discussing several issues at the same time.  Here they are. . ."

2) Name each line of thought that you are able to identify.

For example, a facilitator might have said to the parking garage managers, "I think you are discussing four issues.  The first issue is, 'How to deal with customers who lose tickets.'  The second is, 'Will cashiers cooperate?'  Third, 'Should you reconsider the *very idea* of payment by machines?' And fourth is your concern about the reliability of the equipment."

As a listening skill, *tracking* is described on page 49.  It's a valuable method to use when a discussion is at its most competitive and its most unruly – when people are least likely to be listening to each other.  These are precisely the times when directive methods like *sequencing* don't work.  When everyone is intent on pushing individual agendas, suggestions by the facilitator are hard to hear and respond to.  At such times, a facilitator must refrain from prioritizing or structuring the discussion.  Instead, he or she remains neutral and alert to the necessity for supporting every speaker.  *Tracking* reassures everyone that at least *someone* is listening.

A group generally responds to a tracking intervention in one of two ways. The most common response is an *integrative* one.  Someone combines a few of the tracks named by the facilitator and makes a proposal or offers an insightful analysis or raises a provocative question.  In other words, someone integrates and advances the group's thinking.  The other response is a *persistent* one:  someone returns to his or her pet theme.  At times the members will follow that person's lead, in which case the group has created its new focus – at least temporarily.  At other times a quarrel ensues: "I don't *want* to talk about that issue now." In those cases the facilitator can be an honest broker and propose a simple *sequence*.  "Can we spend a few minutes on this issue, then shift to some of the other themes?"

# FACILITATING OPEN DISCUSSION

**COMPLETING A TRACKING INTERVENTION**  After showing a group the set of issues they have been discussing, invite them to add other themes that you might have missed.  Doing this will remove any pressure you may feel to "get it right." There's no need to hold every issue in your memory during the discussion, because the group will improve your list more often than not.

1) Ask, "Have I captured all the themes?"  Expect someone to answer, "No! You missed *my* idea."  If so, correct the omission non-defensively.

2) Summarize: "OK, you have five threads, each important to someone."

3) At this point you would usually invite another round of comments: "Now let's go back into the discussion.  Who'd like to talk?" However, you might instead prefer to use one of the other moves described in this chapter.  For example, "Before we start another round, would you like to organize a sequence for focusing on these issues?"

**ASKING FOR THEMES**  This technique is like *tracking,* except that the issues are identified by group members, not by the facilitator.

1) Say to the group: "You're discussing several issues, all at the same time."

2) Ask, "Can we pause a moment and list the themes being discussed?"

3) Record the themes on a flipchart as they are listed.

4) When the list is complete say something like, "Okay, it's easier now to see the range of ways you're thinking about [this subject.]  If necessary we can step back and prioritize topics.  For the moment, let's resume the discussion.  Who wants to talk?"

**FRAMING**  The essence of this technique is to gently step back from the *content* and remind the group of the *purpose* of the conversation.

1) As with the two preceding interventions, begin by pointing out that several sub-conversations are underway.

2) Say, "Let's remember how this discussion began."

3) Restate the discussion's original purpose.  For example, "Originally, Susan asked for input into next month's agenda.  The conversation has now gone in several directions.  Some might need to be pursued right now; maybe others can be deferred.  Which do *you* think are relevant?"

4) The remaining steps are the same ones taken when a facilitator *asks for themes*.  Record the group's answers, then return to open discussion.

## FACILITATING OPEN DISCUSSION

### STARTING AND ENDING OPEN DISCUSSION

**INTRODUCING AN OPEN DISCUSSION** When a facilitator works with a group for the first time, s/he should briefly explain his or her approach so they can cooperate with it. Unusual interventions like *stacking* and *interrupting the stack* require more explanation than self-evident ones like *sequencing*.

Here is an example of an effective introduction:

> "We're about to spend half an hour in open discussion. My intention is to support a free-flowing interchange while looking for ways to give everyone opportunities to speak when they want to.

> "If more than one person wants to talk at the same time, I'll ask you to raise hands and I'll number you off. That way, you'll know when your turn is coming and you won't have to keep waving your hand to get my attention. If someone makes a statement that produces immediate reactions, I might take a few comments from people who weren't in line to speak. But I'll do that only when it's an obvious choice. And if I *do* let anyone take a cut, I will *definitely* return to those who were in line."

That introduction takes roughly a minute to deliver – perhaps even a minute and a half. That's a long time for a facilitator to be speaking. But unless s/he explains the approach, the group may not be capable of cooperating.

**SWITCHING FROM OPEN DISCUSSION TO A DIFFERENT FORMAT** When a discussion becomes tedious and people appear to be restless or bored, the wisest choice might be to end the open discussion and switch to another format. Alternative formats include working in small groups, individual writing, listing ideas in brainstorm fashion, structured go-arounds, and many more. These are discussed in great detail in Chapter 9.

### CONCLUSION

Open discussion is the most common of all the formats for thinking in groups. But without strong facilitation, an open discussion can become tedious, frustrating, and ultimately non-productive. Harnessing a group's potential to work productively in this format depends largely on the facilitator's mastery of the participatory techniques described in this chapter.

# 9

# ALTERNATIVES TO OPEN DISCUSSION

HOW TO MANAGE GROUP ENERGY
BY VARYING PARTICIPATION FORMATS

- Managing Group Energy
- Types of Participation Formats
- Listing Ideas
- Structured Go-Arounds
- Small Groups
- Gallery Tour
- Individual Writing
- Improving Presentations and Reports
- Trade Show
- Rotating Breakout Groups
- Debate Mode
- Roleplays
- Skits
- Fishbowls
- Ask The Expert
- Scrambler
- Jigsaw
- Enter The Center
- Setting the Frame for a Structured Activity
- Debriefing a Structured Activity

# MANAGING GROUP ENERGY

(1)

## INTRODUCTION

Managing a group's energy is a critical component of a facilitator's role.

For example, when a group's energy is scattered, the facilitator is thinking about how to harness that energy and focus it. When, instead, the energy of a meeting is sluggish, the facilitator will look for an opportunity to lighten things up. When the energy is antsy and impatient, the facilitator will ponder the options for slowing things down and calming the room.

In a nutshell, effective energy management can be the difference between a productive meeting and a mediocre one.

Yet if the skill of managing energy is an important one, it has also been an elusive one, hard to define and harder to teach. Some talented facilitators just seem to know what to do, as though they had special instincts. But many practitioners find the very notion of "energy" to be mysterious – if not downright flaky.

To understand how to manage group energy, the first step is to be able to recognize it. After all, how can a person manage something that can't even be seen? It's necessary, therefore, to define group energy operationally – or in other words, to define it in a way that makes it visible and measurable.

Theoreticians may never agree on whether "energy" is a biological phenomenon, or a chemical one, or a neurological one, or a spiritual one – or whether it even exists at all.

Yet many group members have no trouble sensing energy at their own meetings – even if they don't have good language to communicate about it. They might refer to it as "the vibe in the room," or "the rhythm," or "the mood." Whatever term they might use to describe it, group energy has a palpable existence, and facilitators should pay close attention to learning how to work with it effectively.

The objective of the next two pages is to demystify the concept of "group energy management," by offering a simple way to think about the process and the relevant skill-set. The remaining 29 pages of this chapter provide a sizable collection of useful tools, each supported with detailed instructions.

## MANAGING GROUP ENERGY

**2**

### GROUP ENERGY IN EVERYDAY LIFE

Perhaps the most common examples of "group energy" in everyday life occur during meetings when a speaker is making a presentation to a group of colleagues at work. We have all seen times when everyone in the audience is captivated. People are listening intently, the silence is crisp. And we have all seen it go the opposite way, when a presentation is boring. Group members whisper or doodle, wriggling in their seats or furtively checking their smartphones for text messages or football scores.

In either case – whether the group's energy was focused and alert, or whether it was dissipated and dreary – a stranger standing in the doorway would have been able to read that energy, even with no idea of the topic of the presentation. And what, concretely, would the stranger be seeing?

She'd be seeing some behaviors, and she'd be making inferences about the presence of certain feelings. She would not be able to "see" the feelings, since after all feelings are private, and unless they are spoken aloud, they remain hidden from direct observation. But she could guess at the presence of those feelings based on the behaviors she was observing.

In the example of a captivating presentation, an observer to the group might see some people leaning forward, or nodding, or taking notes with earnest looks on their faces. These are all measurable behaviors. They seem to indicate feelings that might sound something like, "I'm intrigued," or "I'm fascinated," or "I resonate with everything this speaker says." These feelings can't be validated from a doorway, but they are implied or at least hinted at, by the behaviors that *can* be seen.

In the counter-example (a tedious presentation) typical behaviors include fidgeting, multi-tasking, whispering to a neighbor – the classics of low engagement. Again, these are all observable. As for the feelings, they'd be variations of "Yawn . . ." and "When can we get out of here?" Not so easily measurable but nonetheless inferable, because the outward behaviors were reasonably good indicators of what was being felt in the room.

In summary, when we attempt to recognize group energy, we are looking for behaviors that are visible and easily identified – and that indicate, suggest, or imply a set of feelings that we can't see but we can guess at.

# MANAGING GROUP ENERGY

**③**

## A KEY INSIGHT FOR MANAGING GROUP ENERGY

This leads to an important takeaway from the discussion thus far: You can guess at the feelings that influence a group's energy – but you *can't manage* thoughts and feelings that aren't being said out loud. What you *can* manage is the *behavior* that emerges from the private thoughts and feelings.

Thus, in a disengaged group of people who are withdrawn or self-absorbed, the feeling in the room might be "low energy" or "like things are dragging." That should alert a facilitator to do something. But what the facilitator would *actually do* is something that would *change the group's behavior.*

For example, if you were facilitating that disengaged group:

- You could put everyone in pairs or threesomes. This intervention would create an informal, semi-private opportunity for everyone to participate at a vastly higher rate than permitted when listening to a presentation. The group energy during small groups is lively, refreshing, often uplifting.

- Or you could give everyone a very brief "individual writing" assignment. This intervention invites each person to generate and then refine his or her own ideas. The group energy during individual writing is thoughtful, focused, intent.

- Or you could ask people to engage in a brainstorm session. This intervention increases total participation, even while people are encouraged to be generative, associative and loose in the comments they make. The group energy becomes lighter, progressively more playful and, often, more confident in its ability to create a product.

Each of these options will shift a group's energy, by changing the activity they're engaging in – or more precisely, by changing the format of their participation. Changing the format changes the behavior of the group.

In summary, *we can manage group energy by managing the participation format that structures and organizes the group's behavior, from one activity to the next.*

The rest of the chapter builds on this key insight, providing many tools that let facilitators manage group energy with judgment and good technique.

Group participation can be organized in many different ways, and for different purposes. For example, some formats require everyone to speak; others do not. Some encourage informality, playfulness and first-draft thinking. Some support people to share personal feelings. An individual can be positioned to work alone, or with a partner, or with many colleagues all at once. And so on. This chapter describes the purpose, process and ground rules – and provides helpful facilitation technique – for all the participation formats named above.

## LISTING IDEAS

## RECOMMENDED USES

**1.** *Jump-starting a discussion.* Listing ideas will help a group to rapidly identify many aspects of the subject, even when they're just beginning to think about it.

**2.** *Showing the members of a polarized group that there are actually more than two competing opinions in the room.* Listing ideas will draw out a wide range of thoughts on a given topic. This tends to happen even when there is a polarized, us-versus-them atmosphere in the group.

**3.** *Searching for a better understanding of the causes or elements of a problem.* When a problem is more complicated than it originally appeared, use idea-listing to explore questions like, "What's really going on here?" or "What are some influences we have not yet considered?"

**4.** *Generating a list of innovative or unconventional solutions to a difficult problem.*

**5.** *Bringing a large group back together after people have been working in small groups.* Listing ideas is the fastest way to collect the fruits of their various discussions. The group then has more time to go into depth on topics of interest.

**6.** *Providing structure when a topic feels overwhelming, unwieldy, or out of control.* By listing ideas, participants can see the breadth of the whole group's thinking. The list creates a basis for sorting and prioritizing the elements they want to tackle first. Thus, listing ideas is often an important first step in reducing the complexity of a difficult task.

## LISTING IDEAS

## PROCEDURE

1. *Hang large sheets of paper on the wall.*

2. *Ask for a volunteer to serve as the chartwriter.*
   The job of the chartwriter is to write down everyone's ideas without censoring or improving anything.

3. *Explain the ground rules for suspending judgment:*
   - Anyone may put anything on the list that seems relevant.
   - Suspend judgment. No arguing about what goes on the list.
   - No discussion while the listing is underway. Ideas can be discussed later, after the list has been built.

4. *State the group's task in the form of a question.* For example, "What are our options for reducing our budget?"

5. *Give a time estimate for the activity, and have the group begin.*

6. *Have people call out ideas one at a time.*
   - Honor everything everyone says.
   - Use mirroring as often as possible.
   - Summarize complex sentences for the chartwriter.
   - If anyone begins arguing or discussing an item, politely remind the whole group of the ground rules.

7. *Don't panic when the pace slows down.* It usually means people are *thinking,* now that the obvious ideas have been said. Tolerate silences. If you push for more ideas, many people will feel pressured and stop thinking altogether.

8. *Toward the end of the allotted time, announce, "Two more minutes."* This often produces one final burst of ideas.

## LISTING IDEAS: VARIATIONS

### Listing Ideas: Standard Approach

A group generates answers to a question. Ideas are recorded on flipcharts. All ideas are acceptable.

### Brainstorming

Creative ideas – particularly those that are outlandish, or impossible – are eagerly encouraged. Quantity is more important than quality.

### Using Sticky Notes

Members write ideas on stickies, one idea per sheet. All stickies are posted on a wall. Later, ideas can be categorized.

### Small Group Jump-Start

Have members form pairs and discuss a question. Then reconvene the group to build a list of good ideas.

### Brainwriting

Members write ideas on individual sheets of paper. Every few minutes, people trade sheets, read them, and add fresh ideas.

### Multi-Topic, Multi-Station

Flipcharts on different topics are posted around the room. Members may begin at any station. They move to new ones every few minutes.

*Listing ideas* can be done in various ways, all of which elicit divergent thinking. Using these variations keeps the process fresh and interesting.

Note that although there are clear differences in the specific procedures associated with each approach, *suspended judgment* remains the enduring grounding principle.

# STRUCTURED GO-AROUNDS

## RECOMMENDED USES

1. *Opening a meeting.* A structured go-around (also known as a "round robin") is an excellent way to begin a meeting of ninety minutes or longer. It breaks the ice and affirms the value that everyone's participation is welcome and expected.

2. *As the starting point for a complex discussion.* As a discussion unfolds, different perspectives usually become intertwined in confusing ways. To offset this inevitable challenge, it's useful to begin with a go-around so each person can frame the issue on their own terms. That way everyone knows the lay of the land, right from the start.

3. *Making room for quiet members.* A go-around supports those who have trouble breaking into conversations.

4. *Advocacy without argument.* A go-around restrains members from arguing the validity of each others' frames of reference.

5. *Compensating for differences in status and rank.* A go-around provides equal time to all participants, regardless of the degree of their authority in the group.

6. *Stepping back and taking stock.* After a period of confusion, or perhaps after a heated disagreement, it can help to step away from the content, and take a look at how people are working together. A go-around is the perfect option for doing this.

7. *Closing a meeting.* This gives each member a final chance to express thoughts and feelings that might otherwise not be spoken – at least, not in front of everyone.

## STRUCTURED GO-AROUNDS

### PROCEDURE

**1.** *Have group members pull their chairs together to form a circle or a semicircle.* It is important in a go-around that every member see every other member's face.

**2.** *Give a one-sentence overview of the topic to be addressed.* Example: "In a moment, we'll each have a chance to give our reactions to the presentation we just heard."

**3.** *Explain the process.* Example: "We'll go clockwise from whoever speaks first. While someone is talking, no one may interrupt. When you're finished, say 'pass' or 'I'm done,' so the person next to you knows when to begin."

**4.** *If there are specific variations in the ground rules, go over them now.* For example, a facilitator might give participants permission to pass without speaking when it is their turn.

**5.** *After clarifying the ground rules, restate the topic.* People often forget the topic when they are focusing on your review of the ground rules. Now is the time to remind them and provide a more detailed explanation, if necessary.

**6.** *Give people an idea of how much time to take.* Example 1: "Please take about a minute sharing your reactions." Example 2: "Take as much time as you need."

**7.** *While a go-around is underway, do not paraphrase or draw people out.* Each person has the freedom to choose how much s/he wants to say at this juncture. If necessary, you can follow up on key comments later.

# GO-AROUND VARIATIONS

## The Standard Structured Go-Around

Go left or right around the room, from whoever speaks first. Speaker says when s/he is done.

## Toss the Beanbag

When the speaker is done, s/he tosses an object (an eraser, for example) to someone else, who speaks next.

## Seven Words or Less

People end a meeting with no more than seven words. Incomplete sentences are fine.

## Two or Three "Feeling" Words

End a meeting with two or three *feeling words* per person. ("I'm tired but happy.")

## Talking Stick

A member picks up the *talking stick,* then speaks from the heart. No one else may speak until the stick has been set down.

## Popcorn

Everyone takes a turn whenever they choose. When most have spoken, the facilitator asks, "Who still hasn't had a turn?"

These are just a few of the many go-around variations in use today. They all share the purpose of supporting and equalizing participation. They also all share two ground rules: (1) one person speaks at a time, and (2) the person next-in-line has a way to know when his/her turn will begin.

# WORKING IN SMALL GROUPS

## RECOMMENDED USES

1. *Breaking the ice — making it feel safer to participate.* People feel less reticent in small groups, which seem less public.

2. *Keeping the energy up.* It's physically energizing to get out of a chair and move around. Furthermore, working in small groups allows everyone to talk. Active involvement energizes people.

3. *Deepening everyone's understanding of a topic.* In small groups, people have more time to explore and develop their own ideas.

4. *Exploring different aspects of an issue quickly.* Small groups can work on several components of a single problem simultaneously. This use of small groups is efficient, effective, and quite common.

5. *Building relationships.* Small groups provide more opportunity for people to get to know one another personally.

6. *Greater commitment to the outcome.* Small groups support more participation. More participation means more opportunity to influence the outcome. When the outcome incorporates *everyone's* thinking, participants have a deeper understanding of its logic and nuance, and they are more likely to feel committed to its effective implementation. This is what is meant by "ownership" of the outcome.

## BREAKING INTO SMALL GROUPS

### PROCEDURE

**1.** *Give a one sentence overview of the purpose of the next task.* Example: "Now we're going to discuss our reactions to Dr. Stone's last lecture." Leave the instructions vague for now. (Clarify them in Step 4.)

**2.** *Tell the participants how to find partners for their small groups.* Examples: "Turn to the person next to you," or "Find two people you don't know very well."

**3.** *Wait until everyone has formed their small groups before giving further instructions.*

**4.** *After everyone has settled down, clarify the task at hand.* State the topic people will be discussing; then state the expected outcome. Example: "Dr. Stone claimed that married managers and single managers are treated very differently. Do you agree? What has *your* experience been? See if each of you can come up with two or three examples that have arisen at your place of work."

**5.** *If you have any instructions about specific ground rules or procedures, give them now.* Example: "One person should be 'the speaker' while the other person is 'the listener.' Then reverse roles when I give the signal."

**6.** *Tell people how much time has been allotted for this activity.*

**7.** *As the process unfolds, announce the time remaining.* Example: "Three more minutes!" When time is almost up, give a final warning: "Just a few more seconds."

**8.** *Reconvene the large group by asking a few people to share their thoughts and learnings.*

## Casual Conversation

- Two or more participants.
- Informality prevails.
- Usually brief: 3 to 7 minutes.

## 2 – 4 – 8

- Eight participants.
- Round one: four pairs.
- Round two: two foursomes.
- Round three: group of eight.
- Typically 20 to 30 minutes.

## 2 – 4 – 2

- Four participants.
- Round one: two pairs.
- Round two: all four people.
- Round three: two new pairs.
- Typically 15 to 20 minutes.

**SMALL GROUP VARIATIONS**

## Talk, Then Switch

- Two participants.
- One talker, one listener.
- Switch roles at a set time.
- Often brief: 5 to 8 minutes.

## Two Rounds or More

- Two participants.
- Round one: talk, then switch.
- Round two: repeat sequence.
- Typically 10 to 15 minutes.

## Cocktail Party

- Temporary groupings.
- Objective: informal discussion of key themes.
- Participants mill about.
- Typically 20 to 30 minutes.

## Buddy System

- Two or three participants.
- Partners remain together while activities change.
- Can last all day.

## Breakout Groups

- Any number of participants.
- Objective: make significant headway on a task.
- Chartwriting adds value.
- Often 30 to 45 minutes.

**MORE SMALL GROUP VARIATIONS**

## Speed Dating

- Two participants.
- Objective: explore diversity.
- Casual conversation.
- Switch partners every 2-3 min.
- Typically 15 to 30 minutes.

## Activity with Feedback

- Three or more participants.
- Objective: skillbuilding.
- One person observes silently while others do an activity.
- Observer gives feedback when activity concludes.

There are many more ways to work in small groups than most facilitators realize. Variety prevents boredom and keeps people wondering what will come next.

# USING SMALL GROUPS FOR MULTI-TASKING

## BREAKOUT GROUPS

1. Divide the group into *breakout groups* (i.e., committees) and assign a different task to each. For example, suppose the group is planning a conference. They might divide into three *breakout groups*. One makes a list of people to invite; a second group lists topics to discuss; and a third identifies logistics to handle.

2. Have each *breakout group* select people to play any needed roles, such as discussion leader, recorder and report-out presenter.

3. Specify the time limit for working in committee. Then begin. Give a 10-minute warning before ending.

4. Reconvene the large group. Ask for a report from each *breakout group*. Allow 5 to 10 minutes for questions.

## THE GALLERY TOUR

1. Divide the group into *breakout groups,* and assign their tasks.

2. Give flipcharts and markers to each *breakout group* and send them to their "stations." These could be in separate rooms, or in different corners of the same room. Have every *breakout group* record their work on flipcharts and post the charts on nearby walls.

3. When time is up, reconvene the large group. Now form "tour groups." Each tour group should have at least one member from every *breakout group*.

4. Tell the groups to take a 7 to 10 minute tour of each station. Have someone from each *breakout group* explain the charts from that group.

## INDIVIDUAL WRITING

### RECOMMENDED USES

1. *Giving members a chance to collect their thoughts in preparation for open discussion.*

2. *Reflecting privately on something unusual or noteworthy that happened recently in the group.*

3. *Preserving anonymity.* People may hesitate to speak freely when their superiors or subordinates are present, or when they fear other group members will disapprove of their comments. Sometimes members are more willing to share their thoughts when they can submit them anonymously.

4. *Helping people remain engaged when the discussion has bogged down.* Individual writing gives participants a break from the interpersonal intensity of group dynamics, while allowing them to keep working on the issues at hand.

5. *Allowing group members to collect their thoughts and feelings after tempers have flared.* When emotions go out of control, people can benefit from taking five minutes to write about the hurt and anger they may be feeling.

6. *Producing a first draft of a written product, such as a letter or a mission statement.* In this use of individual writing, each person writes a rough-draft version of the product. Then, those who like what they've written can share their drafts with the group.

7. *Providing input to a sponsor or decision-maker who does not attend the meeting.*

8. *Evaluating a meeting when time is scarce but constructive criticism is needed.*

## INDIVIDUAL WRITING

### PROCEDURE

**1.** *Give an overview of the task.* For example, "We're going to take five minutes writing our thoughts about the problems with our performance review process."

**2.** *Ask everyone to take out a pen and paper.* (Note: Bring extra pens and paper. Due to the prevalence of digital devices, many people no longer carry writing utensils to meetings.)

**3.** *Wait until everyone has settled in.*

**4.** *Give detailed instructions about the task.* For example, "We know the performance review process needs to be improved. Your task right now is to clarify what's wrong with it. First, write down two or three problems with the current system. Then jot down your thoughts on why the process has been difficult to change."

**5.** *Let people know whether they will be expected to show their work to someone else.* It is reassuring to say, "You won't have to show this to anyone. This is intended solely to help you clarify your own thinking."

**6.** *Let people know how much time has been allotted for individual writing. Then begin.*

**7.** *Give a one-minute warning when time is almost up.*

**8.** *When time runs out, reconvene the group.* Allow ample time for discussion of the material that was generated during the writing period.

# IMPROVING PRESENTATIONS AND REPORTS

## PROBLEM

## SOLUTION

Disorganized, complicated reports that group members cannot follow.

Encourage the presenter to take a few minutes ahead of time to think through the logic of his or her report.

Tedious, rambling, repetitive reports.

Have the presenter jot down key points on paper before speaking.

Group members do not appear to understand the report's central point.

Encourage the presenter to state the most important point in the first few sentences, then restate it as summary.

People sit passively through a PowerPoint slide presentation, with no indication of reactions.

Break up the presentation with periods of high-engagement activity, such as small group discussions.

People react to a report with a dazed and uncomprehending look, as though it made no sense.

Ask the presenter to set aside time for questions and answers. Then facilitate an actual Q&A session.

Confusion about what the listeners are expected to do with information presented.

Encourage the presenter to tell people what s/he expects them to do with the information afterward.

Reports that barrage the listeners with details, causing people to get overloaded and shut down.

Encourage the presenter to use simple visual aids and replace details with diagrams. Hand-drawn flipcharts often work better than PowerPoint slides.

Presenters keep talking while handing out written materials. Participants stop listening in order to look over the handouts.

Advise the presenter to pause while people look over the material being distributed. Or wait until the report is done before distributing handouts.

# TRADE SHOW

## DESCRIPTION

- *Trade Show* is an audience-friendly method of presenting information to a group. It is useful whenever at least three speakers are expected to make consecutive presentations that will each run 15 minutes or longer.

- Normally multiple speakers give their presentations to the entire audience, sequentially. With *Trade Show,* speakers present to subgroups simultaneously.

- In this format, audience members rotate to a new speaker's station after a set time has elapsed. Speakers then repeat their talk to the new arrivals.

- *Trade Show* has several benefits. The smaller group size enables more participation and deeper discussion. And walking is energizing; it counteracts the mind-numbing effect of "presentation overload."

## INSTRUCTIONS

1. In advance, identify locations where different speakers can create stations for their presentations. Each speaker should have his or her own station.

2. At the scheduled time, send presenters to their stations. Then send group members to stations. Send an equal number of participants to each station.

3. Have speakers give their presentations for a set time, followed by questions and/or discussion, also for a set time.

4. When time runs out, have everyone leave their stations and go to new ones. (Clockwise rotations work well.)

5. Have speakers repeat the same presentation to their new audiences.

6. Repeat steps 3 to 5 as often as necessary, so that all participants have heard all presentations.

7. Reconvene the whole group to debrief.

# ROTATING BREAKOUT GROUPS

## DESCRIPTION

- The design is a sophisticated version of *Trade Show,* modified to allow all participants an equal hand in developing key ideas.

- As with *Trade Show,* form three breakout groups. Each group focuses on one of three distinct questions. Over the course of the activity, every participant will rotate to all three workstations, allowing everyone to work on all three topics.

- Unlike *Trade Show,* however, there is not an expert waiting at each station to guide or influence the group's thinking. The group works on its topic, records its ideas on flipcharts, and then leaves that work for the next group to build on.

- This format offers a superb way to help a group engage in progressively convergent thinking, even while taking advantage of the vitality of the classic breakout-group model.

## INSTRUCTIONS

1. Have the group identify three challenging questions that arise from the topic they are working on.

2. Divide everyone into three breakout groups and send them into three corners of the room — one for each question they named. Hang flipcharts.

3. Once everyone is settled at their stations, have someone volunteer from each group to be the recorder.

4. Provide specific additional instructions as needed, then let everyone get to work for the next 15–30 minutes.

5. When time has expired, send each group clockwise to the next station. *Have them build on the ideas that were developed by the previous group.*

6. When time expires for round two, rotate groups a third and final time.

7. Upon completion, have everyone stand and do a gallery tour of the flipcharts at all stations. Then debrief together.

# DEBATE MODE

## DESCRIPTION

- *Debate Mode* is intentionally designed to emphasize differences between two points of view. Each position is championed by a team. The teams take turns, each making their case, followed by time for "rebuttal" where each side may respond to the other's remarks.

- Formalizing a difference of opinion allows people to clarify the logic of an argument. Each side develops a path of reasoning that they feel can stand up to other's examination and criticism. This means thinking about the issue from both sides.

- Taking the time to explicate the rationale of opposing viewpoints increases people's tolerance for differences while supporting a group to understand each other's perspectives more deeply.

## INSTRUCTIONS

1. Identify two points of view. Choose teams to represent each one (usually 2-4 people).

2. Instruct each team to construct their argument by clearly stating the position and rationale using logical reasoning and evidence, and to be prepared to answer questions and criticism with considered responses.

3. Allow time for the teams to prepare their arguments, and assign the role of speaker.

4. Decide who goes first. Explain the rules and timing: First round - 7 minutes per side, no interruptions. Second round - 5 minutes to respond to the other team's position.

5. Begin the activity and keep time.

6. Optional ending: the whole group decides which team won.

## ROLEPLAYS

### DESCRIPTION

- A roleplay starts with a fabricated scenario, which then unfolds over the course of 15 to 20 minutes. Among its beneficial uses are these: participants can test "what if" ideas; they can try out new skills; or they can put themselves in the shoes of characters they're roleplaying, thus gaining insight and compassion.

- Roleplays should not be designed too elaborately. They are effective only when everyone has a shared understanding of how the activity is going to work, and why. Clear role definitions and a clear explanation of the plot line are essential to success.

- On the other hand, rigid roles set up participants to run out of ideas, and become goofy or overly aggressive. To prevent this common problem, give everyone permission to change their minds as the roleplay unfolds.

### INSTRUCTIONS

1. Start by explaining the purpose of the roleplay. For example, "This activity will help us gain insight into some communication problems between managers and employees."

2. Break into small groups.

3. Assign a role to each participant, and provide some background to bring that role to life. For example, "Your boss gave you an impossible task and you were afraid to challenge him."

4. Give any specific instructions that might be needed. For example, "In this roleplay, you must explain why you did not finish the task, to a boss who may react defensively."

5. Clarify the time limits. Then begin.

6. When finished, reconvene the large group, and debrief the activity.

# SKITS

## DESCRIPTION

- *Skits* is most well-known as an activity for school-aged children. In the adult version, four-to-six-person breakout groups create short comical sketches that pertain to an issue of relevance to the whole group. Fifteen to thirty minutes is allocated for creating the skit, after which the small groups reconvene and perform their skits in front of everyone.

- Because of its connotations as a child's game, the power of *Skits* is undervalued. To illustrate its effectiveness here is a case from real life. At an annual staff meeting, a school principal and some senior teachers donned baseball hats and t-shirts, etc., and pretended to be students griping over a controversial school policy. Everyone allowed themselves to be silly; the audience laughed heartily. Yet the teachers were able to surface the most polarizing issues facing the school.

## INSTRUCTIONS

1. Using a broad theme, (like "Next Year's Budget"), create breakout groups. Give them a time limit to plan their skits, and send them away.

2. Much of the success of *Skits* derives from what happens in small groups during preparation. When dreaming up the skit, it's easy for a group to get into a playful mood. This often unleashes creativity and inspiration. To enhance that effect, kick off the planning session by encouraging participants to have fun with it!

3. Before reconvening, call a break. This gives slower groups a bit more time.

4. After each skit encourage raucous applause. Finish all skits before debriefing any of them.

5. End by asking for a few comments on learnings and other benefits.

# FISHBOWLS

## DESCRIPTION

- *Fishbowls* are done to help build mutual understanding among people whose backgrounds or jobs are significantly different. For example, a fishbowl might help doctors, nurses, and managers to understand each other's viewpoints.

- For a set amount of time, one group (for example, the nurses) sits together in the center of the room and talks among themselves, while others listen in on the discussion. When time is up, a brief whole-group conversation ensues. Then a new group moves into the fishbowl.

- In this way, like-minded participants are afforded a time-limited opportunity to publicly discuss an issue without needing to explain or defend their thoughts against competing perspectives.

## INSTRUCTIONS

1. Introduce the activity by explaining its purpose. For example (to a group of government officials, service providers, and community activists), "This activity will help you better understand each other's priorities and challenges without getting tangled up in debate."

2. Invite one stakeholder group to be "in the fishbowl." Seat them in a circle in the center of the room.

3. Ask those in the fishbowl to discuss a given issue. Set a time limit. Ask all others to remain quiet and listen.

4. When time is up, allow everyone to make comments and ask questions. Optional: Ask those who were in the fishbowl to report on how it felt.

5. Bring the next stakeholder group into the fishbowl, and repeat the process.

# ASK THE EXPERT

## DESCRIPTION

- *Ask the Expert* creates fishbowl-style, one-to-one conversations between a knowledgeable group member and another member who wants to probe that expertise in more depth than an open discussion normally permits.

- At the group's request, an "expert" member sits at the front of the room. Someone poses a question, which the "expert" answers. At this point, the facilitator encourages the questioner to continue, whether by making comments or asking further questions. The interaction typically runs three to five minutes, usually without need of facilitation.

- The process can be repeated – with the same "expert" or a new one – for as many rounds as the group wants.

- Although only one person is actually conversing with the "expert," many others can feel quite stimulated – as though they too were participating.

## INSTRUCTIONS

1. Before starting the activity, confirm the group's interest in the subject matter. This is often best done in advance, by the agenda-planner(s).

2. Encourage the "expert" to sit at the front of the room.

3. Ask if anyone wants the questioner's role. If so, begin. If not, don't push. In some groups people may feel you are imposing artificial differences in status, which they do not support.

4. Once underway, treat the process as a conversation that's happening in someone's living room. Mainly, just let them talk. Exception: if one or both parties get so nervous that they freeze, draw them out.

5. At the four-minute mark, give a one-minute warning.

6. When time is up, ask if someone else wants a turn. Repeat as time permits.

# SCRAMBLER

## DESCRIPTION

- *Scrambler* is a way to organize a small-group activity so that participants can work with many different partners within the frame of that single activity.

- The key is to break the activity into rounds. Upon completion of each round, the members of each subgroup separate from one another and form new subgroups.

- To avoid chaos, the instructions should give participants a clear way to find new partners. Best practice is to first send one person clockwise to the next station; then send another counterclockwise. Have the third person remain seated. If the activity is designed for more than three participants per subgroup, send people two stations to the left, two to the right, and so on.

## INSTRUCTIONS

1. Form groups of three. Then have everyone number off (#1... #2... #3...) within their small groups.

2. Assign roles, describe the activity in suitable detail, and let the action begin.

3. When time is up, ask everyone who is a #1 to stand up. Send them clockwise to the next group.

4. Now ask the #2s to stand. Send them *counterclockwise* to the next group.

5. All #3s remain in place.

6. Repeat Step 2, reassigning new roles to each individual. For example, if the #1s were listeners before, this time the #2s would be listeners.

7. Repeat Steps 4 to 6 once more.

8. Reconvene the group, and debrief.

# JIGSAW

## DESCRIPTION

- *Jigsaw* is a small-group procedure that allows multiple stakeholders to spend time first with members who share their interests, and then with members who may have different priorities – thus influencing and being influenced by all points of view.

- People begin this activity in the full group, where they define key themes related to the meeting's broader goals.

- Next, they form small groups with others who are interested in exploring one of the key themes.

- After time has elapsed, everyone reorganizes into *jigsaw groups,* which are composed of representatives from the various *interest groups.*

- In *jigsaw groups* they report and discuss key ideas that arose during the work done in the *interest groups.*

## INSTRUCTIONS

1. Identify the topic to be worked on.

2. Have participants distill the topic into themes that interest them.

3. Have everyone form small groups based on their interest in a theme. Give these *interest groups* a relevant task, such as, "Discuss the issues you find most challenging to deal with."

4. When a set time runs out, have everyone form *jigsaw groups.* Each *jigsaw group* should contain one representative from each *interest group.* For example, if there were five *interest groups,* each *jigsaw group* would have five members.

5. In *jigsaw groups,* report on discussions that took place in the *interest groups.* Further discussion is optional.

6. Reconvene the whole group, and debrief the activity.

## ENTER THE CENTER

### DESCRIPTION

- *Enter the Center* is a specialized type of fishbowl, with ground rules that have been modified to support diverse stakeholders to engage in meaningful dialogue.

- Like a fishbowl, a few people sit in the center of the room and talk, while the others sit in an outer circle and listen but do not speak.

- Unlike a fishbowl, however, the outsiders can participate by *entering the center,* standing behind one of the speakers and tapping that person on the back. This requires the speaker to relinquish his/her seat to the newcomer.

- *Enter the Center* is especially useful for dialogue and deliberation on controversial issues. Because of the slightly ritualized nature of this process, participants often speak with sincerity or passion when they take their turns.

### INSTRUCTIONS

1. *Arrange chairs into two concentric circles.* The inner circle should seat one or two representatives from each stakeholder group, plus the facilitator. The outer ring should have sufficient chairs to seat all other participants.

2. Explain that only those who sit in the inner circle can speak. Those in the outer circle can speak only by replacing someone from the inner circle.

3. Invite one or two people from each stakeholder group into the inner circle.

4. Explain that anyone wanting to speak should come forward when ready, stand silently behind someone's chair, and tap that person's shoulder. After speaking once more (if s/he wants to), the seated person has to move to the outer circle.

5. Clarify the time limits – usually 60-90 minutes. Then begin.

6. During the dialogue, intervene only if a ground rule is being broken. Otherwise let the process be self-managing.

## Walk and Talk

Send everyone outdoors, in pairs, to discuss a topic while taking a 30-45 minute walk. (The topic can be the same for everyone, or not.)

## Speakers & Panels

Educate a group by bringing in outside speakers – either individually or as panelists. Also, consider opening the session to invited guests.

## Cafe Mode

Meet at a nearby cafe. Sit in pairs, threes or fours, at different tables. Informally drop in on each other, whenever it feels right.

## CHANGE OF PACE

## Watch a Video

Go online and find one or two inspirational videos that can stimulate conversation. Hook up your laptop to a projector, and enjoy! Popcorn optional.

## Field Trips

Arrange for your group to visit a program, business or community that exemplifies "best practices" relevant to your group's objectives.

## 90-Minute Offsite

For one segment of a day-long meeting, switch rooms. Or move to another nearby location, like the diner across the street. Keep working on the content of your agenda.

Working together in a group for long hours is taxing, even draining. Participation formats like these – which add novelty, physical movement, or a change of scene – are invaluable as an energizing supplement to productivity.

— Community At Work —

# Setting the Frame for an Activity

1. **State the Purpose in One Sentence:**
   "The issue we're now going to work on is . . ."

2. **Organize the Participants:**
   "Find two partners you don't know well . . ."

3. **Wait Until the Buzz Subsides.**

4. **Summarize The Process:**
   "Two people will talk, one person will listen . . ."

5. **Specify the Ground Rules:**
   "When it's your turn as listener, you will . . ."

6. **Note the Allotted Time for the Activity:**
   "Here's how long this will take . . ."

When a facilitator introduces a new activity, many group members won't fully pay attention to what they're being asked to do, especially if the activity makes them feel a bit self-conscious. The logical progression shown above is crisp and concrete – so that even those who are somewhat distracted or self-absorbed will be able to grasp what's expected of them.

# DEBRIEFING A STRUCTURED ACTIVITY

## WHY

Structured activities, like *listing ideas* or *breaking into small groups,* usually produce a wide range of perspectives. At the completion of a structured activity, it is usually worthwhile to provide time for reflecting on the discussion as a whole. For example, people might make observations like, "I never realized that there were so many different ways of looking at this issue!" or, "Now I'm starting to understand why this is such a problem."

This step is particularly important when people have been working in separate groups. It creates an immediate context for resuming work together, thus restoring the group's integrity as a single entity.

## HOW

1. Before starting, select a question from the following list. All such questions work equally well.

   Now that [the given activity] is complete,
   • How did this go for you?
   • What have you learned?
   • What concerns has this raised for you?
   • What feelings did this bring up for you?
   • What are you noticing about this group?
   • What do you think of our prospects for success?
   • Have you heard anything fresh and new?
   • How do you react to hearing so many different points of view?

2. Ask for a few participants to respond to the chosen question. Alternatively, have a *go-around* so everyone can respond.

3. Upon completion of Step 2, proceed to the next item on the agenda. Alternatively, have the group discuss, "Where do we go from here?"

# 10

# EFFECTIVE AGENDAS: DESIGN PRINCIPLES

FRAMEWORK FOR DEFINING, SEQUENCING AND COMMUNICATING THE GAME PLAN

▶ Building Blocks of an Effective Agenda

▶ From Building Blocks to Logic Model

▶ From Sections to Sequence

▶ Six Agenda Templates

▶ Communicating the Game Plan

▶ Agenda Planning Roles

▶ Involving Participants in Agenda Design

▶ Design Principles:  Summary and Integration

## SURE-FIRE METHODS
## FOR CREATING A PATHETIC AGENDA

☑

1. Time the agenda right down to the minute, and assume the meeting will start exactly on time.

2. Assume that everybody will know what you're trying to accomplish at the meeting – if they don't, they'll ask.

3. Plan to spend the first half of the meeting prioritizing what to do in the second half of the meeting.

4. Keep the meeting interesting by making sure the people who give reports use overheads and pie charts.

5. If you've got an agenda of difficult and important items, improve efficiency by skipping breaks and shortening lunch.

6. When the most important discussion is likely to be emotionally charged, save it for last. Maybe the group will be more ready to deal with it by then.

7. Since everyone prefers their meetings to stay on track, assume that no one will raise a topic that's not on the agenda.

8. When you know the agenda is too packed, assume the meeting will run overtime. But don't tell anyone in advance. People sometimes do their best thinking under pressure.

9. To maintain your flexibility, don't put the agenda in writing.

10. Don't waste time planning an agenda. Things never go the way you expect them to.

# BUILDING BLOCKS OF AN EFFECTIVE AGENDA

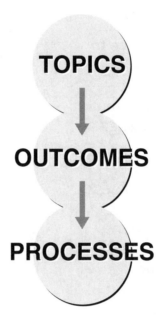

**TOPICS**

**OUTCOMES**

**PROCESSES**

The work of a meeting consists of three components: the topics to be discussed, the desired outcomes for each topic, and the processes needed to achieve the desired outcomes. These three components can be thought of as the *building blocks* of meeting planning.

Each *topic* to be discussed can be viewed as a segment of the meeting. For example, if the group were going to discuss three topics – a marketing issue, a staffing issue, and a budget issue – each topic would be discussed separately and should thus be treated as a distinct segment.

The *desired outcome* of each topic can be viewed as the goal for that segment of the meeting. For example, the desired outcome of discussing the marketing issue might be a plan for developing a new website.

The *process* refers to the activity (or set of activities) the group will do to achieve the desired outcome. Such activities include brainstorming, categorizing, debating, and many more.

# FROM BUILDING BLOCKS TO LOGIC MODEL

|  | **SECTION 1** | **SECTION 2** |
|---|---|---|
| **TOPICS** | Planning the move to our new headquarters. | Recruiting & hiring the receptionist. |
| **OUTCOMES** | Stages and important steps are established. | • Job description OK'd.<br>• A lead recruiter has been assigned. |
| **PROCESS** | 1. Brainstorm stages.<br>2. Prioritize.<br>3. Breakout groups to define steps.<br>4. Gallery tour.<br>5. Open discussion.<br>6. Decisions. | 1. Review last year's documents.<br>2. Suggest changes.<br>3. Decide.<br>4. Ask for volunteer to do recruiting. |
|  | **2 HOURS** | **10-15 MINUTES** |

One of the core tasks of an agenda planner is to turn the three building blocks of each section of a meeting into a *logic model* for that section. Thinking this through proceeds along the following lines:

1. *Topics:* What topics do we want to address?

2. *Outcomes:* What are our desired outcomes for each of those topics?

3. *Process:* What activity (or set of activities) will best support the group to achieve each desired outcome – and how much time should be estimated for each activity?

These steps in building a logic model are challenging to do well, yet they can make the critical difference between a productive meeting and a useless one. (Chapter 11 provides concepts and tools for defining outcomes. Chapter 12 does the same for process design.)

# FROM SECTIONS TO SEQUENCE

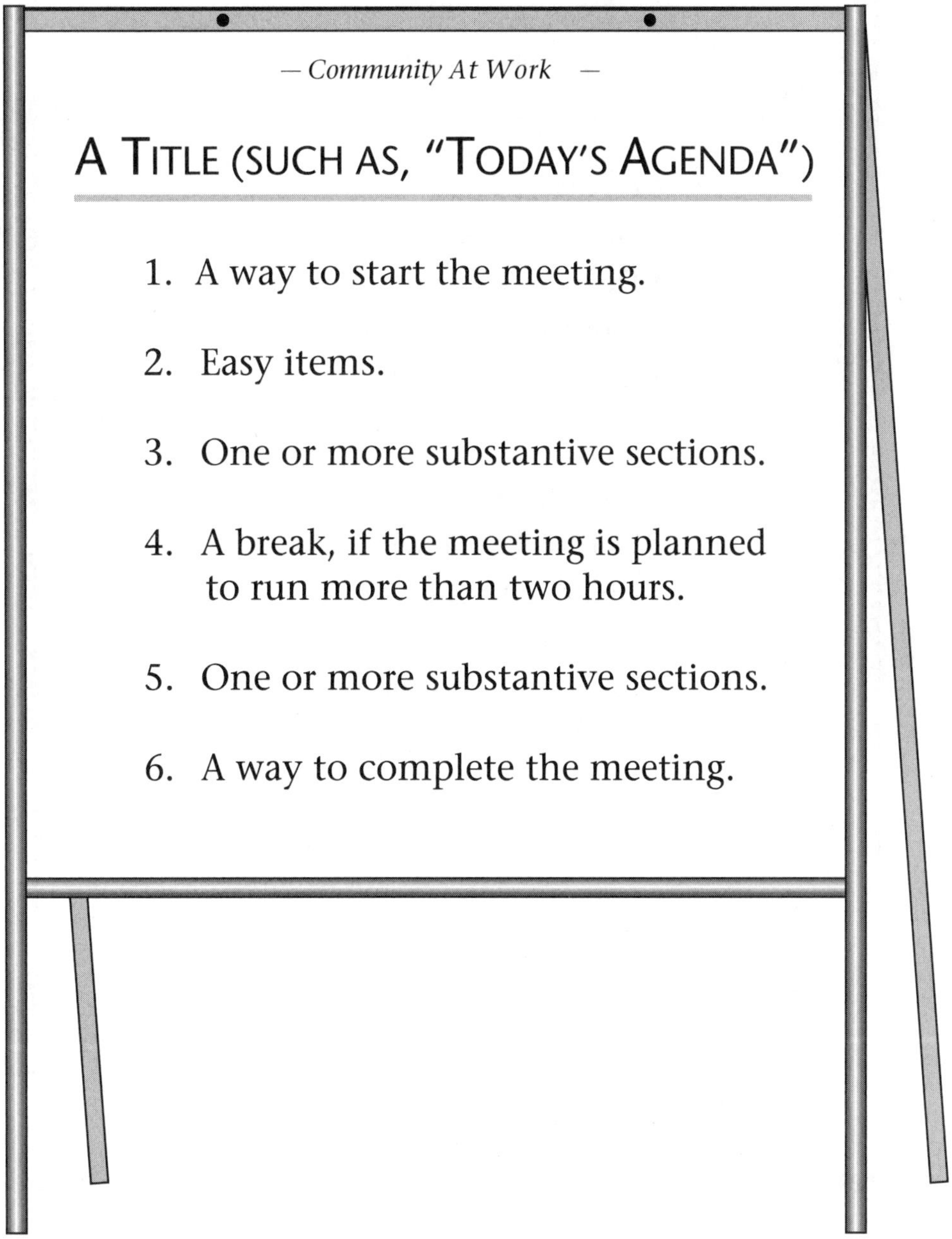

*— Community At Work —*

## A TITLE (SUCH AS, "TODAY'S AGENDA")

1. A way to start the meeting.

2. Easy items.

3. One or more substantive sections.

4. A break, if the meeting is planned to run more than two hours.

5. One or more substantive sections.

6. A way to complete the meeting.

After the meeting designer has built the logic model for each section of the meeting, the next step is to organize the sections into a sequence. The picture above shows a generic approach. The following pages offer six more.

*— Community At Work —*

## QUICK BUSINESS & MAJOR TOPICS

1. Check-in and Agenda Review

2. Quick Business

3. First Major Topic
   - State today's meeting goal.
   - Describe the process to be followed.
   - Proceed until goal is met.
   - Identify action plans.

   *— Break —*

4. Second Major Topic
   - State today's meeting goal.
   - Describe the process to be followed.
   - Proceed until goal is met.
   - Identify action plans.

5. Meeting Evaluation

**BEST USE**: This format is used for ongoing management-team meetings at which decisions are needed for several major items the same day.

**TIMING**: *Quick Business* in this format often takes 30-45 minutes. The items can be handled in a line-'em-up, knock-'em-down fashion. Each *Major Topic* will run 30 minutes or longer. Overall, a meeting with more than one *major topic* should be designed to last at least 2.5 hours. *Major topics* require more attention to process design than *quick business* items. Most *quick business* items can be handled by a simple open discussion.

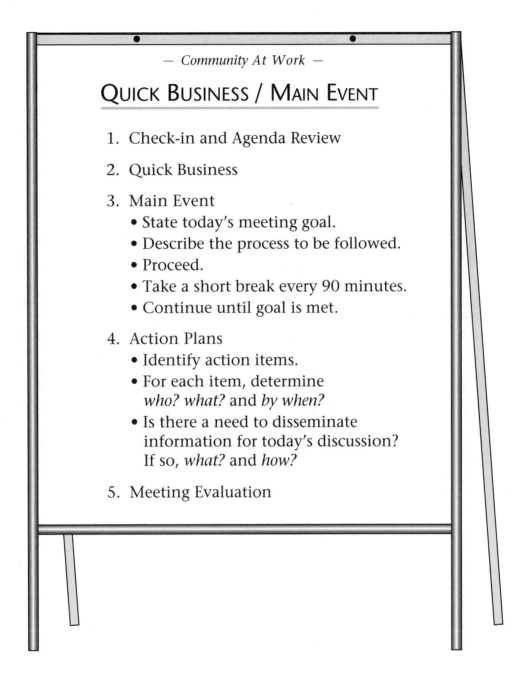

*— Community At Work —*

## QUICK BUSINESS / MAIN EVENT

1. Check-in and Agenda Review

2. Quick Business

3. Main Event
   - State today's meeting goal.
   - Describe the process to be followed.
   - Proceed.
   - Take a short break every 90 minutes.
   - Continue until goal is met.

4. Action Plans
   - Identify action items.
   - For each item, determine
     *who? what?* and *by when?*
   - Is there a need to disseminate
     information for today's discussion?
     If so, *what?* and *how?*

5. Meeting Evaluation

**BEST USE**:   This format works best when a group has been convened to problem-solve a complex issue that has a clear end-goal.  Examples include developing a strategic plan, setting an annual budget, or planning a sizable layoff.  This type of meeting requires a well-thought-out process design.

**TIMING**:   These meetings typically last 3-6 hours per session.  The project often runs for several weeks or more.  *Quick business* is best done by giving each person 5-7 minutes to use as s/he wishes.  Unfinished items are recorded on a back burner, to be dealt with offline or at the next meeting.

*— Community At Work —*

## OLD BUSINESS / NEW BUSINESS

1. Adoption of Last Meeting's Minutes

2. Announcements and Reports

3. Old Business
   - Begin with oldest outstanding item recorded in *the minutes,* which lists items tabled from prior meetings.
   - Deal with the item or table it again.
   - Continue until every *old business* item is either handled or tabled.

4. New Business
   - *New business* items must be listed on the agenda ahead of time.
   - All *new business* items must be handled or tabled until next meeting.

5. Meeting Evaluation

**BEST USE**:   This format – a simplified Robert's Rules –  is used in volunteer organizations, especially in board meetings.  Since members are not regular co-workers, they tend not to spend much time thinking about the agenda items between meetings.  Therefore, the minutes from prior meetings are used as the key tool to structure the agenda.

**TIMING**:   The meeting lasts as long as it takes to complete old business and new business.  Under time pressure, groups tend to defer many items.

*— Community At Work —*

## LINE 'EM UP & KNOCK 'EM DOWN

1. Check-in

2. Announcements

3. Today's Business Items
   - List all items.
   - Rank items by priority.
   - Begin with highest-priority item.
   - Clarify desired outcome.
   - When discussion is complete, identify and record any next steps.
   - Continue process until all items are dealt with, or time runs out.

4. Review Next Steps

5. Meeting Evaluation

**BEST USE**: This format is often used at an ongoing staff meeting, at which most business items are straightforward. This format requires no advance planning, and therefore the desired outcome must be clarified in real time during the meeting. When complex topics are raised, they may be discussed as input, but they are rarely decided at the meeting.

**TIMING**: This type of meeting is usually scheduled to last 1 hour. *Today's Business Items* should run for a set time – typically 45 minutes.

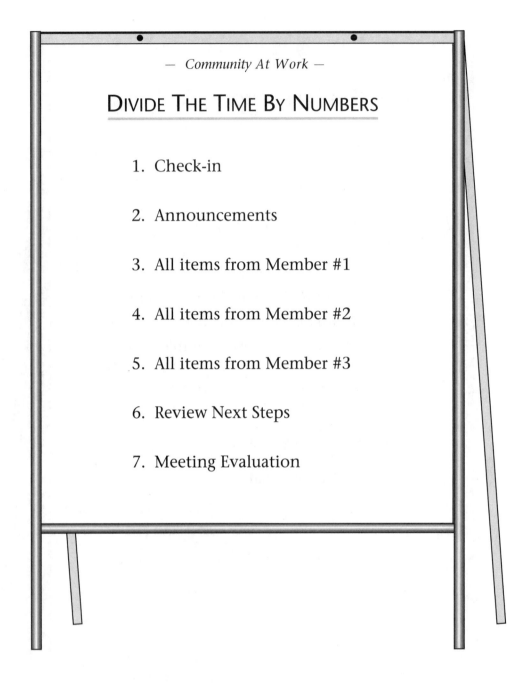

— *Community At Work* —

## DIVIDE THE TIME BY NUMBERS

1. Check-in

2. Announcements

3. All items from Member #1

4. All items from Member #2

5. All items from Member #3

6. Review Next Steps

7. Meeting Evaluation

**BEST USE**: This format is especially suitable for groups whose members have different areas of responsibility. It can be used both to obtain input and to make decisions. However, to be effective, this format requires each member to prepare in advance by defining goals for each topic s/he raises.

**TIMING**: Each group determines for itself how much time to allot each member. Everyone receives equal time unless someone negotiates for more.

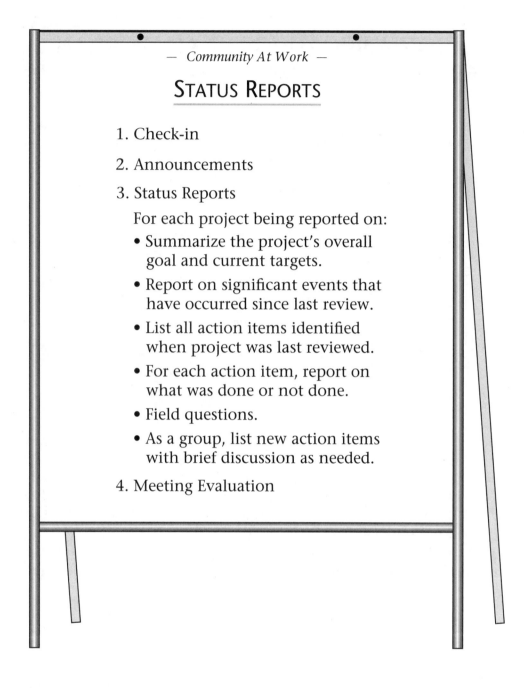

— *Community At Work* —

## STATUS REPORTS

1. Check-in

2. Announcements

3. Status Reports

   For each project being reported on:

   • Summarize the project's overall goal and current targets.

   • Report on significant events that have occurred since last review.

   • List all action items identified when project was last reviewed.

   • For each action item, report on what was done or not done.

   • Field questions.

   • As a group, list new action items with brief discussion as needed.

4. Meeting Evaluation

**BEST USE**: This format is useful for meetings of project teams. It's also useful for program staff meetings at which most staff members are working independently, and want to keep one another updated.

**TIMING**: Status reports should take no more than 10-15 minutes per report. Half that time should be spent discussing action items. A meeting should take less than 1 hour. Have some people report every 2 or 3 meetings.

# COMMUNICATING THE GAME PLAN

**JUNE 15 AGENDA**

1. PRELIMINARIES
2. REPORTS
3. TOPIC ONE
4. TOPIC TWO
   — BREAK —
5. TOPIC THREE
6. TOPIC FOUR
7. NEXT STEPS

An important aspect of agenda design is the way the agenda is documented. Simply put, the agenda must be *well communicated.* People can't follow a plan they don't understand. Psychologically there is a lot going on at the start of a meeting; it's hard to capture people's full and undivided attention. Therefore, the agenda document must be simple, clear, and easy to grasp.

While the picture shown above is generic, it illustrates many features of a clear, simple agenda:

- The page has a title, and the title includes a date.

- The opening of the meeting is noted, e.g. *"Preliminaries"* or *"Overview."*

- Sections are labeled by topic, and listed in the order they will be worked on. (The assumption is that the meeting leader will describe the logic model for each section, along with any other needed context-setting information, when that point in the meeting arrives.)

- The break (if there is one) is shown.

- The end of the meeting is noted, e.g. *"Next Steps"* or *"Closing Comments."*

# AGENDA PLANNING ROLES

| THE FACILITATOR | THE PERSON-IN-CHARGE |
| --- | --- |
| Explains the importance of reserving time to plan the agenda. | Decides how much time to invest in agenda planning. |
| Asks the person-in-charge to list all possible topics. | Identifies possible topics and decides which to include. |
| Asks the person-in-charge to set the *overall goal* for each topic. | Clarifies the *overall goal* for each topic. |
| Encourages the person-in-charge to define *meeting goals* for each topic. | Sets the *meeting goal* for each topic on the agenda. |
| Suggests thinking activities for the group to engage in during each segment of the meeting. | Considers facilitator's suggestions, weighs trade-offs (quality vs time expenditure), and decides for each segment. |
| Puts together a draft agenda, complete with time estimates. | Makes any revisions to the draft and validates the final agenda. |
| *Does not* present the agenda at the meeting. (The person-in-charge is the owner of the outcomes.) | Presents the agenda at the meeting and explains the objectives for each item. |

# INVOLVING PARTICIPANTS IN AGENDA DESIGN

## BUILDING A WHOLE AGENDA

When no one has pre-planned a meeting, or when members want to do their planning as a group:

1. List potential agenda topics.

2. Prioritize topics.

3. Set desired outcomes for the highest priority topic.

4. Establish a process for working on that topic – for example, open discussion? Small groups? Other?

5. Do the work for that topic.

6. Repeat Steps 3–5 as time permits.

## WORKING WITH PLANNERS

Some groups want to have a say in the selection of topics while leaving the details of meeting design to one or more planners:

1. At the end of a meeting, or by email after the meeting, have group members suggest topics for the following meeting.

2. Planners set desired outcomes for each topic, communicating with other members as needed.

3. Planners take full responsibility for process design for each topic.

4. An agenda is posted ahead of time, and comments are invited.

## RATIFYING PRE-WORK

When limited meeting time is available and the group still wants a high level of agreement on meeting content:

1. Post the agenda at the start of a meeting or circulate it beforehand.

2. Begin the meeting by asking each individual for agreement to proceed. Obtain affirmations from everyone.

3. If changes are suggested, facilitate a decision-making process. (This can prevent more serious disputes from undermining the meeting later.)

4. Mark the posted agenda to show new agreements. When ratified, proceed.

# DESIGN PRINCIPLES: SUMMARY AND INTEGRATION

An agenda is a dual-purpose tool. On the one hand, it's the game plan for the meeting: a theory of how a meeting will unfold. It consists of an organized sequence of meeting segments. Each segment has its own logic model: a topic, one or more desired outcomes, and a process for reaching the outcome. On the other hand, it's a document that communicates the game plan to participants. As such, it has to be clear and simple – easy to grasp.

Keeping both purposes in mind, here are the design principles, step by step, that you can use to create an effective agenda:

## AGENDA DESIGN

**STEP 1** Determine who the agenda planner(s) will be, and whether and how to obtain input from other participants.

**STEP 2** Identify the topics to be discussed at the meeting.

**STEP 3** Define the desired outcomes for each topic. (See also chapter 11.)

**STEP 4** Create a process that enables the group to achieve the desired outcomes for each topic. (See also chapter 12.)

**STEP 5** Completing the first three steps produces a logic model for each section of the meeting. Put the sections into the order in which they will be worked on, at the meeting.

**STEP 6** Create a simple, clear document – printed or on a flipchart – that communicates the game plan to participants.

- Title the page.
- Label the opening of the meeting with a short phrase, such as, *"Introductions and Overview"* or *"Preliminaries."*
- Then list sections by topics, in the order they will be worked on.
- Show the break (if one is anticipated).
- Label the ending of the meeting with a short phrase, such as, *"Next Steps"* – or – *"Closing Comments."*

# 11

# EFFECTIVE AGENDAS: DESIRED OUTCOMES

CONCEPTS AND METHODS
FOR SETTING OBJECTIVES

- ▶ **Overall Goals and Meeting Goals**

- ▶ **Seven Types of Meeting Goals**

- ▶ **Setting Outcomes for a Meeting**

- ▶ **Defining Desired Outcomes:
  Questions to Ask a Person-in-Charge**

## OVERALL GOALS AND MEETING GOALS

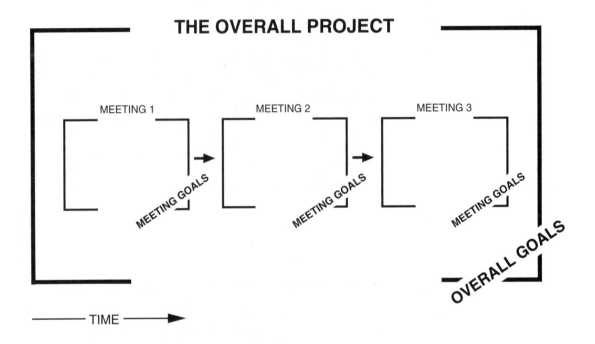

### THE OVERALL PROJECT

MEETING 1    MEETING 2    MEETING 3

MEETING GOALS    MEETING GOALS    MEETING GOALS

OVERALL GOALS

TIME

This graphic is known as a *Multiple Time Frames* map.*  It was developed by the authors to depict the nesting of short-term goals within long-term goals.

As shown, the *overall goal* of a given project may take several meetings to achieve.  By comparison, each meeting can be seen on its own terms, as a context within which the group can make progress toward the overall goal, by achieving two or three narrow *meeting goals*.  As the following pages will clarify, *meeting goals* are specific, well-defined, realistic goals, designed to be achieved in the time frame of a single meeting.

\* The graphic is also known as a *Milestone Map*.  See S. Kaner and D. Berger,
 *Roadmaps for Strategic Change*, unpublished manuscript, 2006.
 Contact authors for more information.

## OVERALL GOALS AND MEETING GOALS

— Community At Work —

### THE OVERALL GOAL FOR THIS TOPIC

What *final result* do we want to achieve in order to be *completely done* with this topic?

### THE MEETING GOAL FOR THIS TOPIC

What *narrowly-defined, specific objective* do we want to achieve for this topic at an *upcoming meeting*?

Defining the desired outcomes for each topic on the agenda is the most difficult task in planning a meeting. At the core of this difficulty is the necessity to distinguish between the *overall goal* for the topic and the *meeting goal* for that same topic.

# OVERALL GOALS AND MEETING GOALS

FIRST MEETING

**CASE STUDY**

A popular local sporting goods store went through a period of expanding rapidly – from five shops to 100 across the country.

Previously they had been able to handle all their human resource needs with one HR employee. Now they needed a real, full-blown HR department.

To design the new HR department and make it operational, the owner put together a project team, led by an HR consultant.

The owner mandated the team to focus on three topic areas:

- *departmental functions*
- *staffing*
- *the budget*

The owner also provided overall goals for each of those three areas.

For *departmental functions* the overall goal would be to define the HR goals, roles, and key systems.

For *staffing*, the overall goal would be to recruit and hire an HR manager and staff.

For *the budget* the overall goal would be to produce a realistic first-year budget.

At the team's first meeting they addressed each topic area as follows.

To begin thinking about *departmental functions*, the consultant prepared a deck of slides that explained the key duties and services

most HR departments are responsible for providing.

For the portion of the meeting that focused on *staffing*, the consultant recommended that they focus first on hiring a manager. They agreed, and they created a first draft of a plan for recruiting the manager.

For *the budget*, the consultant produced a list of typical expenses. He then assigned several individuals to go and find out the actual dollar amounts that were associated with each item on his list of expenses.

Everyone felt the meeting had been well-planned and productive.

| TOPIC | OVERALL GOAL | MEETING GOAL |
|---|---|---|
| Departmental functions | Define HR goals, roles and key systems needed. | Introduce team to key HR services and duties. |
| Staffing | Recruit and hire an HR manager and staff. | Draft a plan for recruiting an HR manager. |
| Budget | Produce a realistic first-year budget. | Assign individuals to research the major costs. |

## OVERALL GOALS AND MEETING GOALS

**LATER MEETING**

**CASE STUDY**

Three months later, the HR Department design team had reached the mid-point of its mandate.

By now, most of the work was being performed by individuals at their desks – reading, writing, or talking on the phone.

But the team did meet for at least an hour each week, with members attending by conference call if not in person. And once a month they held a half-day session to do problem-solving and decision-making.

Now it was time for the monthly meeting.

As always, their agenda was organized around the three topic areas they had agreed to focus on.

With regard to the topic of *departmental functions*, the work had progressed to the point where they were ready to hire a contractor to design the data systems for several key functions: job classification, hiring, promotions, termination, and benefits. At this meeting, the group examined proposals from three competing firms: Oracle, PeopleSoft, and a start-up vendor who seemed to be offering more service at a lower price. The goal for this meeting was to select the winning firm.

Regarding *staffing*, they'd made good progress on the development of job descriptions for every role. It was time, everyone agreed, to get out there and hire a good manager.

By the end of today's meeting, the goal was to finalize the manager's job description so they could pass it along to the head hunter used by their company for senior hires.

As for *the budget*, that was the area in which they felt they'd made the most progress. A draft budget had been circulated to the company's VPs two weeks ago and their comments had been collected. At today's meeting, the goal was to review the input and begin revising the budget to reflect what they were learning.

Once again the meeting came off without a hitch, and once again everyone was proud to be part of a process that was so well organized.

| TOPIC | OVERALL GOAL | MEETING GOAL |
|---|---|---|
| Departmental functions | Define HR goals, roles and key systems needed. | Approve contractor to design key data systems. |
| Staffing | Recruit and hire an HR manager and staff. | Finalize HR Manager job description for headhunter. |
| Budget | Produce a realistic first-year budget. | Digest VPs' comments on draft budget, and begin thinking about next draft. |

The *meeting goal* for any given topic is the specific, narrowly-defined objective for working on that topic at a meeting. There are seven distinct types of meeting goals. For example, say the topic is "Next Year's Budget," and the overall goal is "Finalize the Budget." A group could set a narrow meeting goal that belonged to any of the types shown above. The next page demonstrates this point vividly.

# SEVEN TYPES OF MEETING GOALS

EXAMPLES

Suppose a large project team is working on "next year's budget." That would be the *topic*. Suppose also that their *overall goal* is "Finalize and obtain approval for next year's budget." Now imagine the project manager is planning for upcoming meetings, at which some of the team's meeting time will be spent doing budget work. Here are examples of *meeting goals* that are representative of each of the seven *types of meeting goals* described in this book:

| TYPE OF MEETING GOAL | EXAMPLE |
| --- | --- |
| SHARE INFORMATION | Bring everyone 'up to speed' on past budgeting decisions, by reviewing key numbers and assumptions from the past three annual budgets. |
| ADVANCE THE THINKING | Create 3 scenarios for reducing non-salary expenses by 20-30 percent. |
| PROVIDE INPUT | Obtain opinions and rationales on whether to (a) reduce expenses, or (b) increase revenues, or (c) do both. |
| MAKE DECISIONS | Finalize the categories of expenses that (a) will be reduced compared to last year; (b) will not be reduced; (c) will be forecast to grow. |
| IMPROVE COMMUNICATION | Clear the air of lingering frustrations that originated with a serious budget-planning error. |
| BUILD CAPACITY | Take a few hours to train the whole group in accounting principles relevant to our budgets. |
| BUILD COMMUNITY | Celebrate good cost-reduction ideas by giving out inexpensive, fun prizes and posting goofy pictures. |

## MEETING GOAL:  SHARE INFORMATION

**DESCRIPTION**    When someone makes an announcement, a report or a presentation, his or her meeting goal is to *share information.*

**EXAMPLE**    A project team is going to start working on their budget.  Their overall goal for that topic is, "Finalize the budget for this project."  To achieve this goal, the project manager anticipates that the group will work on the budget over the course of the next three meetings.  At the first of these three meetings, the project manager's objective is to make sure everyone understands how project budgets are constructed at this company.  Her plan is to show people financial data from three comparable projects that were completed last year.

**KEY INSIGHT**    For anyone who is getting ready to share information, it's normal to think mainly about the best way to communicate that information.  Should I make slides?  With graphics?  Should I turn them into handouts?  How much time do I have?  It's also normal to see the recipients of this information as "the audience."  And most group members have a matching perception:  they *do* see themselves as the audience, being "talked at" by a "presenter."  The resulting dynamics are often numbing.  In practice, however, this presenter-audience mindset is neither helpful nor accurate.  When information is being shared in the workplace, recipients are not an audience to be entertained, they are the *end-users* of that information.  Meeting planners who understand this can build in opportunities, like quick conversations in pairs, for group members to *digest* what they are hearing, *so they can apply it when and how they need to.*

## MEETING GOAL: PROVIDE INPUT

**DESCRIPTION**   When someone brings a topic to the group for feedback or suggestions, and s/he only wants comments, not decisions from the group, then his/her meeting goal is for the group to *provide input.*

**EXAMPLE**   Continuing from the preceding page, the same project team is working on the same budget.  The overall goal for this topic is, "Finalize the budget for this project."  This time, however, the planner has a different meeting goal.  He wants to find out how people will react to three different budget scenarios.  He doesn't want a decision, he wants their opinions.

**KEY INSIGHT**   When participants understand that they are being asked to provide their input, not to make decisions as a group, they spend less time trying to persuade their colleagues to change their minds.  Instead, the savvy ones focus on influencing the person who asked for input.  More often than not, this person is their boss.

Sometimes participants don't realize that the goal is to *provide input.*  They might instead think they have been invited to participate in making decisions.  So they put effort into critiquing and debating, with the hope of creating support for their ideas.  When the boss then proceeds to make a unilateral decision after obtaining everyone's input, those who mistakenly thought they were decision-makers often become frustrated and demoralized.  The well-known complaint, "Why ask for my opinion if you don't want to use it?" reflects this confusion.  Fortunately, most occurrences of this problem can be prevented.  Just make it clear that the meeting goal is to *provide input*, not to *make decisions.*

## MEETING GOAL: ADVANCE THE THINKING

**DESCRIPTION**   Most projects involve several stages of work, and normally, many steps of thinking are embedded in each stage.  Yet progress usually entails taking one step at a time.  A planner who understands this principle can become more precise in setting realistic and useful objectives.

**EXAMPLES**   Here is a sample of ways to *advance the thinking* at a meeting:

- Define a problem
- Analyze a problem
- Identify root causes
- Identify underlying patterns
- Sort a list of ideas into themes
- Evaluate options
- Draw a flowchart
- Identify core values

- Create a milestone map
- Create a work breakdown structure
- Conduct a resource analysis
- Conduct a risk assessment
- Define selection criteria
- Rearrange a list of items by priority
- Identify critical success factors
- Edit and/or wordsmith a statement

**KEY INSIGHT**   This meeting goal has a high likelihood of producing engaged, thoughtful behavior by group members.  It's important, of course, that the particulars of the objective are logical.  (For example, when a problem has not yet been well-defined, it would not be logical to have the group evaluate possible solutions.)  It's also important to communicate the objective clearly.  And group members must understand that the meeting goal is to think, not to make decisions.  When those conditions are met, many people enjoy the chance for conversations that use their brains productively.

## MEETING GOAL: MAKE DECISIONS

**DESCRIPTION** Some decisions are simple to make, others are very difficult. Either way, when a planner wants a group to address an issue and *bring it to closure at the next meeting*, the meeting goal is to *make a decision*.

**EXAMPLE** Simple decisions are those that are easy to think about – either because the stakes are low or because the issues are straightforward and familiar, with predictable consequences. For example, a majority of decisions in most budget-planning processes are routine confirmations of ongoing programs and salaries. Those are often made quickly without much analysis. Difficult decisions, by contrast, are those that must be made in the face of uncertainty, or to resolve competing priorities, or when many interdependent variables are in play. For example, a budget decision to cut a program or reduce payroll usually requires much more analysis and consideration.

**KEY INSIGHT** The deep question is, "What decision rule will we use to make this decision?" For simple decisions it usually doesn't matter whether the decision is made by a single person with authority, or by a majority of the group, or by consensus of the entire group. Either way, if the decision is easy to make, the group's behavior will probably be affable and mildly detached – basically, a let's-get-on-with-it attitude. However, for difficult decisions, the difference in impact on group behavior is huge. When the boss is the decider, groups often hold back from saying some of what they are really thinking. (*"What's the point?"* is a common refrain.) Whereas if the whole group has to reach an agreement, get ready for the *Groan Zone!* People who have to decide on tough issues are more likely to feel compelled to build shared understanding of the complexities involved.

## MEETING GOAL: IMPROVE TEAM COMMUNICATION

**DESCRIPTION**   When a meeting planner wants the members of a group to strengthen their working relationships by sharing feelings and/or dealing with interpersonal tension, the meeting goal is to *improve team communication.*

**EXAMPLE**   A project team missed an important deadline.  The sponsor summoned them to his office so he could tell them in no uncertain terms that he was displeased with their performance.  Everyone sat in silence.  Privately, some people blamed the data coordinator for falling behind.  Others blamed the project manager for creating an unrealistic timetable.  Still others had their own pet theories of why this project was not succeeding.  No one discussed their feelings openly at subsequent project meetings, but morale plummeted.  Finally the group scheduled a "team-building" session to raise these issues and clear the air.

**KEY INSIGHT**   This is a challenging meeting goal to execute.  It means, essentially, having group members step away from task-related issues, to talk instead about their feelings and their relationships with one another.  This calls for everyone to behave very differently than they normally would in a group setting.  Deeper, more authentic self-disclosure is needed.  So is the willingness to give and receive feedback.  Participants have to override their natural tendencies to be protective in the giving of feedback and defensive in the receiving of it.  This is no simple matter – many of us are reluctant, for all sorts of personal and cultural reasons, to "get touchy-feely" with our colleagues at work.  It's not reasonable to simply announce, "OK, everyone, let's clear the air" and expect people to open up and say what they're really feeling.  That could work, but not usually.  Rather, it takes a skillful, well-planned approach – first to create a safe, supportive foundation, and then to gently nurture self-disclosure and interpersonal feedback.

## MEETING GOAL: BUILD TEAM CAPACITY

**DESCRIPTION**   Capacity-building is rarely viewed as something that can be done at a run-of-the-mill meeting.  Instead, it is usually seen as classroom training offered by the training department, and attended by individual members for their own personal development.  When instead *building capacity* is treated as a meeting goal for a whole team, it becomes apparent that there are many beneficial areas for group improvement.  Problem-solving and decision-making capabilities; increased knowledge of major trends in the team's industry sector; acquisition of methods or best practices that are especially relevant to this team's objectives – these are just some of many options a meeting planner can consider, to *build team capacity*.

**EXAMPLE**   A team for a large project made two unsuccessful attempts at developing their budget.  The project manager determined that key members did not understand basic accounting principles, causing them to become lost and confused during relevant discussions.  She decided to invite someone from the accounting department to spend a few hours with the group, teaching the relevant essentials of accounting.  Later, everyone looked back on that session as the turning point in their budget conversations.

**KEY INSIGHT**   Capacity-building experiences are bonding experiences. They instill confidence that learning has taken place, and hopefulness that the learning will be applied.  They provide shared concepts, shared language and a sense of "we've-been-through-something-together."  To reap the benefits, of course, requires a plan for applying what was taught at the learning session.  If that's done effectively, it will strengthen the maturity and competence of the group as a whole, with ripple effects on innumerable individual behaviors.

## MEETING GOAL:  BUILD COMMUNITY

**DESCRIPTION**    When a meeting planner wants to promote camaraderie, strengthen the bonds among people who work together, and generally boost morale, the meeting goal is to *build community.*

**EXAMPLE**    The project team decided that they would have a little celebration when they finalized their budget.  They did not consider the achievement to be so major as to justify a grand celebration, yet neither did they want it to pass without some formal acknowledgment.  The project manager decided to invite the project sponsor to come to the last hour of a late-afternoon meeting, at which time the group would enjoy some light food and libations while the budget was presented to the sponsor for his final approval.  By design, the sponsor would have seen the budget ahead of time.  His main reason for coming to the meeting was to contribute to the goal of building community, which he did by offering some words of praise to the group – and by staying around to socialize.

**KEY INSIGHT**    Community building is not normally considered to be a legitimate meeting goal.  It is often relegated to team building off-sites and fancy dinner ceremonies.  This is a misconception of what community building is all about.  Morale will stay higher when community building is integrated into the everyday flow of work.  Team achievements and life events (like birthdays) can be celebrated delightfully in 5-10 minutes.  Other ways to build community include volunteering as a group, sharing reactions to momentous current events, and doing simple creative energizers.  The key is to place community building goals onto the agenda, and treat them just like every other meeting goal.

*— Community At Work —*

# SETTING OUTCOMES FOR A MEETING

Facilitate the person-in-charge to:

1.  Identify all topics for the meeting.

2.  Select one to start with.

3.  List possible overall goals for that topic.

4.  Decide on an overall goal for that topic.

5.  Explore which type of meeting goal seems most suitable. Choose one.

6.  Define the meeting goal precisely. *

Repeat Steps 1 to 6 with a new topic.

\* Example: If the type of meeting goal is *Provide input* (as chosen in Step 5), then the precise meeting goal might be something like, *Provide input about Questions X and Y but not Z* (as defined in Step 6.)

Facilitators should keep in mind that this template is generic. When using it in real life, the person-in-charge will probably hop around from one step to another – or even from one topic to another – without completing the steps in the formal sequence. If this happens, follow his or her lead! Everyone has their own individual style of thinking.

## DEFINING DESIRED OUTCOMES
### FACILITATIVE QUESTIONS TO ASK A PERSON-IN-CHARGE

### OVERALL GOALS

- What does success look like?

- How will you know when you're done?

- Fundamentally, what do you want to accomplish?

- Just to clarify, you're saying you'll all be done when . . .?

- What makes this important?

- What are you shooting for here?

- Tell me more about what you are trying to achieve.

- Suppose you had all the time and money you'd need. What do you *really* want to happen?

- Tell me more about your vision of the future.

### MEETING GOALS

- What deliverables do you want this meeting to produce?

- What part of this is urgent?

- What issues will need to be discussed in the future?

- Logically, what needs to be handled first?

- Let's try breaking your overall goal into a few rough stages.

- At the end of this meeting, what do you want people to come away with?

- What could be done after the meeting?

- What could be done before the meeting?

- What could be done by people who are not at this meeting?

- What discussion needs everyone's involvement?

# 12

# EFFECTIVE AGENDAS: PROCESS DESIGN

## DESIGNING ACTIVITIES TO ACHIEVE THE MEETING GOALS

- ▶ Two Common Misconceptions About Process Design

- ▶ Process Design Options

- ▶ Combining Formats into a String

- ▶ Using Strings to Enhance Open Discussion

- ▶ Keeping the Energy Fresh in a Meeting

- ▶ Insightful Process Design

- ▶ Making Time Estimates for Activities

- ▶ Typical Strings for Seven Meeting Goals

- ▶ Summary

- ▶ Properties of an Effective Agenda

# INTRODUCTION TO PROCESS DESIGN

*A COMMON MISCONCEPTION*

## AGENDA FOR A MEETING

BEGINNING of MEETING

BEGINNING of TOPIC

BEGINNING of TOPIC

BEGINNING of TOPIC

| TOPIC 1:<br>BUDGET REVIEW | → | TOPIC 2:<br>HIRING POLICY | → | TOPIC 3:<br>TRAINING PLAN |
|---|---|---|---|---|

END of TOPIC

END of TOPIC

END of TOPIC

END of MEETING

—— TIME ——→

When most people think about what will happen in a meeting, they think about the topics they expect to be covered at that meeting. For example: "First, we should review the budget. Then we should go to our hiring policy. After that, we can resume work on next year's training plan."

This illustrates a confusion about *process* that is prevalent in the minds of many meeting goers. When they speak about the process of a meeting, they're actually referring to the *sequence* of topics that will be covered at that meeting. "We'll begin with Topic 1 and we'll work on it until we finish with that topic. Then we'll move to Topic 2 and work on *that* until we're done with it. Then we'll go on to Topic 3."

# INTRODUCTION TO PROCESS DESIGN

*A MORE USEFUL CONCEPTUALIZATION*

## AGENDA FOR A MEETING

BEGINNING of MEETING

BEGINNING OF A SECTION

**TOPIC 1:
BUDGET REVIEW**

**PROCESS:
REPORT —> Q&A**

MEETING GOAL:
INFORMATIONAL

BEGINNING OF A SECTION

**TOPIC 2:
HIRING POLICY**

**PROCESS:
LIST —> PRIORITIZE**

MEETING GOAL:
ADVANCE THINKING

BEGINNING OF A SECTION

**TOPIC 3:
TRAINING PLAN**

**PROCESS:
GO-AROUND**

MEETING GOAL:
PROVIDE INPUT

END of MEETING

TIME ——>

As illustrated in the diagram above, each section of an agenda has its own logic model:

- A topic,
- The meeting goal for that topic, and
- The process for reaching that meeting goal.

When a meeting designer understands the structure depicted by the diagram, s/he can design processes for a meeting with more imagination and with a greater expectation that participants will understand what is expected of them. This translates into a higher likelihood that the desired outcomes for each meeting goal will actually be reached – especially when the goals are ambitious and / or the problems are complex.

## INTRODUCTION TO PROCESS DESIGN

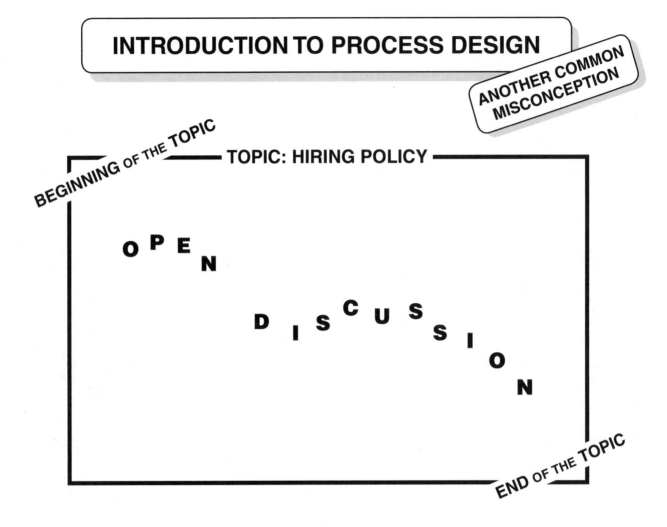

ANOTHER COMMON MISCONCEPTION

BEGINNING OF THE TOPIC

TOPIC: HIRING POLICY

OPEN DISCUSSION

END OF THE TOPIC

When a topic is introduced at a meeting, most groups automatically slip into *open discussion*.  And they typically continue having that discussion until they feel ready to finish with that topic – at which point they move to the next topic and begin *another* discussion.

One might think that *open discussion* would encourage spontaneity and interaction.  And it does – for quick thinkers and eloquent speakers.  For everyone else, *open discussions are not so inviting.*  Yet many leaders persist in using *open discussion* as their default mode for eliciting participation.  Why do they do that?  Is it because they consciously, intentionally want to put performance pressure on their groups?  Probably not.  It's more likely that they just don't realize they have options.

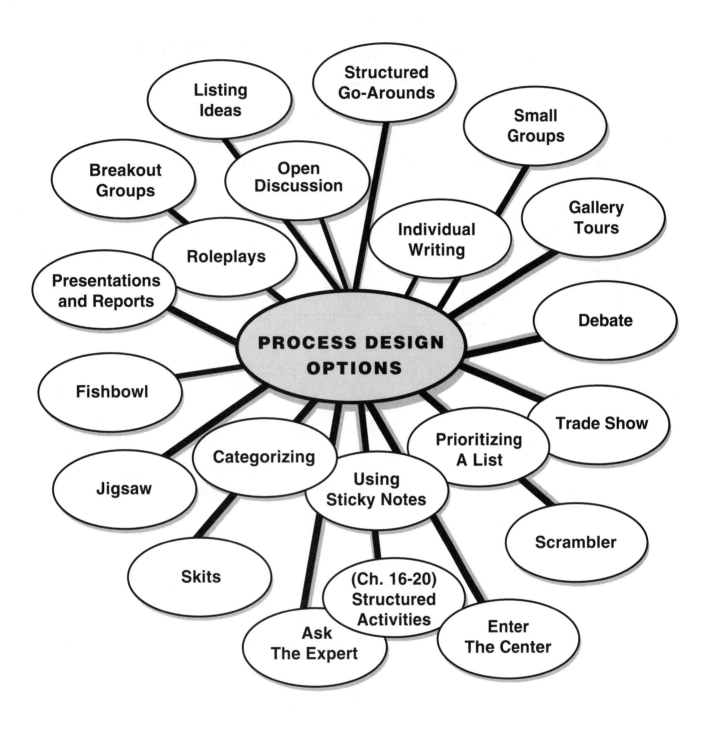

This diagram is provided for easy reference to an agenda designer. To encourage the optimal level of participation during any given section of a meeting, the agenda designer(s) can choose among a wide variety of simple formats, as discussed in chapters 6 through 9. Or s/he can select or create structured activities that have specific objectives, like those in chapters 16 through 20.

## COMBINING FORMATS INTO A STRING

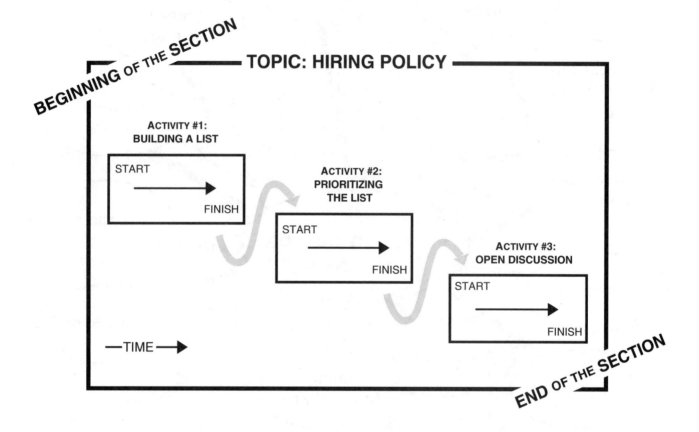

Many people don't realize it is possible to subdivide the thinking time on any topic into different styles of activity. As the diagram makes clear, *open discussion* is one approach to structuring participation in a group; there are many others. Thus, *building a list* and *prioritizing the list* are both participation formats, just as *open discussion* is.

The broad topic – "hiring policy" – remains the same from one activity to the next. It is the *participation format* that keeps changing.

This way of sequencing an activity is called a *string*.

## USING STRINGS TO ENHANCE OPEN DISCUSSION

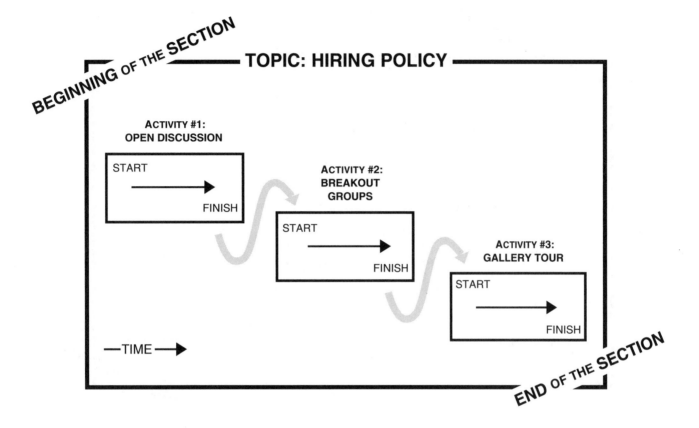

The diagram on the previous page showed a string in which *open discussion* came third, after work on "hiring policy" had already been done in two other formats. It is just as easy to design a process that leads with *open discussion*. That format is then followed by others, such as *breakout groups* (as shown above) or *pairs* (not shown).

Numerous other strings are available to mix *open discussion* with other formats. A group could *begin* with a *structured go-around* and *then* move into *open discussion*. Or the first step could be *threesomes*, or *individual writing* or a more sophisticated format like a *skit* or a *debate* or a *fishbowl*.

## KEEPING THE ENERGY FRESH IN A MEETING

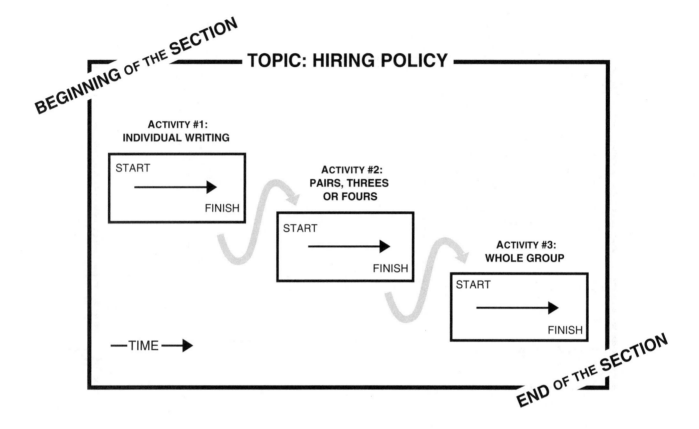

The simplest way to boost energy in a meeting is to give participants frequent opportunities to work individually, in pairs, in threes and in fours. These easy-to-organize, casual, small group formats are crucial for keeping everyone's battery charged.

Using strings that shift back and forth – sometimes working in the whole group and sometimes working in small groups – is truly a "best practice" for facilitators to utilize. Although it seems almost too basic to take seriously, the fact is that this underlying structure will significantly upgrade the "felt experience" of a meeting's quality and productivity.

## INSIGHTFUL PROCESS DESIGN

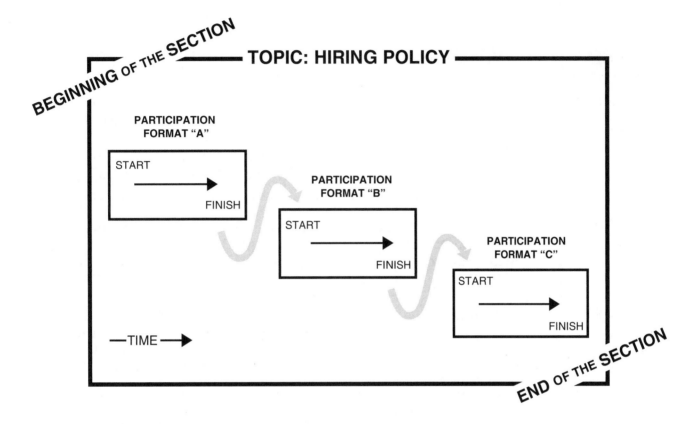

Using strings that vary the *participation formats* during a meeting strengthens participation in many ways. The tight structure of the activities assists people in preserving their focus and staying clear about the short-term objectives of their participation. And the variety supports people to maintain their energy.

Furthermore, your group will have a continuing experience of starting something and finishing it: starting and finishing; starting and finishing; starting and finishing. People have the experience of moving forward step by step, and of getting things done.

*This is how momentum builds.*

# MAKING TIME ESTIMATES FOR ACTIVITIES

| PROCESS | TYPICAL TIME | TIPS FOR ESTIMATING TIME |
|---|---|---|
| SMALL GROUPS | 6-15 minutes | Decide how much speaking time to allow for each person. Multiply by the number of people in the group. Allow 3-4 minutes for instructions and the shuffling needed to form small groups. |
| GO-AROUNDS | 5-20 minutes for an 8-person group, depending on topic | Assume 30 seconds per person for a simple question, and 2 minutes per person for a more evocative topic. |
| LISTING IDEAS | 7-10 minutes | The time limit for listing ideas is entirely arbitrary. However, more than 10 minutes without discussion is difficult for many to tolerate. |
| INDIVIDUAL WRITING | 5-10 minutes | Allow 5 minutes for writing that is a "warm-up" to something else. Allow 10 minutes for writing that has a substantive purpose. |
| OPEN DISCUSSION | 15-30 minutes | If high involvement is desired, assume the discussion will hit its stride after 5-10 minutes. When an open discussion runs longer than 20-30 minutes, attention will flag. |
| BREAKOUT GROUPS | 30-90 minutes | Decide how much time to allow the groups to work. Then add 10 minutes for the shuffle to and from the breakout areas. |

A TYPICAL STRING
# MEETING GOAL 1: SHARE INFORMATION

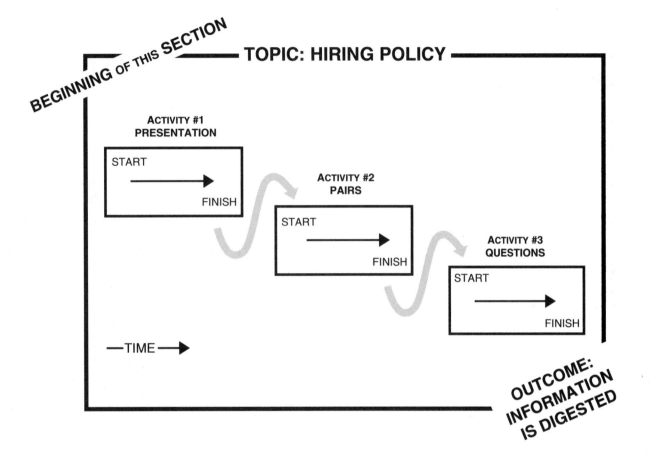

When the meeting goal is to *share information,* the group slips naturally into "audience mode."  Basically, most people sit back and listen, and perhaps a couple of members ask questions.

The string shown above shifts that energy.  By having everyone turn to a person nearby and react to what they've heard, all group members are guided to engage with the substance of the presentation.  Invariably, this leads to more questions – and more interesting questions – when the whole group is reconvened.

If a meeting designer has a reason to pull for even more participation, s/he could use a *structured go-around* as the third format in the string.  Or, s/he could use *individual writing* as the format – asking participants to write anonymous questions, which are then drawn from a hat.

A TYPICAL STRING

# MEETING GOAL 2: PROVIDE INPUT

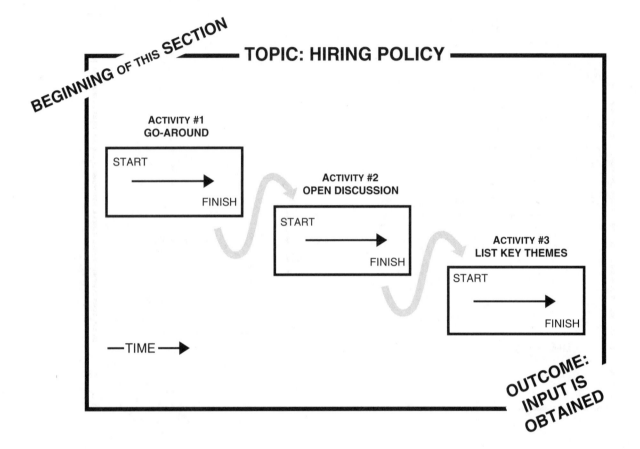

When the meeting goal is to have the group *provide input,* the most straightforward way to manage a group is with a simple *go-around.* That gives everyone a chance to speak up and influence the decision-maker. If a meeting designer wants members to react to each other's inputs, a string like the one shown above will encourage participants in that direction. Alternatively, the designer could start the process with a *list-building* activity, such as listing pros and cons of the idea for which input has been requested.

If the meeting designer wants to intensify the quality of input, s/he could include *debate* as one of the formats, or send people into *breakout groups* to develop different perspectives more thoroughly.

A TYPICAL STRING

# MEETING GOAL 3: ADVANCE THE THINKING

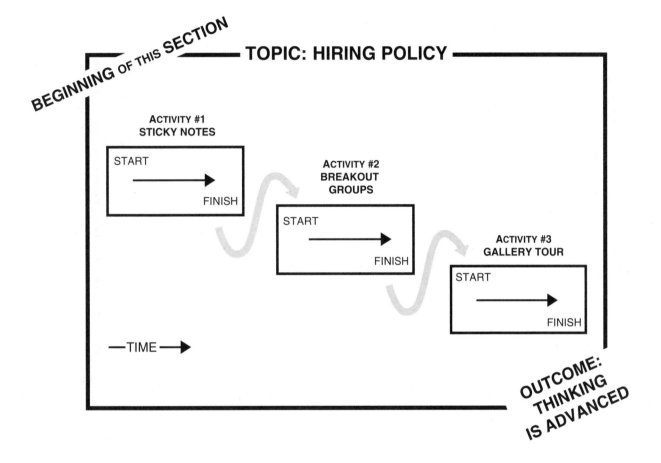

*BEGINNING OF THIS SECTION*

**TOPIC: HIRING POLICY**

**ACTIVITY #1
STICKY NOTES**

START → FINISH

**ACTIVITY #2
BREAKOUT
GROUPS**

START → FINISH

**ACTIVITY #3
GALLERY TOUR**

START → FINISH

← TIME →

*OUTCOME:
THINKING
IS ADVANCED*

When the meeting goal is to *advance the thinking,* participants often tackle the objective with enthusiasm. (For many people, it's fun to think together when they know their work isn't heading straight to a decision.) The string shown above is one of an enormous number of combinations that might be useful – whether to define, analyze, reframe, narrow, resolve or evaluate the issues at hand.

Many of the activities offered in chapters 18-20 match up quite well with this meeting goal. So do several other well-known problem solving tools not included in this book, such as force field analysis. If a process can be adapted for use by groups, it probably belongs on the list of activities that can *advance the thinking* when appropriate. In general, choose formats that (a) stimulate multiple perspectives and (b) utilize those multiple perspectives to perform the type of thinking required.

A TYPICAL STRING

# MEETING GOAL 4: MAKE DECISIONS

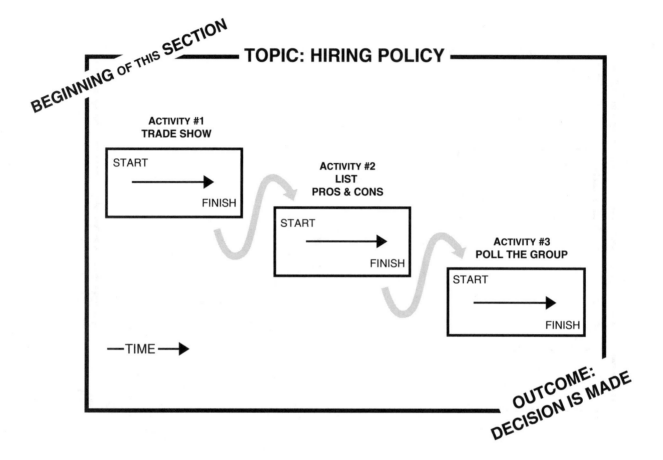

BEGINNING OF THIS SECTION

TOPIC: HIRING POLICY

**ACTIVITY #1**
**TRADE SHOW**

START

FINISH

**ACTIVITY #2**
**LIST**
**PROS & CONS**

START

FINISH

**ACTIVITY #3**
**POLL THE GROUP**

START

FINISH

—TIME—➤

OUTCOME:
DECISION IS MADE

When the meeting goal is to *make decisions,* a group's level of engagement can vary quite a bit. For a low-stakes decision, a meeting designer would want the group to dispense with the issue quickly and painlessly. When the stakes are high, or when the decision must resolve a contentious problem, it's likely that the group will spend time in the *Groan Zone,* a likelihood that the meeting designer should anticipate.

The string above was designed for a decision that required agreement from the whole group. First, three proposals were offered, in a *trade show* format. Next the group *listed pros and cons* of each proposal. Then the group was polled, using *Gradients of Agreement* (chapter 23.) The first two formats built shared understanding, and the third tested for the degree of convergence among the group.

A TYPICAL STRING

# MEETING GOAL 5:
# IMPROVE TEAM COMMUNICATION

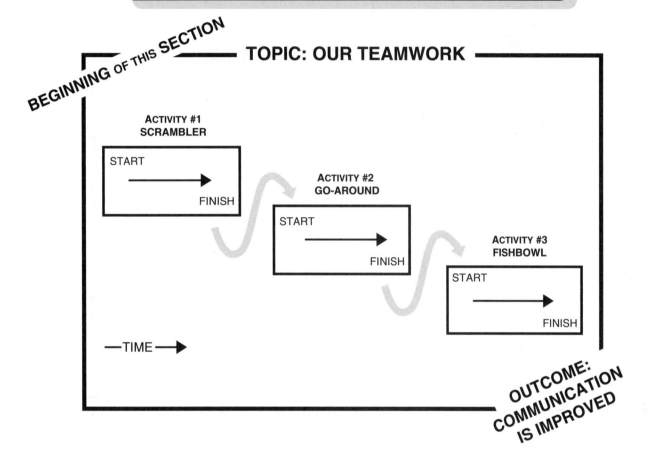

**TOPIC: OUR TEAMWORK**

BEGINNING OF THIS SECTION

OUTCOME: COMMUNICATION IS IMPROVED

When the meeting goal is to *improve team communication,* many team members can be expected to behave cautiously, shying away from the potentially difficult interpersonal interactions that might be necessary.

The string above was designed to optimize safety. A *scrambler* is just a high-structured way to provide people with the privacy that comes from working in threes, and it's ideal for encouraging personal sharing. The *go-around* completes the cycle of self-disclosure, and prepares the group to take the next step toward giving and receiving feedback. By then, a variety of interpersonally-oriented activities could work. The *fishbowl* shown above can be used with several options from chapter 19 – such as *If I Were You* and *Couples Counseling.* And once the trust level has been strengthened, the simple choice – *open discussion,* with shifts into *pairs* now and then – is often the one that "feels right" to the team.

A TYPICAL STRING

# MEETING GOAL 6: BUILD TEAM CAPACITY

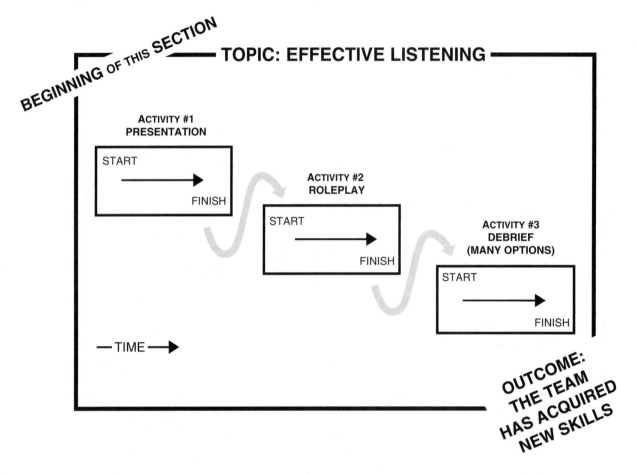

*BEGINNING OF THIS SECTION*

TOPIC: EFFECTIVE LISTENING

ACTIVITY #1
PRESENTATION

START

FINISH

ACTIVITY #2
ROLEPLAY

START

FINISH

ACTIVITY #3
DEBRIEF
(MANY OPTIONS)

START

FINISH

— TIME —▶

*OUTCOME:
THE TEAM
HAS ACQUIRED
NEW SKILLS*

When the meeting goal is to *build team capacity,* the natural tendency of most group members would be to approach the agenda with all the positive and negative attitudes associated with classroom learning. In essence, people can be captivated by the prospect of learning something that is interesting and new, and they can be easily bored if the teaching mode is simply to pass out handouts and show lots of slides.

The string above demonstrates that a training approach can be taken even within the confines of a regular staff or managers' meeting. A brief *presentation* can frame a subject, after which a 10-minute *roleplay* – or a *case study,* or a *skit,* or any high engagement *structured activity* – can put people in an experiential-learning frame of mind. A debrief can be done in *small groups,* in a *go-around,* in an *open discussion,* or by *building a list.*

A TYPICAL STRING

# MEETING GOAL 7: BUILD COMMUNITY

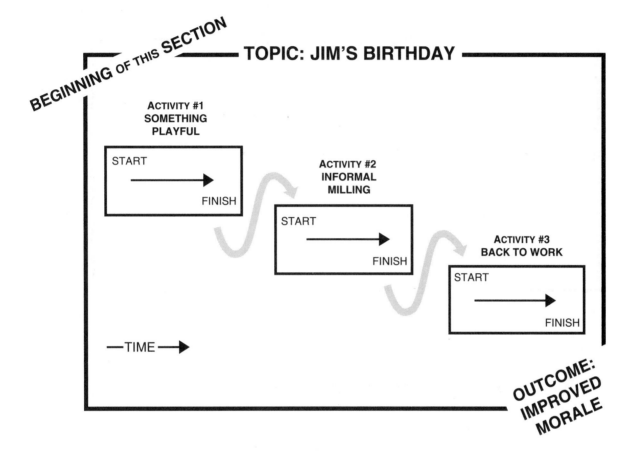

When the meeting goal is to *build community,* the purpose is to promote camaraderie, strengthen bonds, and boost morale. Groups typically split 70-30 between those who are happy to have a few minutes of fun, and those who are reticent to spend meeting time on anything that isn't serious business. But even the grumpiest members can usually tolerate something playful if it happens in a five-to-ten minute time frame. For example, a happy birthday celebration never gets censored. Neither does a *go-around* that gives group members a few minutes to share their reactions to a dramatic current event.

The string above illustrates a useful principle: a few minutes of *informal chat* is an excellent transition from an activity that builds community back to the conventional agenda items. Thus, schedule the community-building activity to occur just before a break, whenever possible.

# PROCESS DESIGN FOR AN EFFECTIVE AGENDA

SUMMARY

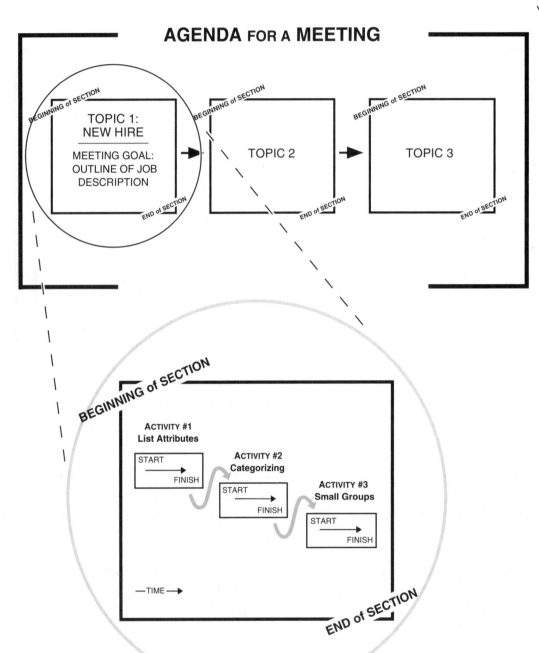

**AGENDA FOR A MEETING**

When a meeting goal pulls for high involvement, a planner can string together three or four different activities to produce the desired outcome. For example, if a meeting goal is to *advance the thinking* on a job description, a group could list attributes of the job; then categorize the list into themes; then break into small groups to write up each theme. This way of sequencing activities is called a *string*.

# PROPERTIES OF AN EFFECTIVE AGENDA

☑

☐ Every topic to be covered at the meeting is clearly identified.

☐ Both the *overall goal* and the *meeting goal* for each topic have been defined. These may or may not be written onto the agenda, but they can and will be explicitly stated as needed.

☐ Each meeting goal is supported by a process that has been designed with the intention of encouraging an appropriate level of involvement. The process consists of one or more activities. When no single activity would achieve the meeting goal, a series of activities are combined into a *string*.

☐ Realistic time estimates have been made for each activity. The estimated times may or may not be posted, but they are stated when the process is described.

☐ The agenda begins with two grounding items: a frame – usually an overview that lets everyone know roughly what to expect for the rest of the meeting – and a brief welcoming activity, like a check-in.

☐ The agenda ends with a way to provide participants with a sense of completion: a summary of accomplishments and a review of next steps, an evaluation of the meeting, or an opportunity for everyone to make a closing remark.

☐ A scheduled 10-minute break occurs whenever a meeting runs longer than 2 hours.

☐ The agenda is written and accessible – either as a printout distributed to everyone or as a flipchart posted on the wall.

# 13

# DEALING WITH DIFFICULT DYNAMICS

SUPPORTIVE INTERVENTIONS
THAT DON'T MAKE ANYONE WRONG

- **Difficult Dynamics Produce Difficult People**
- **Communication Styles That Bug People**
- **Supporting Diverse Communication Styles**
- **Whole Group Interventions for Difficult Communication Styles**
- **Injunctions Against Thinking in Public**
- **Developing Supportive Group Norms**
- **Handling Out-of-Context Distractions**
- **Using a *Check-In* to Build Community**
- **Reducing Deference to a Person-in-Charge**
- **Strengthening Relationships**
- **Forming Personal Bonds**
- **Giving and Receiving Feedback**
- **Stepping out of the Content and Talking about the Process**
- **Continuous Improvement of Meetings**

# DIFFICULT DYNAMICS PRODUCE DIFFICULT PEOPLE

When the objectives of a discussion are straightforward, people can tolerate each other's idiosyncrasies without too much difficulty. If someone is a bit pushy, for example, the group will probably just look past it. However, when the objectives require hard thinking, people have a harder time communicating. Periods of misunderstanding and confusion are common, leading to feelings of frustration and impatience.

Staying focused at such times is an enormous challenge. Clear-headed thinking deteriorates as emotional urgency intensifies. Some people get so exasperated and overwhelmed they can barely pay attention. Others feel compelled to take over the leadership of the discussion, whether or not they know how to do it effectively. Some people just want to withdraw and get away. And others, feeling their anger rise, struggle privately to stay cool when what they *really* want to do is pick a fight.

Despite the rise in tension, many people continue making efforts to stay present and committed to the task. They keep trying – but they're trying under pressure. This can't help but affect their moods, their communication styles, and their thinking abilities. Their behavior toward others may be less than sensitive. They might blurt out their ideas with less tact than usual. They might go on and on – oblivious to the effect they're having on their audience – because they feel they're on the verge of an important line of thought. These are a few of the countless examples of the symptoms people exhibit when trying to contribute their best thinking under stress.

The expression of these symptoms makes many people uncomfortable. If there is a facilitator, people usually look to the facilitator to "save them" from their anguish. For example, many people expect a facilitator to interrupt those who talk too long and silence them. Alternatively, some facilitators think it is appropriate to talk to "the difficult person" during a break to request that s/he tone it down. So-called solutions like these are based on a faulty line of analysis – namely, that eliminating a symptom will somehow remove the cause of the distress.

This chapter offers the reader a different perspective. Difficult dynamics are treated as group situations that can be handled supportively rather than as individual personalities that need to be fixed.

# COMMUNICATION STYLES THAT BUG PEOPLE

## *Many Groups Have Someone Who . . .*

❏ Repeats ideas that someone else has already expressed.

❏ Quibbles over minor details.

❏ Openly expresses strong emotion.

❏ Takes the discussion to a very abstract level.

❏ Uses jargon that is difficult to understand.

❏ Continually raises a pet issue no matter what topic is being discussed.

❏ Criticizes without offering constructive suggestions.

❏ Complains about how little progress the group is making.

❏ Repeats his or her own point over and over again.

❏ Argues as a way of clarifying an idea.

❏ Brings up obscure problems that waste time on insignificant tangents.

❏ Makes long-winded speeches.

❏ Cloaks disagreements with insincere sugar-coating.

❏ Talks in a too-loud voice, as if everyone else were hard of hearing.

❏ Apologizes for everything s/he says.

❏ Blames other people without acknowledging his or her own part.

❏ Nitpicks whenever someone uses an analogy to make a point.

❏ Just sits silently and rarely contributes.

❏ Acts smug and self-assured, as if s/he knows everything.

❏ Whispers to someone sitting nearby, while someone else is talking.

## *Which of these Styles Bug You?*

# SUPPORTING DIVERSE COMMUNICATION STYLES

## Instructions

1. Read the handout titled *"Communication Styles That Bug People."* Identify styles that might irritate *you*.

2. Form small groups. With your partners, discuss your personal reactions to the communication styles that annoy you.

3. In the space provided below, write down anything about your own communication style that might bother someone else.

4. At your discretion, share your reflections with your partners.

5. Discuss: When group members send one another subtle messages of disapproval and annoyance because of their diversity of communication styles, what consequences are created?

6. Return to the large group and discuss: When individuals are suppressed because their styles are "unacceptable," what are the costs to the group as a whole? How can group members become more tolerant of diverse communication styles?

## Bothersome Aspects of My Own Communication Style:

- 
- 
-

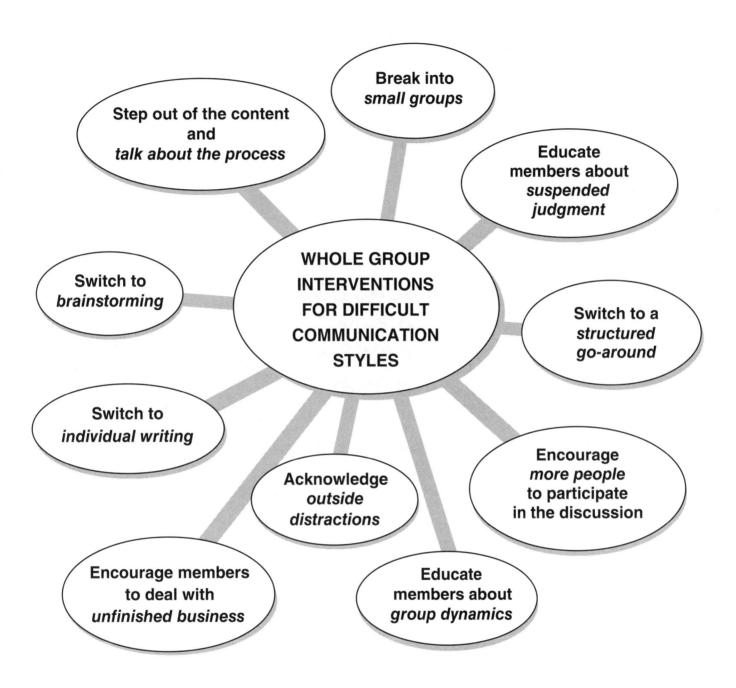

Facilitators who use the interventions shown here can handle many irritants and snags without abandoning the commitment to be respectful and supportive with *every* group member.

"Impossible!!"

"Stop wasting our time."

"That has nothing to do with what we're talking about."

"Your idea doesn't make sense."

"Getting pretty intellectual here, aren't we?"

"Hurry up – we're running out of time."

## INJUNCTIONS AGAINST THINKING IN PUBLIC

"Where'd *that* come from?"

"You're not being clear."

"You're confusing people."

"You're making me think too hard."

"That's crazy!"

"Don't ramble."

"You keep going off on tangents."

"Haven't we already been around that block?"

"Enough joking around – let's get back to business."

"You're repeating yourself."

"Please, no sermons."

"Please wrap it up – you're taking too long."

"Get to the point!"

"Don't confuse me with the facts."

"Let's keep it simple."

"That's ridiculous."

"If you'd been listening, you wouldn't have to ask that question."

"Stop beating around the bush."

"Can you say more about that?"

"I know exactly what you're talking about."

"I'm not quite sure I followed you. Could you repeat what you said?"

"Hold on! I think she has a point here."

"I know this might be difficult for you …"

"Before we change the subject, let's make sure everyone gets a chance to speak."

THE SUPPORTIVE ATTITUDE IN ACTION

"Go ahead. I'm all ears."

"What's *your* opinion?"

"Interesting!"

"Wow!"

"Take your time."

"What would be an example of that?"

"Go for it!"

"Does anyone have more to add?"

"Is *this* what you're saying?"

"I heard *that.*"

"I can see you're having a hard time putting this into words. Keep trying."

"That must have felt *bad.*"

"Even though we don't see eye to eye on this issue, I'm glad you keep standing up for your point of view."

# DEVELOPING SUPPORTIVE GROUP NORMS

## WHY

Many groups have not developed respectful, supportive group norms. Their members do not talk to each other in the responsive, encouraging style shown on the preceding page, *The Supportive Attitude in Action*.

Instead these groups develop norms that stifle spontaneity and discourage first-draft thinking. Members make statements like those found on page 202, *Injunctions Against Thinking in Public*.

Such groups have very little capacity to overcome difficult dynamics. Instead they become trapped in recurring patterns of frustration, conflict, and withdrawal. To overcome their patterns, it is essential for these groups to change their norms and develop cultures that are more supportive. This exercise is a strong first step in that direction.

## HOW

1. Have everyone look over *Injunctions Against Thinking in Public* (p. 202) and privately identify messages that might be intimidating to receive.

2. Form groups of three.

3. Have each person think out loud about how s/he would be affected by being on the receiving end of those messages.

4. Now have everyone read *The Supportive Attitude in Action* (p. 203).

5. Have each person describe how it feels to be on the receiving end of the supportive attitude and how it feels to be on the giving end.

6. Invite everyone to jot down answers to this question: "What changes would I be willing to make in my own communication style, to help the group develop a more supportive atmosphere?"

7. Reconvene the large group and invite people to share their reflections.

# HANDLING OUT-OF-CONTEXT DISTRACTIONS

## THE SITUATION

Current events sometimes interfere with a group's ability to concentrate. After a terrible storm, for example, people need to talk about their flooded basements and leaking roofs. After an election, people need to discover how they feel about the potential impacts. During an organizational transition – a massive layoff, say – people need to let off steam and express their angst.

What should a group do when faced with distractions like these? Many people believe that the best response is to ignore their existence. This belief is grounded in value judgments, however, not empirical fact. Realistically, the presence of a serious distraction will lower a group's efficiency *regardless of what group members are officially allowed to talk about.*

This activity gives people the chance to spend a well-structured period of time talking about what's really on their minds. After a round of expressing themselves, they are often better able to concentrate on the work at hand.

## THE TECHNIQUE

1. If it's obvious that the group is having trouble focusing on the topic at hand, suggest that people talk about whatever might be the source of distraction. For example, "I notice we're having a hard time concentrating on this subject, and I'm aware that [the recent event] is on a lot of people's minds. Could we step back and spend a few minutes talking about [the event]?"

2. Secure agreement from the group to proceed.

3. Pose an open-ended question, such as, "What *are* people feeling about [the event]?" Ask everyone to respond.

4. When everyone has spoken, suggest a sequence for making the transition back to the main topic. For example, "What if we spend a few more minutes in this conversation, then take a short break and return to the main topic after the break?"

## THE CHECK-IN
### A PERSONAL WAY TO BEGIN MEETINGS

## PURPOSE

A *check-in* is simply a *go-around* that occurs at the beginning of a meeting. People are invited to share their moods and to briefly identify anything that might affect their participation. Each person takes a turn to say, in essence, *"Here's how it feels to be me today."*

Everyone faces non-work-related problems now and then. They range in degree from mild ("I'm having a bad hair day") to severe ("My mother is dying"). A check-in allows people to tell each other what they're facing, in a way that informs without being obtrusive. For people who will devote most of their discussion time to work-related issues, this helps them get to know one another in greater depth as multi-dimensional human beings.

Furthermore, a check-in sets the norm of full participation, by having each person speak before the work has even begun. Once a person has spoken in the group, s/he is much more likely to speak up again.

## PROCEDURE

1. Introduce the check-in as a time for everyone to briefly share "what mood you're in" or "whatever is on your mind, especially anything you feel like sharing that might be affecting your mood." Any context is fine, work-related or not. If anyone questions the purpose, explain that it helps many people to share a little of their personal context in order to make a better transition from *outside* the meeting to *inside* the meeting.

2. Ask for a volunteer to go first. As with all go-arounds, ask this person to say, "I'm done" or "pass" when s/he is finished checking in.

3. If someone interrupts another group member's check-in, politely interject. Say something like, "Sorry, excuse me, this isn't the time for conversation. Let's just give each person space to check in without comment."

4. When everyone has checked in, you might opt to make a comment that acknowledges a theme you've just heard. For example, "It sounds like many of you are feeling pressured this week. Maybe we can go a bit easy on ourselves today." Then move into the business section of the agenda.

A *check-in* builds group cohesion. It lets everyone participate in a common activity right from the first moments of a meeting.

People use it to let each other know that they may still have feelings lingering from the previous meeting.

It helps the group to be patient with someone who is having a "bad hair day."

## REASONS FOR DOING A CHECK-IN

Everyone occasionally has to deal with a severe "outside problem," like the death or illness of a loved one. A *check-in* lets people inform the group, without making a big issue of it.

It provides a transition from "outside the meeting," to "inside the meeting." It helps members shift the focus of their attention by expressing something in order to let go of it.

A regular *check-in* is a solid investment in the long-term development of mutual trust.

A *check-in* is simply a *go-around* that occurs at the beginning of a meeting. People are invited to share their moods and to briefly identify anything that might affect their participation. Each person takes a turn to say, in essence, *"Here's how it feels to be me today."*

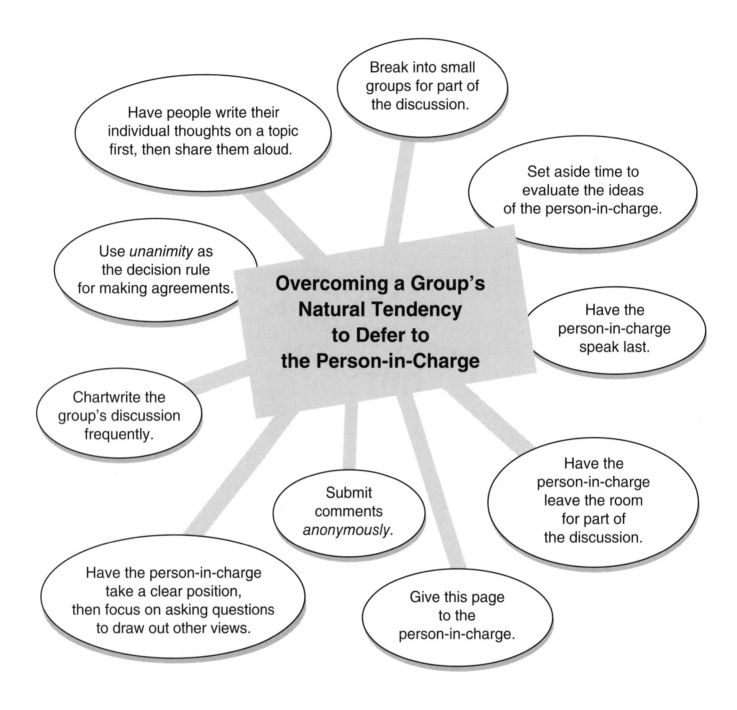

Have people write their individual thoughts on a topic first, then share them aloud.

Break into small groups for part of the discussion.

Set aside time to evaluate the ideas of the person-in-charge.

Use *unanimity* as the decision rule for making agreements.

**Overcoming a Group's Natural Tendency to Defer to the Person-in-Charge**

Have the person-in-charge speak last.

Chartwrite the group's discussion frequently.

Submit comments *anonymously*.

Have the person-in-charge leave the room for part of the discussion.

Have the person-in-charge take a clear position, then focus on asking questions to draw out other views.

Give this page to the person-in-charge.

In many groups, people automatically defer to the person-in-charge. Often a facilitator's best intervention is to choose whichever option seems simplest and least disruptive. But if the goal is to instill participatory culture, a better option might be to *identify the tendency, and educate the group*. Acknowledge that it takes courage to speak truthfully in a hierarchy. Form small groups to discuss what might be said differently if the person-in-charge were not in the room. Then debrief in the large group.

# STRENGTHENING RELATIONSHIPS

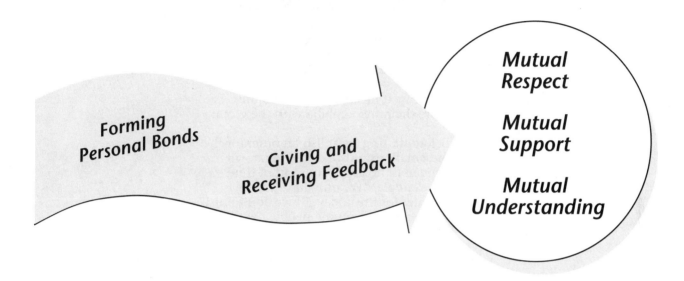

People who know one another are more likely to overcome their differences and find common ground than people who remain strangers to one another.

This principle is noticeable in business and in politics, where leaders often make a practice of building friendly relationships with their colleagues and the families of their colleagues. It holds true for grassroots movements, where activists – progressives and conservatives alike – intentionally design events to provide participants with a mixture of community building and social action. Yet this principle is undervalued in the realm of group decision-making. Bringing photographs of one's family members to a meeting, for example, or taking time to tell each other a little about the neighborhood where one grew up – these activities are hard for some people to imagine in the context of group decision-making.

The facilitator's task is to seek opportunities to strengthen relationships, in order to counterbalance the struggles that make collaboration so challenging. Participants need relief, even if temporary, from long, frustrating meetings. More important, broadening the context of working relationships allows people to see one another as real people, not just as "opponents" or "allies." Relationship building strengthens the foundation of mutual understanding.

# FORMING PERSONAL BONDS

## ANECDOTES & MEMENTOS

1. Ask everyone to bring something personal to share at the next meeting – a memento, a photograph, or an anecdote.

2. At the next meeting, ask for volunteers to share their memorabilia with the group.

3. Before starting, establish an order for the presentations. Also, clarify what will happen if the group runs out of time. For example, "We only have thirty minutes for this today. If we don't finish, we'll do the remaining people next time."

4. Give each presenter five minutes to speak. Allow time for two or three questions. Then switch to someone new.

## TWO TRUTHS AND A LIE

1. Describe the activity.* Explain that all members will tell the group three things about themselves: two truths and a lie. The lie must be a bald-faced lie, not a half-truth. For example, someone who has one brother may not say, "I have two brothers." S/he *could* say, "I have twelve brothers."

2. After all have told their tales, have everyone quickly raise hands to indicate which "fact" they think was the lie. Ask, "How many people think the lie was such-and-such?"

3. Have the person reveal the lie. Then call on the next person to take a turn.

4. After everyone has gone, applaud those who did the best job of fooling the group.

## THE SUPPORT SEAT

1. Arrange the chairs in a semi-circle, and put one chair in front, facing the rest.

2. Describe the activity. Explain that each person will sit in the support seat for 20 minutes, while colleagues ask about the person's life away from work. Members may ask whatever they wish. The person in the center can always say, "I prefer not to answer that question."

3. Ask for a volunteer to sit in the center.

4. Anyone can ask the first question, plus one follow-up question. S/he must then pass until everyone has had a turn.

Note: This activity is often spread over several meetings.

* This activity is a variation of "Two Truths and a Lie" presented by Bill Schmidt, instructor in Organizational Psychology at the Wright Institute, Berkeley, California, 1993.

# GIVING AND RECEIVING FEEDBACK

## OBSERVATIONS AND INTERPRETATIONS

1. Ask everyone to find a partner.

2. Allow each person five minutes to give his or her partner feedback as follows: First: "Something I *observe* about you is..." Then: "What I make up in my head about this observation is..."

3. When five minutes have passed, remind each pair to switch roles. The speaker becomes the listener, and vice versa.

4. Optional: When time is up, ask everyone to find a different partner. Repeat Steps 2 and 3 with the new partner.

5. Return to the large group and debrief.

## APPRECIATIONS

1. Count the number of group members and subtract one. Then give each person that many sheets of blank pages. For example, each person in a seven-person group would receive six sheets.

2. Ask everyone to write one thing they appreciate about each group member. It can be something simple, or something more personal and thoughtful.

3. When everyone has written one message to each member, ask everyone to fold their messages, stand up, and put each note on its proper chair.

4. When all messages have been delivered, have people return to their seats and read.

5. Debrief, allowing at least 15 minutes.*

## HOW DO I COME ACROSS?

1. Describe the activity. Explain that one person will ask the group, "How do I come across in our meetings? What are my strengths and weaknesses?" People can respond with statements like, "You are the only person who really listens to everyone's opinions." Or, "I see you protecting Jim whenever he misses his deadlines."

2. Ask for a volunteer. Set a firm time limit for this person to hear how s/he comes across. Allow at least 15 minutes.

3. While people state their perceptions, make sure the recipient listens without speaking. When time is up, give him or her at least 5 minutes to respond.

4. Move to another volunteer. If members prefer to continue interacting with the first person, set another limit.

* Source: Nancy Feinstein, PhD organization development specialist, as told to Sam Kaner, May 1995.

## STEPPING OUT OF THE CONTENT AND TALKING ABOUT THE PROCESS

### THE SITUATION

Meetings sometimes get bogged down for reasons that aren't clear. For example, suppose a few people keep raising a topic that has already been put aside. At such times, a facilitator may be tempted to ask, "What's going on here? We appear to be stuck. Does anyone have any ideas why?"

One might expect such a comment to help a group reflect on their process. But it seldom works. The sudden "level shift" is usually too confusing. A few people may respond to the question, but many will keep discussing the original topic. The problem is that some people don't realize they are being asked to step back from the discussion and talk about their process.

### THE TECHNIQUE

1. *Describe what you are observing.* "This morning everyone agreed not to interrupt anyone while they're speaking. Yet this afternoon many people are talking over one another. I'm also noticing some other signs of stress, such as [examples of what you have observed]."

2. *Ask for validation.* "Is anyone else noticing this?" Or "Are others seeing something similar?" For those who have a tougher time thinking in terms of group process, the responses to this simple question can provide examples of what "stepping away from the content" looks like.

3. *Encourage reflection.* "What reactions are people having to this?" Or "What thoughts and feelings are coming up for you?" Or "Does anyone have a sense of what this is about?"

4. *Encourage and draw out the different perspectives.* Don't try to problem solve or bring people to a shared agreement. Raising awareness is exploratory.

5. When people seem ready to return to the original topic, ask: "Before we go back to our topic, are there any final reactions to what has just been said?"

6. *Optional:* Call a short break to let the planner(s) reconsider the agenda.

# CONTINUOUS IMPROVEMENT OF MEETINGS

## STRENGTHS AND IMPROVABLES

1. Hang two sheets of paper. Title one page "Strengths." Title the other page "Improvables."*

2. Ask someone to call out a strength. Then ask someone else to call out an improvable. Build the two lists simultaneously.

3. Encourage participants to speak frankly in the spirit of constructive learning.

4. While the lists are being made, the ground rule of suspended judgment is in effect – no defending, explaining, or apologizing.

## LEARNING FROM LAST WEEK'S EXPERIENCE

1. Ask participants to look back on the previous meeting and recall anything that made them feel uncomfortable.

2. Brainstorm a list: What can we do to handle this better in the future?

3. If everyone agrees to abide by one or more items on the list, fine. Often, however, agreement does not come easily because unresolved feelings may still be present. Rather than attempt to force an agreement prematurely, treat Steps 1 and 2 as a consciousness-raising activity. Often, simply naming a problem goes a long way toward changing it.

---

\* Many facilitators substitute symbols for the words "Strengths" and "Improvables."
The plus-sign "+" and the Greek letter delta "Δ" (symbol for change) are both common.

# 14

# CLASSIC FACILITATOR CHALLENGES

HANDLING DIFFICULT DYNAMICS
THAT ARISE IN MANY MEETINGS

▶ **Thirty Universal Problems
Faced by Facilitators**

▶ **Typical Facilitator Mistakes
When Handling These Problems**

▶ **Effective Facilitator Responses
For Each Situation**

# CLASSIC FACILITATOR CHALLENGES ①

| PROBLEM | TYPICAL MISTAKE | EFFECTIVE RESPONSE |
|---|---|---|
| DOMINATION BY A HIGHLY VERBAL MEMBER | Inexperienced facilitators often try to control this person. "Excuse me, Mr. Q, do you mind if I let someone else take a turn?"<br><br>Or, even worse, "Excuse me, Ms. Q, but you're taking up a lot of the group's time . . ." | When one or two people are over-participating, everyone else is under-participating. So, focus your efforts on the passive majority. Encourage *them* to participate more. Trying to control those who dominate just sends more attention in their direction. |
| GOOFING AROUND IN THE MIDST OF A DISCUSSION | Try to "organize" people by getting into a power struggle with them. Raise your voice if necessary. Single out the ringleaders.<br><br>"All right everyone, let's get back to work." (Or better yet, "Focus, people, focus!") | Often a break is the best response. People become undisciplined when they are overloaded or worn out. After a breather, they will be much better able to focus.<br><br>Alternatively, ask for advice: "Is there something we ought to be doing differently?" |
| LOW PARTICIPATION BY THE ENTIRE GROUP | Assume that silence means consent. Don't ask whether everyone understands the key issues. (That just wastes time unnecessarily.)<br><br>"Great work so far, everyone. We're getting a lot done." Don't question whether what's getting done is substantive and inclusive or merely cosmetic. | Always be suspicious of low participation. Unexpressed anger or fear often inhibit free expression. If people do not appear ready to share their feelings, shift from *open discussion* to a less stressful format. Build a list or work in small groups. Or try a new activity, like a *fishbowl* or a *scrambler.* Or call a break. |

# CLASSIC FACILITATOR CHALLENGES   ②

| PROBLEM | TYPICAL MISTAKE | EFFECTIVE RESPONSE |
|---|---|---|
| SEVERAL DIFFERENT TOPICS BEING DISCUSSED AT THE SAME TIME | "Jim, that sounds like a different topic to me."<br><br>"Can we please try to stick to one topic at a time?"<br><br>Select a sub-topic to focus the conversation. Propose it with confidence to break through the din: "Hold on, folks, let's focus on . . ." | Use *tracking*: Name the various topics in play. "Let me see if I can summarize the key themes being discussed."<br><br>Use *linking*: "Can you help us link your idea to the central issues before us?"<br><br>Create a *parking lot* for ideas and issues to return to later. |
| MANY PEOPLE INTERRUPTING ONE ANOTHER, IN COMPETITION FOR AIRTIME | Take control. Don't be shy about interrupting the conversation yourself, in order to exhort people to be more respectful.<br><br>Select one person to speak, but give no indication of whose turn will come next. That would undercut spontaneity. | If you must interrupt to restore decorum, say something like, "Pat, I'm going to cut in here. First, let's be sure your point is being heard." Next, paraphrase Pat's point. Then organize the discussion by offering a ground rule or two. Then use *stacking*, *tracking*, and *sequencing*. |
| PEOPLE TREAT ONE ANOTHER DISRESPECTFULLY | Ignore it altogether. Why throw fuel on the fire?<br><br>Pretend that posting a ground rule imploring people to "be respectful" will somehow create respectful behavior. | Increase the frequency of your paraphrasing. People under pressure need support.<br><br>If proposing a ground rule to control this dynamic, make time for people to reflect on their behavior, so they say what they want to change. |

# CLASSIC FACILITATOR CHALLENGES

③

| PROBLEM | TYPICAL MISTAKE | EFFECTIVE RESPONSE |
|---|---|---|
| THE HOT LUNCH HAS ARRIVED EARLY. IT SMELLS DELICIOUS. | Stick to your agenda. The food will keep.<br><br>Give people a small group activity immediately. That way you can get some food while it's still hot. After all, you will be working all the way through lunch. | Face it: once a visceral presence has entered a room – whether lunch food or a birthday cake or a fire drill – the chance to do good work has been pre-empted for now.<br><br>Use the intermission to figure out how to recapture the mood from the morning. |
| NOT ENOUGH WALL SPACE TO HANG THE FLIPCHARTS THAT RECORD WHAT PEOPLE SAY. | Use an easel that holds a flipchart pad. When you fill a page, just flip it over and start a fresh page. What's the problem?<br><br>If the wall isn't any good, don't use flipcharts at all. Instead, use pre-constructed slides. That will send a clear signal to everyone not to add their own ideas to a presentation that is already canned. This will eliminate the need for flipcharts.<br><br>Complain throughout: "This meeting would have been a lot better if they'd given us a better room. Sorry, everyone. Though just to be perfectly clear, this was not my fault." | If the room uses long rectangular tables, you can stand them on their ends and position them side by side. Completed charts can be hung over bookshelves, on top of paintings, over chair backs … virtually anywhere.<br><br>Use Google Docs™ or any virtual meeting software that enables everyone to see the same written words on their laptop screens.<br><br>The best practice is to know your room in advance and work with meeting planners to ensure that they gain a full return on their investment by securing a room that will support the work they want their group to accomplish. |

# CLASSIC FACILITATOR CHALLENGES

④

| PROBLEM | TYPICAL MISTAKE | EFFECTIVE RESPONSE |
|---|---|---|
| MINIMAL PARTICIPATION BY MEMBERS WHO DON'T FEEL INVESTED IN THE TOPIC | Act as though silence signifies agreement with what's been said.<br><br>Ignore them and be thankful they're not making trouble. | Propose a discussion: "Does this topic affect me? Does it matter?" Warm up in pairs, so people can honestly explore their stake in it.<br><br>Later, ask the planners to assess reasons for the group's passivity. Plan next meeting accordingly. |
| POOR FOLLOW-THROUGH ON ASSIGNMENTS | Give an ineffective pep talk.<br><br>Ignore it.<br><br>Excuse it: "Oh well, we didn't really need that information anyway." | Assign the work to teams.<br><br>Build in a report-back process at a midpoint before the assignment is due. This gives anyone having trouble a chance to get help. |
| FAILURE TO START ON TIME AND END ON TIME | Announce, "We're going to start in five minutes." Then, five minutes later, repeat. But this time, replace "five minutes" with "just a few more minutes."<br><br>Wait for the arrival of the "people who count," but don't bother waiting for anyone with lower ranking.<br><br>When it's time to end, go overtime without asking. If anyone has to leave, let them tiptoe out so they don't disturb anyone. | Option 1: Start the meeting when it is scheduled to begin. (Principle: *Keep your word.*)<br><br>Option 2: Wait for everyone to arrive. People learn that one person's tardiness wastes other people's time. (Principle: *Every person's attendance is valuable; protect the integrity of the group.*)<br><br>Note: Make sure it is the person-in-charge, not you, who sets the policy and enforces it.<br><br>If meetings chronically run late, improve your agenda planning. |

# CLASSIC FACILITATOR CHALLENGES

(5)

| PROBLEM | TYPICAL MISTAKE | EFFECTIVE RESPONSE |
|---|---|---|
| TWO PEOPLE LOCKING HORNS | Put the focus exclusively on the interaction between the two disputing parties, as though no one else in the room has an opinion on the issue at hand.<br><br>Or, treat the two like children. "Come on, you two, can't you get along?" | Reach out to others: "Who else has an opinion on this issue?" or "Are there any other issues that need to be discussed before we go too much further with this one?"<br><br>Remember: When the majority is passive, focus your attention on *them*, not on the over-active few. |
| ONE OR TWO SILENT MEMBERS IN A GROUP WHOSE OTHER MEMBERS PARTICIPATE ACTIVELY | Put the quiet person on the spot. "Mr. Z, you haven't talked much today. Is there anything you'd like to add?"<br><br>Assume their silence means that they have no opinions. Keep moving. They will speak if they want to. | "I'd like to get opinions from those who haven't talked for a while."<br><br>Breaking into small groups works even better, allowing shy members to speak up without being pressed to compete for airtime. |
| SIDE CONVERSATIONS AND WHISPERED CHUCKLES | Ignore the behavior and hope it will go away.<br><br>Chastise the whisperers, in the belief that humiliation is an excellent corrective. | Playfully and politely, find a way to connect with the whisperers and encourage them to refocus.<br><br>Ask if the subject could be shared with the whole group.<br><br>If the problem persists, assume there's a reason. Are people bored? Do they need a break? |

# CLASSIC FACILITATOR CHALLENGES

**6**

| PROBLEM | TYPICAL MISTAKE | EFFECTIVE RESPONSE |
|---|---|---|
| FACILITATOR EMBARRASSED AT MAKING A MISTAKE | Keep a stiff upper lip. To show weakness will make you lose face with the group.<br><br>Away from the group, put it out of your mind. Have a drink to unwind. Brooding serves no useful purpose. | We all make mistakes. Be authentic with the group, but don't overdo it. Acknowledge your error and keep working.<br><br>Learn from your mistakes by talking about them with like-minded peers or a coach. |
| FACILITATOR IS ANNOYED – OR – DISTRUSTFUL – OR – FEARFUL – OR – COMPETITIVE WITH A SPECIFIC GROUP MEMBER | Use your feelings as evidence that something is wrong with the other person. Take them aside and try to support them to change. Offer them feedback, so they can understand why they bother you so much.<br><br>Freeze them out. But don't be too obvious about it – you wouldn't want to appear to have lost your neutrality.<br><br>Commiserate with others who are also made uncomfortable by this person.<br><br>Ignore your feelings and hope they will dissipate. | Feeling irritated or fearful or competitive with someone is a natural human response. It's in our role as facilitator to take responsibility for those "triggers." Here are two in-the-moment remedies:<br><br>• Call a break and take time to calm yourself.<br><br>• Catch up with the person later and make an effort to learn more about them.<br><br>Those two responses may be helpful under pressure. But to genuinely become more accepting of others requires a commitment to personal growth and self-awareness. This calls for an ongoing practice, like journaling, meditation or therapy. |

# CLASSIC FACILITATOR CHALLENGES

⑦

| PROBLEM | TYPICAL MISTAKE | EFFECTIVE RESPONSE |
|---|---|---|
| A DISCUSSION RAMBLES WITH NO CLEAR PURPOSE OR STRUCTURE. | Don't interfere. Sometimes people just need a chance to let off steam.<br><br>On a break, politely scold the boss for not showing more leadership & charisma. | Ask someone to clarify the objectives for the discussion.<br><br>Use *stacking* and other active listening skills to gently organize the flow of conversation. |
| FACILITATOR IS UNCOMFORTABLE WITH SILENCE | Fill the space by stating your own opinion. This gives the group something to react to.<br><br>Tell a funny story. Nothing breaks silence better than a good joke.<br><br>Say, "Come on people, *someone* must have an idea!" | Silence often indicates that *people are thinking.* Before doing anything, wait at least 15 seconds. If no one speaks up, either of these will work:<br><br>• "Any new thoughts?"<br><br>• "Would someone please restate the objective of this discussion?" |
| PEOPLE SEEM OVERWHELMED BY THE RANGE OF "OPEN THREADS" IN A SINGLE DISCUSSION | Say, "Let's focus on one theme at a time – which one should we start with?" Then go with the choice of whoever speaks first.<br><br>Halt the discussion – it's too confusing. Sort the themes into categories, prioritize them, and then take a break. | Ask people to call out themes currently being discussed. This lets people step back for a moment so they can see the forest as well as their own favorite trees.<br><br>The listening skills *tracking* or *summarizing* can accomplish the same objective. |

# CLASSIC FACILITATOR CHALLENGES

**8**

| PROBLEM | TYPICAL MISTAKE | EFFECTIVE RESPONSE |
|---|---|---|
| SOMETHING UPSETTING HAPPENED EARLIER, AND THE MEETING IS NOW GOING BADLY | Keep pushing on like nothing has happened. Naming it would make things worse.<br><br>Call out the troublemakers and ask for their apologies, so the group can forgive them and move on. | Encourage the group to step away from the content and talk about what happened.<br><br>Timing options include:<br>• right after the incident<br>• after a break<br>• end of the meeting<br>• start of the next meeting |
| EAGERNESS TO MOVE AHEAD WITHOUT FURTHER HELP FROM A FACILITATOR | Insist they will get much better results if they make more use of you.<br><br>Remind them that this is your job they're talking about, and times are tough. | Assure the planners that the decision to bring you back next time is theirs to make.<br><br>Be sure to have an evaluation activity to end the meeting.<br><br>If the planners opt to part ways, encourage them to schedule a debriefing session with you at a later time. |
| THE BOSS IS TAKING UP TOO MUCH AIRTIME | On a break, tell the boss to talk less and listen more.<br><br>In the whole group, point out this dynamic and assume people will change it, now that they are aware of it. | Focus on the key question(s) and switch to small groups or go-arounds in order to obtain a broader range of views.<br><br>In some groups, the boss wants to empower his / her employees. In this case, help the group step back and look at their authority dynamics. |

# CLASSIC FACILITATOR CHALLENGES

(9)

| PROBLEM | TYPICAL MISTAKE | EFFECTIVE RESPONSE |
|---|---|---|
| A KEY INFLUENCER HAS TO ARRIVE LATE, OR LEAVE EARLY | Go ahead and do the work. If the key person isn't there, too bad. Snooze, you lose.<br><br>Support the group to express their complaints at being disrespected. They wouldn't say these things with the person in the room so use this time to let off steam. | Avoid getting deep into discussions that might turn out differently if the missing person were in the room.<br><br>To optimize the use of time, ask the group to identify what can be done in the key person's absence. If there's no group work to be done, most folks are glad to turn to their backlogged emails. |
| SOMEONE MAKES A COMMENT THAT SOMEONE ELSE FINDS TO BE OFFENSIVE | This is a significant challenge for facilitators. No matter what you do in response, someone will probably perceive it as a serious blunder.<br><br>• If you *don't* confront the offending remark directly, part of the group will see you as being too passive – or worse.<br><br>• If you *do* confront the remark directly, a different part of the group will see you as advancing your own agenda or bowing to pressure from a special interest faction. | Depending on a group's culture and values, one of these might be useful:<br><br>• "Are there any responses to what Steve just said?"<br><br>• "Steve, are you open to feedback on what you just said?" (This works only in groups who practice giving and receiving feedback.)<br><br>• Wait to see the impact of Steve's comment. If there is one, point it out and have the group discuss it.<br><br>Dealing with this issue probably won't be pleasant – but ignoring it might turn out even worse. |

## CLASSIC FACILITATOR CHALLENGES

(10)

| PROBLEM | TYPICAL MISTAKE | EFFECTIVE RESPONSE |
| --- | --- | --- |
| A PARTICIPANT SHARES A VIEW WITH FACILITATOR IN PRIVATE, BUT NOT AT THE MEETING | Say, "I've spoken to people outside the meeting, so I know you're not all saying what you're really thinking. Let's get real, okay?" | Don't push. Trust develops over time; risky perspectives surface later than safe ones.<br><br>As a first step, suggest a small group activity that allows for the missing perspective to emerge informally. |
| AN IRRESISTIBLE DISTRACTION HAPPENS OUTSIDE THE MEETING ROOM | Raise your voice, and ask others to speak louder too.<br><br>Lean out the window and shout, "Hey cut it out down there! We have a meeting going on here!" | Acknowledge the distraction.<br><br>For short-lived distractions, take a break.<br><br>For lengthy distractions, change rooms or reschedule the meeting. |
| PEOPLE KEEP CHECKING THEIR SMARTPHONES | Call out anyone who does it and berate them for being rude.<br><br>Let it happen, but roll your eyes with exasperation and sigh loudly when it does.<br><br>Get with the times! Facilitate by email and text messages. | When the meeting begins, ask for agreement on dealing with digital distractions.<br><br>Offer longer breaks, extra breaks, or longer lunch.<br><br>When you notice someone surreptitiously checking email, even after the group has agreed not to do that, say, "Well, I can see the digital distractions have begun. Let's get to a break as soon as we can." Optionally you might add, "Meantime, screens down please." |

# CLASSIC FACILITATOR CHALLENGES

11

| PROBLEM | TYPICAL MISTAKE | EFFECTIVE RESPONSE |
|---|---|---|
| QUIBBLING ABOUT TRIVIAL PROCEDURES | Lecture the group about wasting time and "spinning our wheels."<br><br>Space out; doodle; think to yourself, "They're just not motivated to get anything done right now. Whatever." | Reframe it as a challenge worth tackling:<br><br>• "Sal has asked why we have to do [procedure X] this way. Can anyone suggest a different way to do it?"<br><br>• Build a list of options, or facilitate a brief discussion. |
| SOMEONE BECOMES STRIDENT AND REPETITIVE | At lunch, talk behind the person's back. Tell the person-in-charge that s/he must take more control.<br><br>Confront the person during a break. When the meeting resumes, raise your eyebrows or shake your head whenever s/he misbehaves. | People repeat themselves because they don't feel heard. Summarize the person's point of view until s/he feels understood.<br><br>Encourage participants to state the views of group members whose views are different from their own. |
| SOMEONE DISCOVERS A COMPLETELY NEW PROBLEM THAT NO ONE HAD PREVIOUSLY NOTED | Try to come up with reasons to discourage people from opening up this new can of worms.<br><br>Pretend not to hear the person's comments. | Wake up! This may be what you've been waiting for: the doorway into a new way of thinking about the whole situation. |

# Part Three

# SUSTAINABLE AGREEMENTS

# 15

# PRINCIPLES FOR BUILDING SUSTAINABLE AGREEMENTS

MAKING DECISIONS THAT INCORPORATE EVERYONE'S POINT OF VIEW

- ▶ **What Makes an Agreement Sustainable?**

- ▶ **Case Example: A Typical Tale of Woe**

- ▶ **Case Example: Success Story**

- ▶ **Business-as-Usual Compared with Participatory Decision-Making**

- ▶ **Two Mind-Sets:** *Either / Or* versus *Both / And*

- ▶ **Both / And Problem Solving Principles**

## WHAT MAKES AN AGREEMENT SUSTAINABLE?

IDEALIZED SEQUENCE

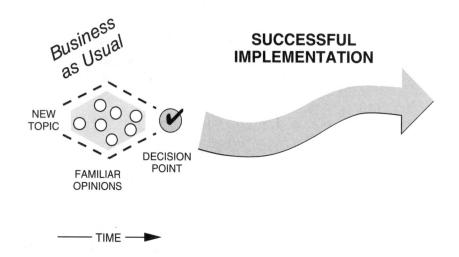

The diagram shown above represents an idealized sequence of the relationship between the discussion that precedes a decision, and the implementation that follows a decision. The discussion is quick and direct, and the implementation is straightforward.

Many people – perhaps most people – really do believe in this model. No struggle. No *Groan Zone*. Just a clean, linear, predictable forward movement from the inception of an idea to the end of its implementation.

And the reason the model is so widely credible is simple: *most of the time, it works!* In other words, most of the decisions a group makes *are* routine. The issues are familiar, the solutions are obvious, and the implementation can be accomplished with a bare minimum of planning and organizing.

Not all problems are routine, though. And what most people don't realize is that *this model does not work when the problem is a difficult one.*

# WHAT MAKES AN AGREEMENT SUSTAINABLE?

**TOUGH PROBLEMS DON'T SOLVE EASILY**

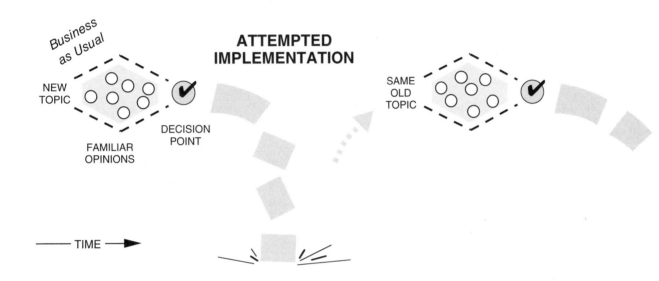

When a group attempts to solve a *difficult* problem as though it were a routine problem, they will very likely make a decision that simply does not work. The implementation will break down, and the group will find itself, sooner or later, back where it began.

Attempts to solve a tough problem with a business-as-usual discussion frequently produce "pseudo-solutions" – ideas that sound good at the time, but are ridiculous in retrospect. Here are some common pseudo-solutions:

- Agree on the top 20 priorities
- Delegate a job to someone who is already too overworked to do it
- Establish a policy that has no accountability built into it
- Create a committee to do the same work all over again
- Create a program and don't fund it
- Make an agreement that will be vetoed by someone who is not present
- Agree to "try harder" from now on

Pseudo-solutions don't solve anything; they merely provide participants with an illusory feeling of closure, so people can believe they accomplished something without having to go through the *Groan Zone.*

# UNSUSTAINABLE AGREEMENTS

A TYPICAL TALE OF WOE

It's a mistake to expect a business-as-usual discussion to solve a difficult problem. Here's a case in point.

## CASE STUDY

The owner of a large urban department store had a problem: his salespeople were consistently late for work. The owner had tried everything he could think of – fines, threats, pleading – but nothing worked. So he called a storewide staff meeting to tackle the problem.

The meeting began in good spirits. Many participants had an opinion about what the "real problem" was, and they were eager to state their views.

There appeared to be two camps. One group, including most floor managers and supervisors, believed that the owner hired too many students to work part-time. Students, they said, are transient – not committed to the long-term health of the business. If supervisors were free to hire more full-time employees, they could instill the staff with more loyalty, better morale, and higher standards of discipline.

The other group, including most salespeople, said that the problem was caused by the way they were paid. They were on commission, and very few shoppers appeared before mid-morning. Therefore, said the salespeople, they rarely earned any money for the first hour of the day. They recommended that those who opened the store should be paid a few extra dollars per day for their work.

The store owner listened as the two sides debated each other. After a while, people's patience began to wear thin. No one seemed to be changing their mind, and the group hadn't found any new ideas. The group saw no point in continuing. Someone said, "Everyone can't always get what they want. Sometimes there are winners and losers, and we just have to bite the bullet." So the owner said, "Here's my proposal. For the next four months, everyone who works on the first floor will be paid extra for coming on time. If it works, I will do it storewide. If it doesn't work, I will switch policies and hire more full-time employees. How does this sound?" A few people said, "Fine" or "Let's try it." The owner asked for objections, got none, and said, "All right, we're agreed."

After the meeting most people felt that the salespeople "won" and the managers "lost." The salespeople were glad for the extra pay and pleased that their concerns had been heard. But the supervisors were irritated. They felt the owner had not respected their judgment and that their authority had been undermined.

Over the next few months, the part-time students were treated very poorly. If someone asked to work Thursday and Friday, that person was scheduled to work Monday and Tuesday. If they asked to work evenings, they got mornings. The students reacted predictably: by taking long breaks; by spending too much time on personal phone calls; by calling in sick at the last minute; by quitting on two days' notice. The full-time sales staff saw what was happening and reacted by complaining more than ever. Morale on the first floor dropped to an all-time low.

Four months later, the owner ended the experiment and told the managers to hire more full-time staff. They were relieved. Now, with a better workforce, they could move forward on their goals of improving morale and loyalty and instilling higher standards of discipline. But the sales staff were resentful. They felt they'd been robbed of extra income by a management that had sabotaged the agreement. They told newly hired employees, "Don't trust your boss; he is a jerk." Tensions lingered for years. And the original problem – coming to work late – grew even worse, and was never resolved.

## SUSTAINABLE AGREEMENTS

*SUCCESS STORY*

A participatory decision-making process can produce meaningful, integrated, broadly supported solutions to exceedingly difficult problems. The keys are to resource it properly, and stay committed to the process.

**CASE STUDY**

In Mendocino County, California, local authorities brought together a group of loggers, environmentalists, and government officials to try to resolve a longstanding quarrel over the fate of privately owned redwood groves.

Until 1975 the property tax on privately owned forest land was based on the number of standing trees. The more trees on your property, the more tax you paid. To give the lumber companies an incentive to replant, all redwood trees under forty years old were exempt from the tax. But this policy had an unintended consequence: it created an incentive to cut down all older redwood trees, including ancient redwoods, whether or not the wood was in demand.

Environmentalists proposed taxing *all* redwoods, regardless of age. Lumber companies opposed this proposal. They argued that it would discourage them from replanting. Further, it would induce them to cut down even more trees – fewer standing trees would mean fewer taxes. Many residents of Mendocino County were advocates for preserving old-growth forests, and the county politicians felt pressured to find a workable solution.

Accordingly they created a task force with representatives from all factions. The task force was charged with developing a proposal for revising the tax code. The proposal would then be submitted to the California State legislature for approval.

The first meetings of the task force were polarized. The loggers insisted that the environmentalists' proposal would wreak havoc on the local economy, which depended heavily on the viability of the lumber business. Environmentalists retorted that the lumber companies were mercenary and short-sighted, and that they failed to protect the needs of the local ecosystem.

Many observers doubted that the group could produce a proposal that would make it through the legislative gauntlet. (Ten committees had to approve the bill – providing special-interest lobbyists ample opportunity to stall a proposal they didn't agree with.) But the conveners of the task force were determined to overcome the odds. They provided encouragement and staff support, so the group could keep working to find a solution that would be agreeable to all parties. They knew that letting

the dispute persist would lead to costly legal battles, a divided community, and various potential disruptions in the local economy.

Over the next few months, the task force met regularly. They gradually relaxed their posturing and became more willing to search for common ground. As they became more familiar with each other's points of view, their discussion became more interesting and more insightful.

It took them several months, but they found a creative framework: What if they stopped calculating property tax based on standing trees and switched to a tax based on *cut lumber?* This would discourage lumber companies from logging more than they could immediately market. By removing the tax on standing trees, land owners were no longer penalized for preserving ancient redwoods.

They developed a formal proposal and sent it to the legislature. Since it was supported by all sides, the proposal sailed through all ten legislative committees without opposition. The bill passed quickly, became law, and the entire community benefited.

\* This case study was told to Sam Kaner by a former lumber industry lobbyist who was a member of the task force described here.

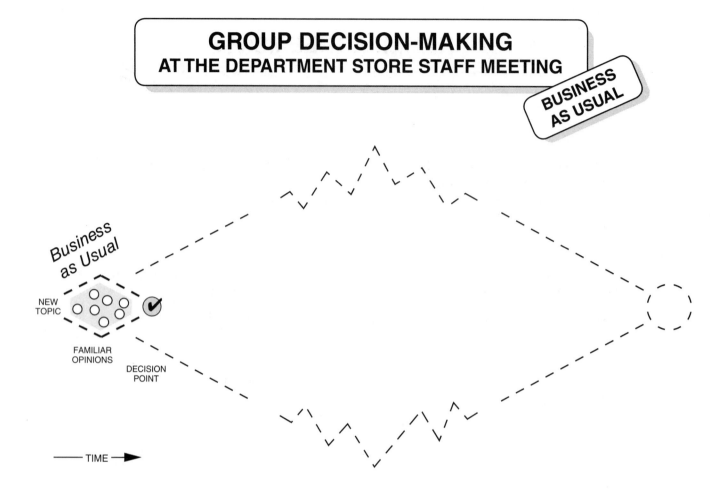

**GROUP DECISION-MAKING**
**AT THE DEPARTMENT STORE STAFF MEETING**

BUSINESS AS USUAL

Business as Usual

NEW TOPIC

FAMILIAR OPINIONS

DECISION POINT

TIME →

What went wrong at the department store staff meeting?  Not only did the participants fail to solve the tardiness problem, but their course of action bred long-lasting animosity and cynicism.  The above diagram offers insight into the reasons their meeting produced such poor outcomes.

Not realizing how much effort it would take to find a sustainable agreement, the group engaged in a *business-as-usual* decision-making process.  They considered only familiar options, not creative ones.  No one, for example, raised the possibility of opening the store an hour later; or offering free cappuccino to early-morning shoppers.  Rather than search for alternatives, the group focused on two conventional approaches:  people stated their own points of view without thinking too deeply about the larger implications of their opinions, or they repeated their arguments until nothing new was being said.  No one attempted to take the other side's needs into account. The owner expected to reach closure at that meeting, so he suggested a proposal and then made a superficial effort to check for group agreement. Thus, the group reached a quick decision – quick, but entirely ineffective.

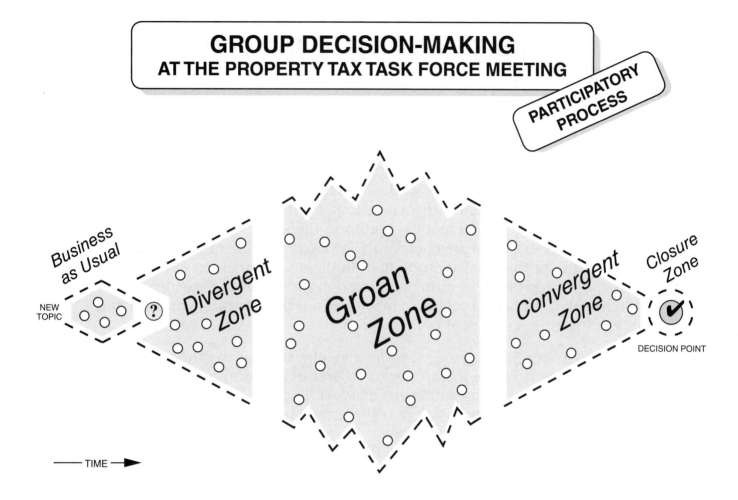

What made the second case turn out so differently? After all, the problem itself was much more difficult: the stakes were higher, the competing interest groups were more powerful, and the overall structure for reaching closure was incomparably more complicated. Yet the parties were able to find a creative solution that was genuinely acceptable to all sets of stakeholders. The diagram above is a rough schematic representation of the type of decision-making process *this* group engaged in.

This group did not try to solve the problem in a meeting or two. Instead they created a structure that supported them to persist for as long as it took to find a good solution. As for decision authority, it was clear that the final concept would need endorsement from all parties – or it wouldn't become law. Challenging though that may have seemed, this very requirement was what let them survive their factional animosities. They had to struggle, sometimes for entire meetings, to make sense of each other's viewpoints. But gradually they grew able to understand one another. This led to their discovery of a concept / solution that incorporated everyone's point of view.

## TWO MIND-SETS FOR SOLVING PROBLEMS

Why did the results of the department store staff meeting turn out so poorly, compared to the results of the property tax task force? Part of the answer to this question is obvious: *they organized themselves differently.* The people at the department store held a single meeting: business as usual. They gave themselves a chance to air familiar opinions; then they brought the issue to closure. In contrast, the members of the property tax task force designed a participatory process that allowed their problem-solving process to unfold in stages. They too began by airing familiar opinions – but they created a structure that supported people to move beyond their starting positions and build a shared framework of understanding.

But this tells us *what* they did, not *why* they did it. Why, in other words, did the two groups organize themselves so differently? The answer is that each group was operating from a different *mind-set* for solving problems: one group had an *Either/Or mind-set*; the other group had a *Both/And mind-set.*

From an *Either/Or mind-set*, solving a problem is a matter of making a choice between competing alternatives. Either you choose option A or you choose option B. Someone wins and someone loses, and that's how it goes. From a *Both/And mind-set*, solving a problem is a matter of finding an *inclusive solution* – one that encompasses everyone's perspectives. Rather than choose between options A and B, you search for a brand-new idea that works for everyone.

Groups that operate from an *Either/Or mind-set* are in a hurry. They want to get the decision over with. After all, what's the point of going over and over the same territory? Once the options have been clarified, further discussion becomes irrelevant. But groups that operate from a *Both/And mind-set* place a higher value on effectiveness than on expedience.

If the original options provide the group with a workable solution, then great! Decisions that can be made quickly *should* be made quickly. But if the original range of options does not provide a workable solution, then more effort lies ahead. The goal in such groups is not merely to reach a decision, but to reach a *sustainable agreement* – that is, to devise a solution that can be effectively implemented and supported by key stakeholders.

Several characteristics of these two mind-sets are contrasted on the next page.

# TWO MIND-SETS FOR SOLVING PROBLEMS

| | EITHER / OR | BOTH / AND |
|---|---|---|
| VALUE SYSTEM | Competitive | Collaborative |
| TYPE OF OUTCOME EXPECTED | Win / Lose | Win / Win |
| ATTITUDE TOWARD "WINNING" | To the victor goes the spoils. | Your success is my success. |
| ATTITUDE TOWARD "LOSING" | Someone has to lose. | If someone loses, everyone loses. |
| ATTITUDE TOWARD MINORITY OPINIONS | Get with the program. | Everyone has a piece of the truth. |
| WHY EXPLORE DIFFERENCES BETWEEN COMPETING POSITIONS? | To search for bargaining chips, in preparation for horse trading and compromise. | To build a shared framework of understanding, in preparation for mutual creative thinking. |
| ESSENTIAL MENTAL ACTIVITY | Analyze: break wholes into parts. | Synthesize: integrate parts into wholes. |
| HOW LONG IT TAKES | It's usually faster in the short run. | It's usually faster in the long run. |
| WHEN TO USE IT | When expedience is more important than durability, *Either/Or thinking* will usually produce satisfactory results. | When all parties have the power to block any decision, and the issue is for high stakes, *Both/And thinking* is usually the only hope for resolution. |
| UNDERLYING PHILOSOPHY | Survival of the fittest. | Interdependence of all things. |

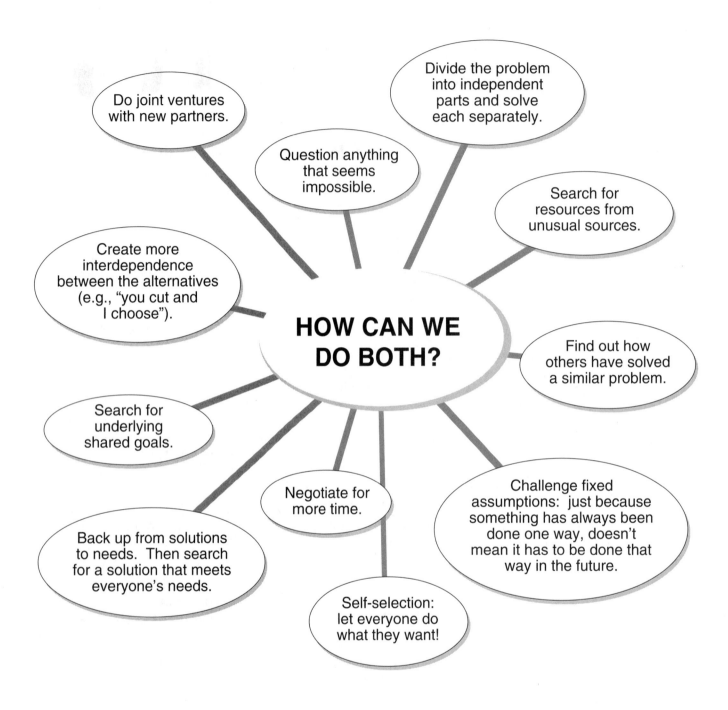

These problem-solving principles help people synthesize seemingly opposing alternatives into an integrated solution. Note that none of these requires group members to use adversarial methods to resolve their differences. *They all lead to solutions that work for everyone.*

# 16

# INCLUSIVE SOLUTIONS IN REAL LIFE

USING CASE STUDIES TO INSPIRE CREATIVE,
NON-ADVERSARIAL PROBLEM-SOLVING

- ▶ **Why Case Studies Are a Strong Asset in the Search for Inclusive Solutions**

- ▶ **Ten Case Studies that Demonstrate the Power of Using Inclusive Principles**

- ▶ **Using Case Studies as a Meaningful Facilitation Technique**

## REAL-LIFE INCLUSIVE SOLUTIONS
### USING CASE STUDIES TO INSPIRE CREATIVE INSIGHTS

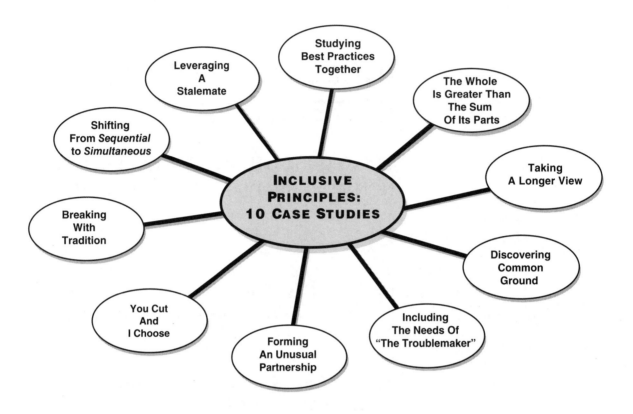

Inclusive, nonadversarial, problem-solving principles are often at the heart of sustainable agreements.

Consider the case of the Mendocino County timber tax committee. After years of disagreement over the rate of logging, they realized that a change in the tax code would benefit everyone. Thus, they switched from taxing *standing trees,* a method used for forty years, to taxing *cut trees.* Underlying this change was a creative problem-solving principle:

> *Challenge fixed assumptions – just because something has always been done one way doesn't mean it has to be done that way in the future.*

Exploring inclusive principles fosters creative thinking. For example, a facilitator might introduce a group to the Mendocino case, discuss it, and then ask, "What are *our* group's fixed assumptions? Are there any *we* can challenge?" Real-life cases often stimulate group members to think this way. Ten great case-examples are presented in the following pages.

--- CASE STUDY ---

# THE WHOLE IS GREATER THAN THE SUM OF ITS PARTS

## PROBLEM

The City of Oakland Unified School District has long attempted to improve education outcomes in a city with high rates of youth unemployment, drop-out before graduation, and teen pregnancy. Past initiatives included beacon schools, family resource centers, and equity budgeting, but the efforts were spotty. Each time, the challenges outlasted the improvements. In 2003 the school district went into receivership and control was handed to the state amid accusations of incompetence and corruption among district leadership.

## SOLUTION

With facilitation support, the whole community worked together to develop a model that combined education and community support. The model is called a *Full Service Community School District*. Programming offers education, health care and other services specific to each neighborhood in which a school is located. Services are offered based on input from residents of that neighborhood and staff. After three years, the results include a substantial rise in graduation rates and significantly fewer suspensions. Also, there are now school-based health centers in all the districts' secondary schools.

## PRINCIPLE

*The whole is greater than the sum of its parts.* Bringing together different parts of the community, including school district officers, people from the neighborhoods, health workers, police, teachers' union members, city officials, church leaders and more, all with different outlooks and differing stakes, will create pressure to serve different needs – and that in turn can generate opportunities to look at the bigger picture and find new, whole-system solutions.

Source: *Junious Williams,*
*Chief Executive Officer,*
*Urban Strategies Council,*
Oakland CA,
and *lead facilitator*
of the 2-year process
that built this model.

CASE STUDY

# LEVERAGE A STALEMATE

## PROBLEM

MacMillan Bloedel, a large Canadian forestry company, was locked in a multi-decade, very public battle with environmental groups over old growth logging practices in British Columbia, Canada. A government task force tried and failed to develop an acceptable land use plan. Too many strong, committed stakeholders! The lumber company opposed having its rights to log constrained. Unions were deeply concerned about job loss. Environmentalists were dissatisfied with the proposed amount of land to be protected. And First Nations communities were deeply troubled at being excluded from decisions affecting their homeland. Fierce protests and boycotts ensued. Communication was adversarial, with each side telling its story to the media in the most compelling way possible.

## SOLUTION

The battle raged on, in the courts and in pitched public protests. Meantime, the hardest working, most engaged people on every side of the dispute inevitably reached a first name basis. This simple human familiarity eventually led to informal conversations, A "conflict free zone" was created where people spoke only of their side's needs and interests. First Nations leaders introduced a treaty process. Thus unfolded the shift from adversarial debate to respectful dialogue. Finally, after years of stalemate, the parties came to a landmark agreement for land use on the Central Coast, with a new protocol between First Nations and the Province of B.C.

## PRINCIPLE

A stalemate is a conflict that perpetuates itself. When walking away means you lose, and neither party is willing to lose, everyone sticks around to protect their side's interests. But *a perpetual conflict is also a perpetual relationship.* Over time, the sides get to know one another as people, even as they continue to disagree. The dispute doesn't change, but the people do. This is a core principle underlying the shift from confrontation to a collaborative mindset.

Source: Ann Svendsen and Myriam Laberge, May 2003, Co-creative power: Engaging Stakeholder Networks for Learning and Innovation, www.collectivewisdominitiative.org/papers/laberge_wholesystems.pdf

# STUDYING BEST PRACTICES TOGETHER

**PROBLEM**

Marshall Medical Center, the largest health care provider in El Dorado County, California, had to upgrade their computer network for *Electronic Medical Records (EMR)*. The physicians formed a task force to choose the product they wanted. The hospital administration did the same. The doctors, who cared about the quality of treatment for their patients, needed an *EMR* system that was *flexible*, to let doctors write comments that described the idiosyncrasies of each patient's unique response to treatment. The hospital aspired to provide the best patient services, most of which depend on insurance company reimbursement. To ensure fast and full payment, *EMR* data had to be *standardized*, to conform to insurance reporting standards. To administrators a system that enabled flexible data entry could be a reporting nightmare.

**SOLUTION**

"Field trip" research teams with both administrators and physicians traveled to other hospitals to learn how other *EMR* systems worked. The teams discovered that some *EMR* products are designed to track a patient's progress through an entire system – from doctor's office to lab to hospital. Data from those settings are different enough that data entry *has to be* flexible. Yet these *EMR* products find ways to translate the data into standardized categories. Thus the Marshall teams saw that their requirements could be met by an *EMR* designed to work across their whole medical system.

**PRINCIPLE**

When people are at odds, they often continue advocating pet solutions back and forth. Instead, send them on a "study mission" to learn how their needs are handled in other contexts. Have them look for *best practices* and *design principles* that might be transferable. This approach reframes *either / or* solutions into the questions, "What works? Why? How?" And the research context lets people dialogue about their needs and requirements, rather than argue about them.

Source: Leah Hall, VP, Performance Excellence, Marshall Medical Center, Placerville CA. 2007

CASE STUDY

# BREAKING WITH TRADITION

## PROBLEM

At San Jose National Bank, many of the employees were women. One year, 10 percent of the staff became pregnant. A high rate of maternity leave would clearly cause a serious drop in productivity. Management pondered the options. Should maternity leave be limited? Should some of the employees be laid off? The expectant mothers recognized that the bank could suffer, but they also felt it was important to be with their babies during their first months of life. Each group understood the other's point of view, but no one felt able to change positions.

## SOLUTION

Mothers were allowed to bring their infants to the office and keep them by their desks. They stayed at work the whole day and tended to their infants' needs as necessary. Their pay was slightly reduced to reflect the actual hours they worked. When the infants became toddlers, they were placed at a nearby day care center sponsored by the bank.

## PRINCIPLE

The solution to this problem was to break with the tradition that parents must choose between working and being with their children. Here, the bank's needs (getting the work done) and the mothers' needs (staying with their infants) were combined. In your situation, is there a tradition that locks you into an *either / or* position? Why is that tradition seen as "sacred"? If it were challenged, what new options might open up?

Source: *San Jose Mercury News*, March 6, 1994.

CASE STUDY

# YOU CUT AND I CHOOSE

## PROBLEM

Representatives from many nations met to develop international policies regarding the mining of oceanic resources. One problem they addressed was how to best allocate underwater mining sites. The Enterprise, a U.N. organization representing poorer countries, charged that rich countries had an unfair advantage. They feared that private companies from wealthy countries could identify the superior mining sites because they had better radar and mining equipment and superior expertise. With this knowledge, the rich countries could propose an unequal allocation of mining resources, and the poorer countries would have no way to evaluate the fairness of the allocation.

## SOLUTION

The representatives decided to ask a private company to identify two mining sites of equal value, using its sophisticated equipment and expertise. The Enterprise would then choose one of the sites for the poorer countries to mine. The private company would get the other one. In this way, the private companies would have an incentive to identify two sites of equal value, thus giving poorer nations the benefit of their expertise.

## PRINCIPLE

This situation involved competition for a fixed resource: high-quality mining sites. The inclusive principle they employed was to tie the interests of the more powerful party to those of the less powerful party. In your own situation, what incentives might induce the more powerful party to participate?

Source: R. Fisher and W. Ury, *Getting to Yes* (New York: Penguin Books, 1983), p. 58.

CASE STUDY

# DISCOVERING COMMON GROUND

**PROBLEM**

A suburb of a large city was becoming more and more racially diverse. Residents formed a community council to preserve the neighborhood's character while simultaneously promoting racial integration. The council suspected that financial institutions were cutting back on their investment in the neighborhood because of the demographic changes. After investigating several local lending institutions, the council found evidence that lenders were indeed using discriminatory tactics. The council demanded more investment in its neighborhood, and it threatened to boycott the lenders. The lenders denied the charges and refused to cooperate with further monitoring.

**SOLUTION**

At first the two sides locked horns and argued over who was to blame for the disinvestment. Their breakthrough came when they realized they all shared a common concern: preserving the neighborhood. Together they founded a local development corporation that promoted commercial revitalization, and they created a foreclosure rehabilitation program for which the lenders raised funds.

**PRINCIPLE**

Affixing blame, polarizing into opposing camps, and calling for help from the powers-that-be is a typical strategy for dealing with the problems created by changing circumstances. In this case, participants followed a different principle. They focused on discovering shared concerns, and they aimed at developing a shared vision. This helped them collaborate effectively and take constructive, self-empowered action.

Source: B. Gray, *Collaborating* (San Francisco: Jossey-Bass, 1989), p. 95.

## CASE STUDY
# INCLUDING THE NEEDS OF "THE TROUBLEMAKERS"

**PROBLEM**

A community had a problem with its high school youth, whose public behavior was becoming increasingly unruly, especially at night. The city administration decided to increase police patrols and impose a curfew for the youth in the neighborhood. Community members rejected this decision. They felt that the curfew would restrict everyone's freedom, and the increased police presence would probably *increase* violence in the neighborhood.

**SOLUTION**

Neighborhood residents, both youth and adults, met and discussed ideas for solving this problem. They decided that a midnight basketball program would provide the youths with an alternative to hanging out and getting in trouble. The community members saw this as a way to improve neighborhood safety without requiring outside intervention. The city administrators were pleased because the program would help keep youth off the streets at night.

**PRINCIPLE**

Normally we try to "fix" the people who make trouble – whether by incarcerating them, hospitalizing them, expelling them, going to war with them, or controlling their behavior. By contrast, it sometimes can be advantageous to treat the "troublemakers" as stakeholders, and involve them in the problem-solving process. If their needs can be understood, they might become allies in transforming the problem.

Source: Marshall Rosenberg's workshop on Compassionate Communication, February 1995, as related by Liz Dittrich to Sam Kaner's *Group Facilitation Skills* class, June 1995.

## CASE STUDY
# FORMING AN UNUSUAL PARTNERSHIP

**PROBLEM**

A small western city had a one-time-only budget surplus. Two groups immediately began vying for the funds. On one side, a coalition of women's groups wished to use the money to expand the city's inadequate day care facilities. On the other side, homeowners and the city's firefighters wanted to upgrade their antiquated firefighting equipment to protect homes and lower insurance costs.

**SOLUTION**

A small portion of the money was used to convert the city's old fire stations into day care centers. A state matching-funds grant was obtained to subsidize the new centers' start-up costs. The majority of the city's surplus was then used to build three new fire stations. The new stations raised the city's fire rating from AA to AAA, thus lowering insurance rates and raising property values – which in turn enabled new equipment purchases.

**PRINCIPLE**

Competing for funding is the normal way to proceed when finances are limited. Yet the groups in this case partnered in order to identify additional resources from sources that were foreign to their own contexts.

Can your group partner with its competitors? Are there other unusual alliances to explore?

Source: M. Doyle and D. Straus, *How to Make Meetings Work* (New York: Jove Press, 1982), p. 56.

CASE STUDY

# TAKING A LONGER VIEW

## PROBLEM

In a rainforest in New Guinea, the indigenous people were approached by a large lumber corporation. The company offered to pay a lump sum for the right to clear-cut the forest and extract the hardwood trees. The deal sounded fantastic to many members of the impoverished forest tribe; they wanted to sell their only marketable commodity in exchange for money, which they could use to buy things they could not produce themselves. Local environmentalists, however, were alarmed; the forests would be completely and irreplaceably destroyed.

## SOLUTION

Environmentalists helped the indigenous people start their own lumber company with a small, portable sawmill that could process trees one at a time. The cut lumber was worth significantly more than the company had offered for the trees, so the people did not feel pressured to log more than was appropriate for the health of the forest. The logging company purchased the lumber, which it then resold at a profit overseas.

## PRINCIPLE

Group problem-solving often seeks simple, direct solutions that focus on the near term, and the immediate need. But it sometimes makes more sense to search for solutions that take a longer view. As this example shows, a consideration of long-term sustainability can surface creative strategies that would not have been discovered in a search for a quick fix.

Source: Told to Sarah Fisk by John Seed, environmentalist and author.

## CASE STUDY

# SHIFTING
# FROM *SEQUENTIAL* TO *SIMULTANEOUS*

## PROBLEM

At Irvine Medical Center, a unit of Kaiser Permanente, administrators wanted to bring down the cost of its most time-intensive surgeries: total hip and knee-joint replacements. The task was daunting because the solution required collaboration among many parties who don't usually interact: specialists who normally compete for resources; non-physician employees whose standardized job descriptions prevented creative thinking; and insurance customers whose models for reimbursement stipulated what types of care were acceptable.

## SOLUTION

An inclusive team examined the surgery process. Efficiencies were gained by identifying parts of the sequential process that could be done simultaneously. Cues were set to let a person know when to begin each task, rather than wait till the prior task was done. Roles were thus fitted together. A "floater" nurse with a flexible job description was added to provide help where needed. Surgeries increased from two to four per day. Average time between procedures dropped from 45 to 20 minutes. Annually, 188 hours of OR time were freed up. At one facility, staff job satisfaction rose by 85%. Kaiser Permanente has widely adopted this strategy.

## PRINCIPLE

Complex processes that require action by specialists from different disciplines are often designed to be performed sequentially. That is, each team begins its step only after prior teams are done with theirs. Such slow, costly processes can often be streamlined by designs that favor more simultaneous action, with faster communication across teams and more role-flexibility. These features – simultaneity, access to information and versatility – are some of the classic characteristics of inclusive, *both / and* solutions.

Source: Building a Collaborative Enterprise, by Paul Adler, Charles Heckscher and Laurence Prusak. In *Harvard Business Review's 10 Must-Reads on Collaboration.* Harvard Business School Publishing Co., 2013

## USING CASE STUDIES

### WHY

This chapter presents capsule summaries of inclusive solutions to difficult real-life problems. Each case demonstrates the use of an *inclusive principle* – that is, a problem-solving principle that enables participants to develop a creative solution that takes everyone's interests into account.

Most groups find it hard to break free of an *either / or* mind-set. To motivate and inspire such groups, some facilitators simply make interesting suggestions, such as "What if you did such-and-such?" or "Here's a way to look at this . . ." But many people perceive such efforts as a move by the facilitator to "join the group." They tend to reject those suggestions out of hand, without regard for their merits.

A strong alternative is to provide real-life examples that demonstrate *both / and* thinking. Discussing a case is often more effective than a lecture. And this approach preserves facilitator neutrality – even as it inspires group members to keep working toward sustainable agreements.

Use the cases on the preceding pages as tools to stimulate discussion.

### HOW

1. Photocopy and distribute some or all of the preceding case studies.

2. Ask everyone to read one or two cases.

3. Have everyone find a partner and discuss their case studies. Ask, "What reactions are you having to what you just read?"

4. After five minutes, reconvene the large group and ask, "Has anyone found a principle that might shed new light on *our* situation?" Allow ample time for discussion.

# 17

# CREATIVE REFRAMING

PRINCIPLES AND TOOLS
FOR BREAKING OUT
OF FIXED WAYS OF THINKING

# TWO WAYS OF LOOKING AT THE SAME PROBLEM

| PERCEIVED PROBLEM | REFRAMED PROBLEM |
|---|---|
| It's them. | It's all of us. |
| It's a problem. | It's an opportunity. |
| Our goal is unachievable. | We don't have our goal broken into realistic steps. |
| Our product won't sell. | We're trying to sell our product to the wrong people. |
| We don't have enough resources. | We are wasting the resources we do have. |
| We need to gather more input. | We need to pay more attention to the input we're already getting. |
| Our employees are incompetent. | Our employees don't have enough time to do a quality job. |
| We don't have enough money. | We haven't figured out how to find new sources of money. |
| We can't get along with each other. | We haven't made the commitment to work through our feelings toward one another. |
| We don't have any power in this system. | We haven't found our leverage points in this system. |
| We don't have enough time to do all of these things. | We have to decide what to do now and what to do later. |

# INTRODUCING REFRAMING TO A GROUP

## WHY

Once someone perceives a problem in a particular way, s/he may find it difficult to see that problem in any other way. Our minds tend to lock into a pattern of thought. For example, many job recruiters routinely decline to hire a talented applicant because of the applicant's appearance; yet in some companies, this habit persists even when recruiting for technical positions, when appearance has no impact on performance.

When tackling difficult problems, most people reach conclusions quickly. They believe they have explored every option for a solution and that it would be pointless to waste more time. The idea that it might be possible to reframe a problem – that is, to dramatically alter their understanding of the nature of the problem – is, for most people, a paradigm shift.

Thus, facilitators who encourage their groups to try creative reframing often find it quite challenging to motivate people to invest the time. This tool effectively helps facilitators overcome that initial wall of resistance.

## HOW

1. Hand out copies of page 254, *Two Ways of Looking at the Same Problem.*

2. Ask people to discuss the differences between a perceived problem and a reframed problem. This concept will be new to many. As part of digesting a new idea, they may say things that sound rigid or naive. Expect remarks like, "To me, this whole idea is ridiculous." Remember to honor all points of view and stay supportive throughout.

3. After several minutes say, "Now let's apply this theory to our own situation. Could someone please state *our* perceived problem?" Write the perceived problem on a flipchart. Then ask the group to brainstorm a list of *reframes* of the problem. Record all answers on flipcharts.

4. After the brainstorm, encourage members to discuss the implications of their new ideas. Say, "As you review this list, what are your reactions?"

# BACKING UP FROM SOLUTIONS TO NEEDS

## WHY

When an argument seems to be going around in circles, it can be *extremely helpful* for everyone to stop arguing over proposed "solutions" and start talking about their individual needs instead.

For example, consider a dispute between three department heads over whether to schedule a key meeting in Boston, Detroit or New York. The problem (where to meet) had three solutions (one city or the other). But beneath the surface of the three solutions were three individuals' needs. One person needed to stay near his New York office because his assistant was on vacation. A second was already committed to attending two other meetings in Boston. A third, based in Detroit, was expecting a drop-in from a regional director; she needed to be available "just in case." Once everyone understood each other's needs, they realized that a meeting on a Saturday or Sunday would work for everyone, no matter *where* they met.

As the example shows, it becomes easier to develop proposals that meet a *broader range of needs* when those needs have been made explicit – and, therefore, understandable to everyone.

## HOW

1. Make sure everyone understands the difference between "their proposed solution" and "their actual need." For example, *holding the meeting in New York* is a proposed solution; *covering for the absent assistant* is a need. Teach your group members this distinction.

2. Ask everyone to answer these questions: "What are my needs in this situation?" and "What do I think *your* needs are?"

3. Continue until everyone feels satisfied that their own needs have been stated clearly. Then ask the group to generate new proposals that seek to incorporate a broader range of people's needs.

# WHAT'S UNCHANGEABLE ABOUT THIS PROBLEM?

## WHY

Habits of thought are as hard to break as habits of any other kind. Suppose, for example, that someone thinks his or her boss is afraid of confrontation. That person may find it very difficult to change this opinion, even if the boss has actually changed.

Entire groups fall into these habits of thought, too. For example, a management team had to refill one staff position five times in less than two years. Yet every time they lost another person, they simply recruited someone else for the job and crossed their fingers. Not until the fifth person left did they consider reorganizing the department and doing away with that job altogether.

*What's Unchangeable About This Problem* allows a group to explore hidden assumptions and biases in the way they have defined a problem. Once a group has identified a self-limiting assumption, they often discover a new line of thought that leads to a creative, innovative solution.

## HOW

1. At the top of a flipchart, write "What's unchangeable about our problem?"

2. List everyone's answers.

3. Ask the group to look over the list and identify any hidden assumptions and biases. Encourage open discussion.

4. Based on these insights, list any aspects of the problem that may be changeable after all.

# TWO REFRAMING ACTIVITIES

## REVERSING ASSUMPTIONS

1. Hang a sheet of chart paper titled, "Assumptions About This Problem."

2. Have the group list assumptions about
   • The causes of the problem
   • The connections between different aspects of the problem.

3. Ask someone to select an item from the list, and reverse it. For example, consider an item like "We are losing our best employees." Reverse this to, "We're *keeping* our best employees."

4. Ask, "How could we bring about this new, opposite state of affairs?" Encourage a brainstorm of answers.

5. Choose another assumption and repeat Steps 3 and 4. When done, discuss ideas that seem promising.

A version of this activity appears in M. Michalko, *ThinkerToys* (Berkeley, CA: Ten Speed Press, 1992), p. 45.

## REMOVING CONSTRAINTS

1. Have the group generate constraints by asking, "What is keeping us from developing the most effective solution to this problem?"

2. Upon completing the list, consider each item one at a time, asking, "What if *this* were not a problem?" For example, "What if we had plenty of funds available? How would we solve our problem in *that* case?"

3. Keep each discussion brief for now. The goal is to scan the list in search of promising options.

4. When finished with the first pass, have the group identify potential high-payoff ideas in preparation for extended discussion.

# TWO MORE REFRAMING ACTIVITIES

## RECENTERING THE CAUSE

1. Ask the group to break the problem into its major components. For example, consider the problem of keeping public libraries open. This might divide into such components as "funding," "usage," "staffing," "civic priorities," and so on.

2. Ask a volunteer to select any component. For example, suppose someone picks "staffing."

3. Treat that selection as the central cause of the problem. Ask, "How might this affect our view of the problem?" For example, suppose "staffing" is viewed as the central cause of the problem. Someone might now suggest a new approach to the problem: perhaps volunteers could help staff the library during busy hours, enabling the library to remain open with less funding.

## CATASTROPHIZING
### (WE'RE DOOMED NO MATTER WHAT WE DO)

1. Ask everyone to think about the problem from their own perspective, imagining anything and everything that could go wrong.

2. Have each person in turn state his or her worst-case scenario.

3. Encourage each new speaker to build on the previous ideas until the situation seems doomed. Whining and complaining are an integral part of the activity at this point.

4. When the humor has subsided, have the group identify obstacles that merit further discussion.

5. Go down the list of obstacles one at a time, asking "Is *this* one capable of producing a catastrophe?" If so, ask, "What could be done to reduce its potential impact?"

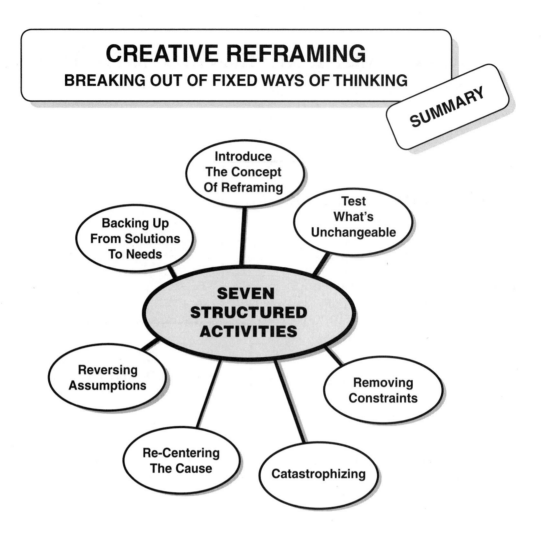

**CREATIVE REFRAMING**
BREAKING OUT OF FIXED WAYS OF THINKING

SUMMARY

Introduce The Concept Of Reframing

Test What's Unchangeable

Backing Up From Solutions To Needs

**SEVEN STRUCTURED ACTIVITIES**

Reversing Assumptions

Removing Constraints

Re-Centering The Cause

Catastrophizing

*Creative Reframing* involves breaking out of our normal categories of analysis and reexamining our beliefs and assumptions. This type of thinking requires us to make a deliberate mental shift in order to look at a problem from a completely different angle. Making such a shift can lead a group to see choices to which they were blind just moments before.

Because it is counterintuitive and "unnatural," *creative reframing* rarely happens spontaneously in groups. A facilitator can guide a group toward this type of thinking in two ways – either with structured thinking activities or through informal technique that helps participants shift their thinking. Examples of the latter are questions like, "Is that the only way to do this?" or "Suppose this had never happened. Would that change your plan?" Simple questions like these can be posed with relatively little forethought. Or, one can use a pre-designed activity like those on the preceding pages.

# Part Four

# FACILITATING SUSTAINABLE AGREEMENTS

# WHAT MAKES AN AGREEMENT SUSTAINABLE?

**SHARED UNDERSTANDING**

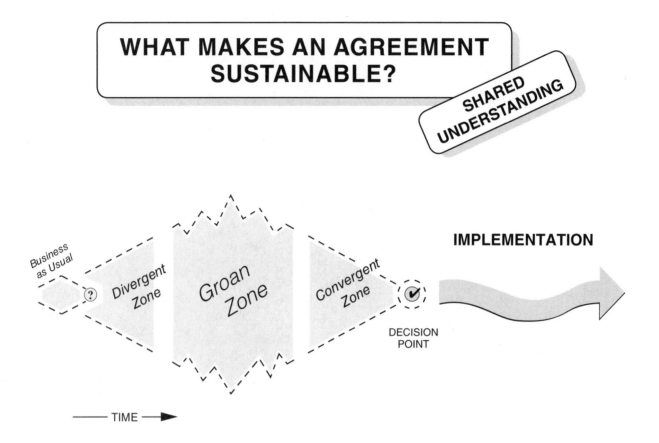

This diagram represents the process of building sustainable agreements. Up to the point of decision, progress is slow, as members of the group struggle to develop a shared framework of understanding. The implementation, on the other hand, is often meaningful rather than painful. Implementing a sustainable agreement is like swimming with the tide instead of against it. People feel confident that their efforts are aiming toward results.

What is it that makes a sustainable agreement sustainable? The answer is that the agreement is based on a solution that incorporates everyone's point of view. Participants would say, "Yes, this works! From my perspective, this proposal actually does solve the problem."

How does a group achieve this? By patient, persistent effort. People keep working to understand one another's goals and needs, their fears and their aspirations. Together, they face conflicts and overcome them. They explore possibilities by putting themselves in each other's shoes. They challenge their underlying assumptions. They search for imaginative solutions. And they share responsibility for reaching a result that works for everyone.

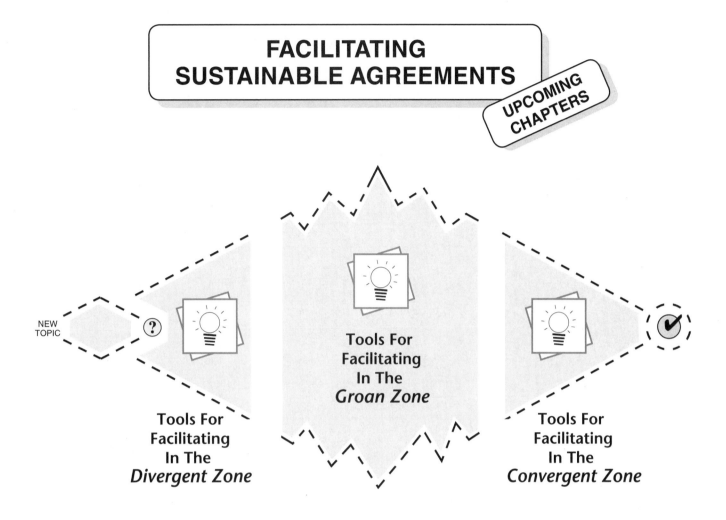

**FACILITATING SUSTAINABLE AGREEMENTS**

UPCOMING CHAPTERS

NEW TOPIC

Tools For Facilitating In The *Divergent Zone*

Tools For Facilitating In The *Groan Zone*

Tools For Facilitating In The *Convergent Zone*

To build sustainable agreements, groups need different types of support at different points in the process.

For example, it is unwise to promote convergent thinking in a group whose members have not yet built a shared framework of understanding. Some participants may not trust solutions proposed by those with competing interests – especially if the two camps seem to misunderstand one another. The facilitator's main objective here would *not be* to push for agreement. It would instead be to keep strengthening communication, helping people listen to one another, until group members could think from each other's points of view. *Then* would be the time to encourage convergent thinking.

Facilitators who understand this principle will vary their approach to match a group's needs in each phase of its work. On this subject, *The Diamond of Participatory Decision-Making* has much to offer. It can inform a facilitator's choice of technique, from one zone to the next. Utilizing *The Diamond* is the theme of the next four chapters.

# 18

# FACILITATING IN THE DIVERGENT ZONE

## PRINCIPLES, TECHNIQUES AND TOOLS TO ENCOURAGE FULL PARTICIPATION

- ▶ **Introduction to the Divergent Zone**
- ▶ **Common Facilitation Techniques**
- ▶ **Responding to Challenging Situations**
- ▶ **Structured Activities**
- ▶ **Summary**

## LIFE IN THE DIVERGENT ZONE

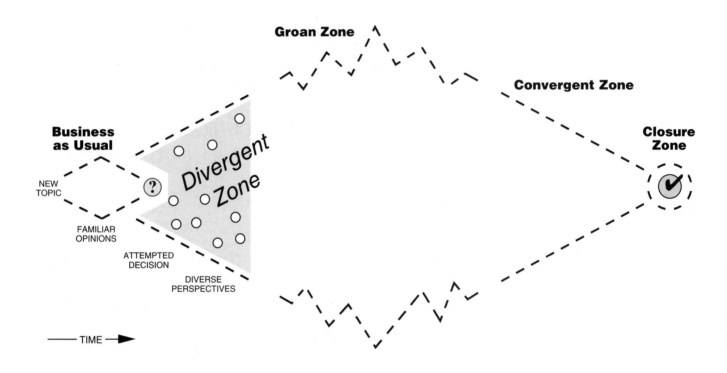

When a diverse group begins work on a complex problem, people's views are not unified. Instead, they vary widely across many parameters: goal(s), priorities, problem definition, critical success factors, options for action, resources needed, people who should be at the table, and many more.

To reconcile these differences, the first step is to make them visible. This typically requires a lot of listing and sorting and defining: all the processes that epitomize divergent thinking! In groups whose members are veterans of the *Divergent Zone*, behavior tends to be guided by principles like *suspend judgment* and *accept different perspectives*. In contrast, many people have not experienced full-on divergent thinking. In those groups, behavior tends to be cautious, reserved – even to the point of withholding – yet impatient with thoughts that are different than the majority's view.

# FACILITATING IN THE DIVERGENT ZONE

FACILITATOR'S OBJECTIVES

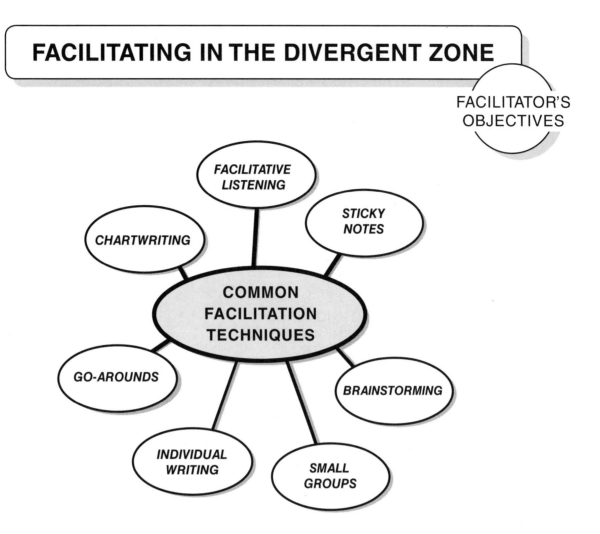

Using a facilitator in the *Divergent Zone* has two purposes: one pertains to the *content* of the issues at hand; the other to *the process of communication.*

Regarding matters of *content,* divergent thinking *expands the range of perspectives and possibilities.* A facilitator can help a group do this by using simple formats and skills like those shown above. Probably the most important of these, for content management, is *chartwriting.* Good recording is the *sine qua non* of effective divergent thinking.

Regarding *the process of communication,* a facilitator is a neutral third party, whose listening skills can make all the difference in building a supportive, respectful atmosphere. Encouraging people, drawing them out, mirroring and validating – these are some of the many basic tools that help people relax, and express what they're really thinking. So do simple formats like small groups, go-arounds, trade show, and a well-managed open discussion.

# FACILITATING IN THE DIVERGENT ZONE

CHALLENGING
SITUATIONS

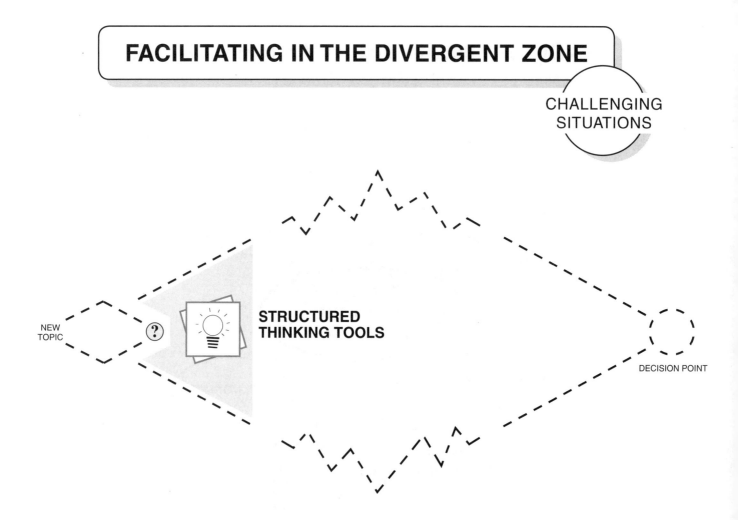

NEW
TOPIC

**STRUCTURED
THINKING TOOLS**

DECISION POINT

The common techniques for facilitating in the *Divergent Zone* (as listed on the preceding page) are adequate for most situations, most of the time. When members feel secure and encouraged to participate, they speak up – especially when they see, via chartwriting, that their own ideas and views are indeed different from those expressed by other group members.

There are occasions, however, when the common facilitation techniques don't have sufficient impact. For example, when there's a wide disparity in education level, subject-matter expertise, or fluency in the dominant language – these and other inequities can influence less privileged members to stay quiet. Similarly, difficult or controversial subjects can be hard to talk about, particularly when taking a position risks offending other participants.

Experienced facilitators can respond to such challenges by complementing their repertoire of fundamental skills with structured activities that are designed specifically to elicit divergent thinking in situations that are challenging. Many such tools are provided in this chapter.

## SPEAK FROM YOUR OWN PERSPECTIVE

### WHY

This is a basic, straightforward activity that encourages participants to offer their own points of view on the topic at hand.

The purpose of this activity is to enable members to quickly gain a picture of the breadth of the group's thinking. By seeing all the parts, the group gains a sense of the whole.

Another purpose of the activity is to legitimize and validate every perspective. By allowing the group to hear each person's contribution, this activity sends the message that "Everyone has something to offer."

### HOW

1. Pose an open-ended question such as:

   - How would you describe what's going on?
   - How does this problem affect you?
   - What is your position on this matter?
   - Why, in your opinion, is this happening?

2. Ask each person to answer the question without commenting on each other's ideas.

3. Optional Step:
   When everyone has had a chance to express their views, ask,
   "Is there anyone absent today who might have a significantly different perspective? What might that person tell us?"

4. Debrief by asking participants for reactions, insights and learnings.

# WHO, WHAT, WHEN, WHERE, AND HOW?

## WHY

When solving problems in groups, people come to the table with *very different questions* based on their individual perspectives. Everyone wants their own questions answered, which prevents them from seeing that others' questions need to be answered, too. This element of divergent thinking is one of the most difficult aspects of group decision-making.

At a recent meeting, for example, one person who was mystified by the budgeting process requested clarifications and explanations repeatedly. Another asked several questions about why certain people had been invited to the meeting while others had not. A third person appeared to understand everything but one little detail, about which he kept asking questions. Each was focused on his or her own questions and could not see that others were struggling with entirely different questions.

This activity supports a group to identify *the whole range of questions* before they get too focused on wrestling with any single question.

## HOW

1. Hang five sheets of paper titled respectively, "Who?" "What?" "When?" "Where?" and "How?"

2. Start by naming the general topic. For example, "We're now going to start planning the annual staff retreat."

3. On the "Who?" page, brainstorm a list of questions that begin with "Who?" For example, "Who will set the agenda?" "Who knows someone who can rent us a conference room?" "Who should be invited?" "Who said we can't spend more than $500?"

4. Repeat Step 3 for each of the other sheets.

5. When all five lists are complete, identify the easy questions and answer them. Then make a plan to answer the rest.

This tool was inspired by an exercise called "Five W's and H" in A. B. VanGundy, Jr., *Techniques of Structured Problem Solving,* 2nd ed. (New York: Van Nostrand Reinhold, 1988), p. 46.

## SPECIFYING REQUIREMENTS

### WHY

To be sustainable, the solution to a difficult problem must reflect the requirements of every stakeholder – which often are quite diverse. As an example, take the case of a meeting held by an appliance manufacturer to discuss the development of a new, low-energy light bulb. The purchasing department wanted the bulb to be built from parts and materials that were readily available. The marketing department wanted the shape of the bulb to fit standard packaging. The engineering department wanted precise timetables from research and development in order to schedule their staff efficiently. And the company president wanted assurance that the new product would be a salable commodity.

For groups like these, the challenge is to take stock of *all* requirements before getting bogged down in specifics. This activity helps a group to gain a preliminary understanding of everyone's conditions for success.

### HOW

1. Hang two sheets of chart paper, one titled "Requirements and Necessary Conditions" and the other "Topics for Further Discussion."

2. Break the group into pairs. Ask each person to take a turn describing his or her own requirements and necessary conditions for success.

3. Reconvene everyone. Give each person three minutes to state his or her conditions and five to take questions. Record each requirement on a chart. Also record questions requiring further discussion.

4. After repeating Step 3 for each person, have the group examine the lists and decide how to organize the subsequent discussion.

# MIND MAPPING

## WHY

A simple example of a *Mind Map* is described in "Step 1" below.

*Mind mapping* supports four different types of thinking: generative, logical, associative, and classifying. Generative thinking is the act of calling out any items while suspending judgment. Logical thinking is the art of reasoning. Associative thinking is a particular type of generative thinking, in which one thought inspires a second thought even though the two are not linked logically. Classifying involves putting items into categories and sub-categories. *Mind mapping* enables a group to do all of them at once.

## HOW

1. First create a simple *Mind Map* to show the group how it works.

   - Choose a topic everyone can relate to, such as, "Improving our work-place." Write those words in the center of a big sheet of chart-paper.

   - Ask the group for subtopics that connect with the main topic.

   - As people call them out, draw branches from the center and label each branch. (For example "Parts we enjoy" could be a branch).

   - Continue a few more times, adding subtopics to the branch as they arise. (For example, "Water cooler chats.")

   - Soon someone will call out an *association* – an idea that is a different branch altogether, such as, "We need a better printer." Draw a new branch for each new association.

   - After a few more subtopics and associations, end the demonstration.

2. Encourage questions about the method.

3. Begin working on the group's actual subject. Allow 15-25 minutes.

4. When the activity is done, encourage discussion of key insights.

Mind Mapping was first developed by the great English psychologist Tony Buzan in 1960. See *The Mind Map Book*: *How to Use Radiant Thinking to Maximize Your Brain's Untapped Potential*, Plume, 1996.

# STARTING POSITIONS

## WHY

This activity is a perfect way to begin dealing with a contentious issue – especially when the conflict is fueled by many opposing perspectives.

When people are brought together to resolve a dispute, many participants arrive with strong opinions and well-rehearsed arguments. They need to be given a chance to express their opinions fully, so they can let everyone else see where they stand.

When people aren't able to speak without being interrupted or discounted, it is predictable that they will insert their positions into the discussion at every opportunity. Conversely, when people *are* supported to state their positions fully, they frequently become more able to listen to one another. This often leads to better mutual understanding, which is a precondition for finding creative solutions to difficult problems.

## HOW

1. Introduce the activity by indicating that there may be several diverse perspectives in the room. Encourage everyone to give each other the time and the attention each person needs to express his or her views.

2. Using a go-around format, ask each speaker to take a turn answering the following questions from his or her individual perspective:

   - What is the problem and what solution is s/he advocating?
   - What are his or her reasons for taking this particular position?

   Note: This step is often done by having each speaker come up to the front of the room and present his or her ideas standing up.

3. When each person has had a turn, ask the group to reflect aloud on what they're learning.

# HOW HAS THIS AFFECTED ME?

## WHY

This activity gives people permission to express their fears, confusions, hurts, or resentments openly.  This supports people to become more aware of what they're feeling so they can discuss the situation in more depth.

Also, this activity enables people to step back from their own individual perspective and see a bigger picture.  It is frequently surprising and highly informative for them to hear what other people are feeling.

## HOW

1. Ask people to reflect on the following questions:

   • "How do I feel about this situation?"
   • "How has it affected me so far?"

2. Ask each person to take a turn sharing his or her reflections and feelings with the whole group.  A go-around format works best for this activity because it discourages back-and-forth discussion.

3. When everyone has spoken, ask the whole group, "Now that you have heard from everyone else, what reactions are you having?"

4. If responses indicate that this activity has surfaced a lot of emotion, encourage the group to do a second go-around.  Say something like, "Use this time to let the rest of us know whatever is on your mind."

5. End by summarizing the main themes.  Validating everyone's self-disclosure helps provide people with a temporary sense of completion, even when the source problems remain obviously unresolved.

# THREE COMPLAINTS

## WHY

Inviting people to complain about their situation gives them the chance to say things that are normally unacceptable. This can be powerful, as often useful information is revealed that would otherwise remain hidden.

Furthermore, when people have a chance to vent their negative feelings instead of stewing in them, they are more able to move forward on a task.

After an activity like this one, it is common for people to make significant progress on the topic under discussion.

## HOW

1. Give the group an overview of the upcoming steps. Then have each individual write on a separate slip of paper three complaints about the situation under discussion.

2. Have everyone throw the slips of paper into a hat.

3. Pull out one note, read it aloud, and ask for comments. The author may or may not wish to identify himself or herself.

4. After three or four comments, pull out another complaint and repeat the process.

5. After 10 or 15 minutes, ask the group how much longer they would like this activity to continue.

6. When time runs out, ask people to close by saying what the experience was like for them.

# UNREPRESENTED PERSPECTIVES

## WHY

People in a group often share so many assumptions in common that they may not recognize their own blind spots. Yet omitting a key perspective can ruin the outcome of an otherwise participatory process.

For example, in the 1980s, urban-based environmental organizations, in collaboration with state and federal agencies, drew up many unpopular and ultimately unacceptable proposals for rural conservation. These plans were rarely supported by the loggers or miners whose livelihoods were being threatened. In many cases, the plans were unworkable because they had been designed without adequate understanding of the needs and goals of the working people in the affected communities.

This activity assists a group to determine whether there are stakeholders whose perspective should be better represented at future meetings.

## HOW

1. List every group of stakeholders that might be affected by this problem. Don't forget to include less-than-obvious stakeholders. For example, does your issue affect trainees? Suppliers? Neighbors? Does it affect the families of employees? For this activity, every affected stakeholder group matters.

2. One by one, go down the list considering each group in the following way: "How does the situation at hand affect this stakeholder group?" Example: "How does our project expansion for next year affect our trainees?"

3. When the list is complete ask, "Has anyone spotted a problem that wasn't previously identified?" and "Is there someone missing from these meetings who should be included from now on?"

## FACILITATING IN THE DIVERGENT ZONE

SUMMARY

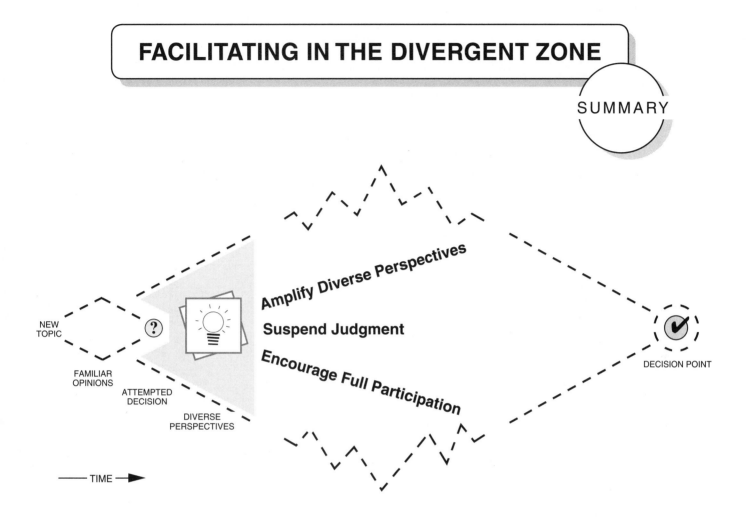

Most groups will go along with almost anything a facilitator suggests in the *Divergent Zone*. For one thing, people generally appreciate the chance to talk. For another, most members are reluctant (at this stage) to challenge the facilitator. However, this compliance can be deceptive. Superficial or pat activities may get everyone talking – but most people will know, when the exercise is done, that they've just had a "fast food experience."

Structured activities are strong and effective for the purposes described in this chapter. But they shouldn't be overused. They're directive and pre-packaged. Often people just want to have a conversation, or call out ideas to a silent chartwriter. Identifying differences doesn't always require a production!

Facilitators can keep it simple with low-key formats like go-arounds or pairs. And they can use non-directive listening skills like paraphrasing, drawing people out, mirroring, encouraging, stacking, validating, and making space. This approach is usually more than adequate to encourage full participation.

# 19

# FACILITATING IN THE GROAN ZONE

PRINCIPLES, TECHNIQUES AND TOOLS
TO BUILD MUTUAL UNDERSTANDING

▶ **Introduction to the Groan Zone**

▶ **Common Facilitation Techniques**

▶ **Responding to Challenging Situations**

▶ **Structured Activities**

▶ **Summary**

# LIFE IN THE GROAN ZONE

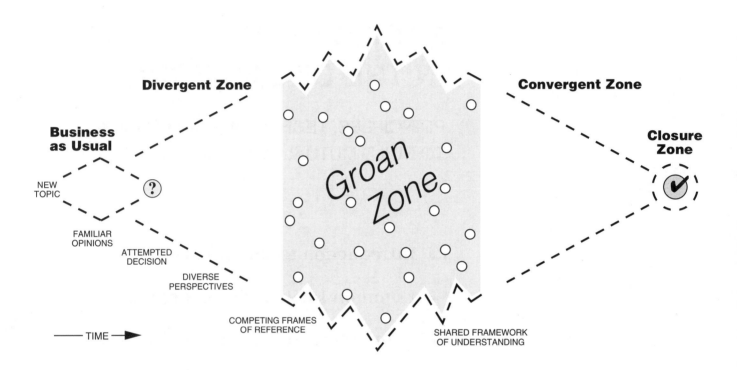

After a period of divergent thinking, most groups enter a *Groan Zone*. It's almost inevitable. For example, suppose a group has just brainstormed a list. In theory, the next task is simple: sift through the ideas, and pick a few to discuss in depth. But in practice that task can be grueling. Everyone has their own frame of reference. Moreover, when people misunderstand one another, they become more confused, more impatient, more self-centered – more unpleasant all around. People repeat themselves, they interrupt, they dismiss other people's ideas and rudely put each other down.

Behaviors like these usually produce even more behaviors like these; it becomes a vicious cycle. Without a facilitator, the cycle often continues its regressive descent until participants give up altogether. At that point, they will agree to almost anything – any half-baked, unrealistic, mediocre compromise – just as long as it will get them out of the room.

# FACILITATING IN THE GROAN ZONE

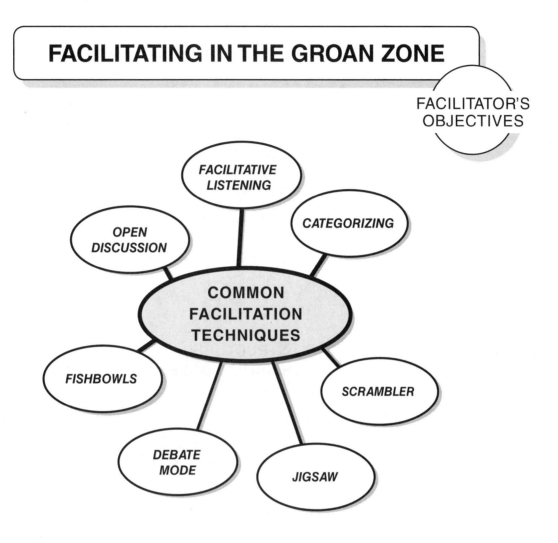

The facilitator's main objective in the *Groan Zone* is to help the group develop a shared framework of understanding. This is anything but easy.

Whether the facilitator is helping one person stand up to pressure from others, or helping two people clear up a misunderstanding between them, it takes a lot of careful, responsive listening. At times, the facilitator may be the *only* person in the room who is listening at all. The classic listening skills – paraphrasing and drawing people out – are indispensable now. So are empathizing, validating differences, helping people listen to one another, linking, and listening for common ground (all described in Chapter 4).

Furthermore, energy management is a critical success factor for facilitating in the *Groan Zone*. To prevent exasperated participants from shutting down, switch participation formats frequently, as discussed in Chapter 9. All the formats shown above are designed to promote mutual understanding.

## FACILITATING IN THE GROAN ZONE

CHALLENGING
SITUATIONS

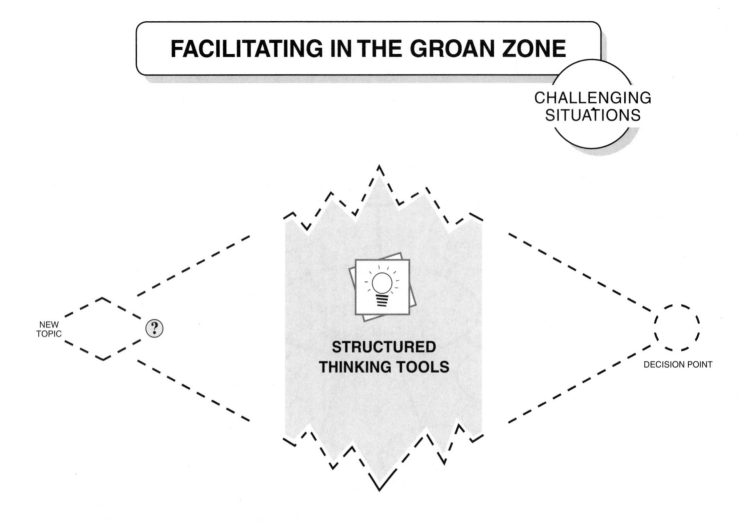

NEW
TOPIC

**?**

**STRUCTURED
THINKING TOOLS**

DECISION POINT

The simplest way to help group members gain a deeper understanding of each other's perspectives is to encourage them to ask direct questions of one another, and listen carefully to the answers. This common-sense approach would be enhanced by using any and all of the standard facilitation techniques listed on the previous page.

But some participants fear that asking questions might seem confrontational or rude, especially when a speaker's statement is difficult to comprehend. Also, many people simply can't sit with the ambiguity of unstructured inquiry and dialogue for very long, whether or not a facilitator is refereeing the process. And most of all, it's hard for everyone – participant and facilitator alike – to tolerate the poor behaviors and emotional turmoil that surface when people feel misunderstood. Under any of these challenging conditions, structured activities provide the added firmness, the safe container, that many participants require in order to settle down and keep working in a *Groan Zone.* Many such activities are presented in this chapter.

## LEARNING MORE ABOUT EACH OTHER'S PERSPECTIVES

### WHY

The most basic method for promoting mutual understanding is to ask questions. Sometimes, however, people hesitate to ask questions about each other's perspectives because questioning is so often perceived as criticism. By providing structure, this activity helps people understand that the questions are not intended as attacks. Using this simple tool builds trust and patience, and it greatly improves mutual understanding.

Some facilitators may hesitate to use this tool, feeling that it burns up precious time. But the alternative – proceeding in the absence of mutual understanding – ends up consuming much more time, with worse results.

### HOW

1. Ask for a volunteer to be the "focal person." S/he begins by saying, "Here's the point I want to make." S/he has three minutes to talk.

2. When s/he is done, invite anyone to ask the speaker a question, such as, "What do you mean by . . . ?" or, "Can you say more about . . . ?"

3. The focal person then answers the first question.

4. Turn to the questioner, and ask, "Is this clear to you now?" If so, continue to Step 5. If not, ask the questioner to state, first, what s/he believes the focal person has said, and then what s/he still finds unclear. For example, someone might say, "I hear the focal person saying that we should all share the cleanup chores equally. But I still don't understand why he feels so strongly about it."

5. When both the questioner and the focal person feel understood, ask for another questioner to take a turn.

6. After three or four people have had a chance to ask questions, ask for another person to volunteer to be the new focal person.

   *The goal of this activity is to promote understanding, not to resolve differences.* This should be emphasized beforehand and, if necessary, throughout the activity.

# IF I WERE YOU

## WHY

Another straightforward way to promote mutual understanding is to have people look at the world through each other's eyes.

Exploring someone else's perspective helps people to suspend their own points of view. This activity thus provides some participants with insights they may not have acquired through conventional discussion.

Furthermore, the process supports participants to feel understood and "seen." If necessary, it allows them the opportunity to correct any misperceptions.

## HOW

1. Have the group choose a statement to work with. The statement should begin with the words, "If I were you . . ." For example, two common choices are, "If I were you, a main concern of mine would be . . ." or "If I were you, one of my goals would be . . ."

2. Write each member's name on two separate slips of paper, and put them into a hat.

3. Have each person draw out two slips, so that each person has the names of two different people. (If a person pulls his or her own name, s/he puts it back or trades with someone.)

4. Give everyone a turn being the focal person. The two people who have that person's name say to him or her, "If I were you . . ."

5. After listening to both people, the focal person may respond.

6. When everyone has had a turn, ask the group members to reflect on the activity and share any new insights they have gained.

# MEANINGFUL THEMES

## WHY

Each participant comes to a meeting with his or her own unique set of interests and concerns. And in many cases, the participant wants to find out where others stand on the area of his or her special concern. For example, one person may need to know whether other members are committed to remaining in the group. Someone else may need to discuss the group's track record on diversity issues. Another member may want to know people's attitudes about retaining a consultant.

Often, however, it is not clear how or when to raise those issues for discussion. Any of these themes might be very meaningful to a few people, yet not particularly important to others. This creates a dilemma. How can a group devote sufficient time to such concerns – enough to prevent individual participants from becoming impatient or withdrawn – yet not so much time that the agenda becomes derailed by topics that seem tangential to other members? This activity offers a method for balancing the two concerns, by enabling members to make a *preliminary assessment* of the attitudes pertaining to their area of interest.

## HOW

1. Begin by having each group member write down one or two questions that, if everyone's answer were known, would enable that group member to participate more effectively. For example, "Do others think we should be prepared to spend a lot of money on this project?"

2. Collect one question from each person and put them in a hat.

3. Draw one sheet of paper out of the hat, read that question, and ask the person who wrote that question to explain, in two minutes or less, why s/he wants to understand everyone's position on that question.

4. Ask for brief responses from everyone: "I feel this way because . . ." When everyone has spoken, draw another question. If time is short, the remaining questions can be carried over to the next meeting.

# KEY WORDS

## WHY

Everyone makes assumptions. People often think that everyone else shares the same assumptions about such things as a word's meaning, an event's likelihood, or someone's motives for their actions – to name just a few. When groups are unaware of their differences in assumptions, they may find it difficult to understand each other's thinking or behavior.

For example, the director of a city agency asked her staff for input on a proposed reorganization. A few people took her request seriously, but many others treated it lightly. This caused turmoil at staff meetings until the explanation was found. Several people had heard a rumor that the director was leaving; they doubted the reorganization would ever occur. The few who worked hard to give input were those who had not heard the rumor. These differences in assumptions were never mentioned, but they influenced everyone's commitment to the task.

*Key Words* helps people explore the meaning of the statements they make to one another. By discussing the meanings of key words, people can identify unspoken assumptions that are causing miscommunication.

## HOW

1. Have the group compose a problem statement. For example, "New computers are too expensive to purchase." Write it on a flipchart.

2. Ask group members to identify the key words in the statement. Underline all key words. For example, "<u>New computers</u> are too <u>expensive</u> to <u>purchase</u>."

3. Have the group identify which word to focus on first. Then ask, "What questions does this word raise?" Record all responses. Then ask, "Does this word suggest any assumptions that can be challenged? For example, is 'purchase' the only way to obtain new computers?"

4. Repeat Step 3 for each key word. Encourage discussion throughout.

This tool was inspired by an exercise called "Lasso" in M. Doyle and D. Straus, *How to Make Meetings Work* (New York: Jove Books, 1982).

# FACTS AND OPINIONS

## WHY

This activity enables a group to trade a lot of information without getting bogged down in a discussion of who is right or what is true.

For example, suppose a group needed to begin thinking about next year's budget. *Facts and Opinions* would help them to generate statistics ("last year we spent $4,000 on legal fees") and speculation ("we might want to initiate two new lawsuits next year") both within a short period of time.

Note that in this example, *Facts and Opinions* postpones the debate over the budget. Instead, the thrust of the exercise is to gather a lot of material on many different subjects. Once group members see the big picture, they can decide which topics to discuss and in what order.

## HOW

1. Hang two large pieces of paper on a wall. Title one "Facts" and the other "Opinions." Also, make available sticky notes in two colors, with enough for every member to receive at least ten of each color.

2. Ask the group members, "What do you know about this topic?" Have each group member write his or her answers on the sticky notes, using one color for "Facts" and the other color for "Opinions." (If asked how to know whether something is a fact or an opinion, answer, "Please decide for yourself. If you're not sure, write it both ways.")

3. Have each person post his or her sticky notes on the wall. The notes should be posted as soon as they are written, so everyone can read the posted notes whenever they like. Reading often prompts new thinking. Participants can continue posting ideas until time is up.

4. After all data have been collected, ask for observations and reflections.

# HOW WILL THIS PROPOSAL AFFECT OUR JOBS?

## WHY

Sometimes a participant is clearly unhappy with a proposal but s/he is having trouble finding words to express his or her concerns effectively. The difficulty may be rooted in the fact that most proposals affect different roles in different ways. When participants do not understand the nuances of one another's roles – a common state of affairs – they may have trouble understanding one another's concerns.

This activity helps the group focus their whole attention on how a proposal will affect each participant. As a result, many confusions and misunderstandings clear up as people gain insight into the subtle realities of each other's situations.

## HOW

1. Identify which members are likely to be affected by the proposal on the floor. Ask for a volunteer to become the focal person.

2. Have a 3–5 minute brainstorm session to list answers to the question: "If we implement our proposal, how will it affect this person's role?" While the brainstorm is in effect, no disagreements are allowed.

3. When time is up, ask the focal person to come to the front of the room. S/he educates the group by elaborating on the items s/he thinks are important for everyone to understand. Encourage participants to ask questions.

4. Have the group choose a second focal person. Repeat Steps 2 and 3.

# TAKING TANGENTS SERIOUSLY

## WHY

Tangents are a major cause of the frustration and confusion of the *Groan Zone*. When someone raises an issue that seems peripheral to the discussion, other participants often become nervous. They don't want the speaker to derail the conversation and take the group off track. But the speaker may believe that s/he has identified a crucial "side problem" that the group must face before the "main problem" can be resolved.

This dilemma comes up regularly. Because everyone has a unique perspective, it's not unusual for one person to spot a hidden problem that no one else has noticed. Group members may think that the speaker is wasting their time on a tangent, when in fact the speaker might be *ahead* of the group in articulating hidden complexities. And when that happens, the group is plunged into the *Groan Zone*.

*Taking Tangents Seriously* mitigates misunderstanding by supporting the group to gain a deeper appreciation of each person's perspective.

## HOW

1. At the beginning of a discussion, or when the first tangential issue arises, post a blank sheet and title it "Side Issues." Add to it as tangents are identified.

2. At every meeting, ask the group to choose one topic from the list and discuss it for 15 minutes.

3. After 15 minutes ask, "Are we done, or would you prefer to extend the time?"

4. When time is up, finish with a quick summary. Ask, "What have you learned? Are there any next steps you should take?"

5. Repeat Steps 2 to 4 at subsequent meetings.

## IS THIS WHAT YOU MEAN?
## NO, THAT'S NOT IT!

### WHY

Anyone whose job involves serious writing knows that clarifying an important thought often takes several drafts. The same is true for ideas that are being birthed in group conversation, rather than in private writing. However, when a group is the medium for doing rough-draft thinking, the potential for misunderstandings and frustration is high.

If group members become impatient, the person trying to express the idea usually just gives up, even when the idea could be very important. This activity counters that tendency, by reversing it. Here, the person taking the risk of looking clumsy (or worse) is permitted to express frustration non-verbally, just as long as his/her energy is not aimed directly at anyone in particular.

### HOW

1. When someone is having trouble consolidating a thought, ask if s/he would like some support from the group.

2. Explain that this activity involves two roles: the *idea-drafter* – the person trying to articulate an idea s/he feels might be important – and the *assistants* – anyone willing to follow the ground rules. (See below.)

3. Ask the *idea-drafter* to tell everyone what s/he is thinking.

4. Next have the *assistants* tell the *drafter* what they understand him/her to be saying ("So is this what you mean . . . ?")

5. Early attempts by the *assistants* will probably miss the mark. The *drafter* can say, "No, that's not it!" (. . . or words to that effect.) The *drafter* has permission to use tone of voice and/or nonverbal gestures to vent exasperation at feeling misunderstood. (In order for this activity to work, everyone must acknowledge that the *drafter* can scowl, etc., without fear of being spurned for rudeness.)

6. In a few rounds, you'll see the idea's depth and insightfulness emerge.

# COUPLES COUNSELING

## WHY

Incessant bickering between two people can be quite disruptive to a group. For any pair caught in this dynamic, their quarreling *might* be rooted in a deep subject-matter disagreement. But it's just as likely that the source of the problem is in their relationship. This activity helps the two parties step back and give each other feedback about the ways they're interacting.

Note that this activity is best done with a well-formed group, not with people who are only together for a few meetings. Note too that the activity can also be done "offline" – in private, between the two parties and a facilitator, without involvement by the other group members.

## HOW

1. Explain that this activity is for only two people at a time. Other group members can expect to sit in respectful silence for the 10-20 minutes this normally requires. A few minutes of debriefing may follow.

2. Have the two participants move their chairs to face each other. Guide them to speak to each other – not to the facilitator. Explain that one person will offer feedback while the other listens, after which they will reverse roles. When one person speaks, the other must not interrupt.

3. Decide who speaks first and who listens first, then invite the speaker to begin. (Note: The first time through, you may need to stop the listener from interrupting.)

4. When the speaker finishes, ask the listener to paraphrase what s/he heard. Then ask the speaker if the listener "got it right." If not, ask the speaker to restate key points. Then ask the listener to paraphrase again.

5. Continue the cycle described in step 4 as many times as necessary, until the speaker feels understood. Then have them switch roles and repeat.

6. Continue switching roles until both people feel complete – or until time runs out. Then offer the larger group an opportunity to debrief.

# IS THERE ANYTHING I'M NOT SAYING?

## WHY

People often refrain from saying what they're really thinking. Sometimes they hold back because the risk is too great. But some people stay silent when they aren't sure if their ideas are worth saying; or when they can't turn the kernels of their ideas into fully formed presentations. In other words, there are many times when group members – if they were given a little support, a little permission, a little nudge – might go ahead and say what's on their mind. Yet without support, they often remain quiet.

This activity helps group members take a look at the thoughts they've been having (but not speaking) during a discussion. It also gives members an opportunity to reflect on whether the group would be served if a person did open up and share his or her perspective.

## HOW

1. Describe this activity. Explain why people can benefit from structured activities that give them permission to speak up. Obtain agreement from the group to proceed.

2. Break the group into pairs. Ask all to answer this question: "During this discussion, have I had any thoughts I haven't said aloud?" Assure people that no one is required to say anything they don't want to say.

3. Next, ask everyone (still in pairs) to answer this question: "Would the group benefit from hearing your partner's thinking?"

4. Return to the large group. Ask for volunteers to share any of their own thoughts that might be useful for others to hear.

## FACILITATING IN THE GROAN ZONE

SUMMARY

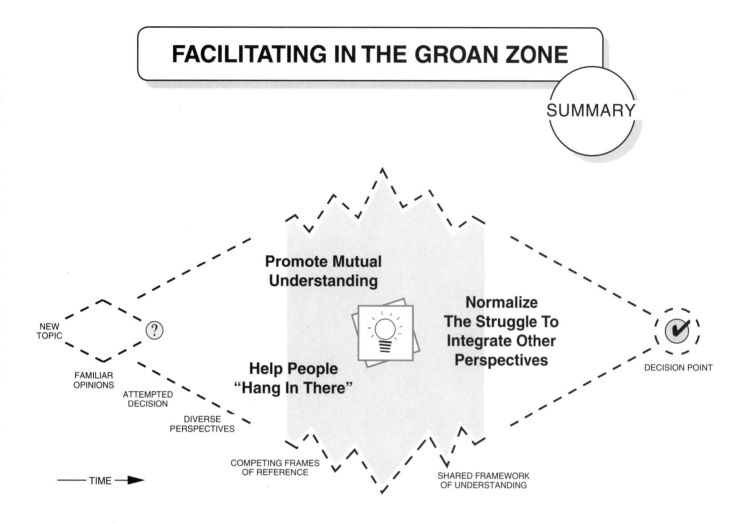

**Promote Mutual Understanding**

**Normalize The Struggle To Integrate Other Perspectives**

**Help People "Hang In There"**

NEW TOPIC

FAMILIAR OPINIONS

ATTEMPTED DECISION

DIVERSE PERSPECTIVES

COMPETING FRAMES OF REFERENCE

SHARED FRAMEWORK OF UNDERSTANDING

DECISION POINT

TIME

Structured activities are directive, they're designed to let people follow clear procedures, and they pull for sincerity, earnestness and relationship building. All these characteristics can ground a group whose communication is poor.

Those qualities can calm a troubled group and keep it focused – but getting agreement to *do* the activity is another matter. In the *Groan Zone,* when trust is low and tensions run high, everyone's ideas are easily misinterpreted – and yours will be too. You might be seen as pushing the group into feelings they don't want to share. Or as manipulating the group in the direction of your own secret biases. Or someone may simply think you're a control freak.

So if you propose a structured activity in the *Groan Zone,* keep in mind that your role is to help, not to be "right." Be patient, be tolerant, be flexible; don't be attached to what you suggest. *Honor objections, and ask for suggestions* – that's how to install a structured activity in this phase of work.

# 20

# FACILITATING IN THE CONVERGENT ZONE

## PRINCIPLES, TECHNIQUES AND TOOLS FOR STRENGTHENING GOOD IDEAS

## LIFE IN THE CONVERGENT ZONE

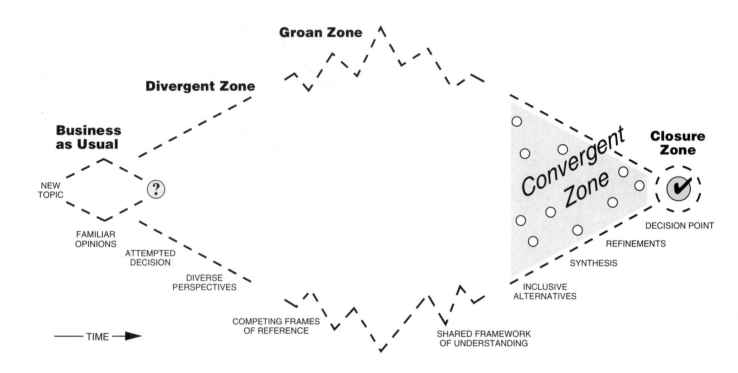

Once a group has developed a shared framework of understanding, everything feels faster, smoother, easier. The pace of discussion accelerates. People say, "Finally, we're getting something done!" Ideas take shape. Vague notions become workable, and goals become detailed plans.

Confidence runs high during this period. People show up on time and stay until the end of the meeting. Between sessions, work that needs to be done gets done.

During this time people engage in problem solving from a place of shared understanding. There isn't nearly as much complexity as in the *Groan Zone*. People are paying attention to each other and the need for facilitation has dwindled. This is a time when people can talk to each other with minimal confusion. They can play with ideas, plan them, and evaluate them.

# FACILITATING IN THE CONVERGENT ZONE

FACILITATOR'S
OBJECTIVES

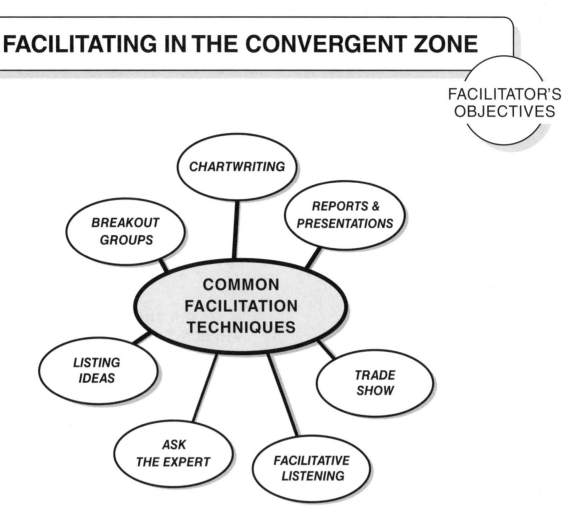

In the *Convergent Zone*, the facilitator's objectives are first, to help the group develop inclusive alternatives; second, to synthesize the alternatives into an approach that will work for everyone; third, to strengthen and refine the practical logic of that approach; and fourth, to plan it and bring it to life.

While much problem-solving may remain to be done, it takes the form of planning, designing, quantifying, evaluating – in other words, rational and logical analysis. The heavy lifting can often be done with formats like *reports & presentations, breakout groups, ask the expert, trade show* and *listing ideas*.

A lot of chartwriting happens in the *Convergent Zone;* seeing one's thinking in print is the easiest way to refine it – and that goes triple for groups! The facilitator's listening becomes focused rather than open-ended, using skills like *listening for the logic* and *summarizing*. Non-directive technique is rarely used, whereas *directive questioning* and *facilitating with a point of view* are common.

# FACILITATING IN THE CONVERGENT ZONE

CHALLENGING
SITUATIONS

NEW
TOPIC

?

STRUCTURED
THINKING TOOLS

DECISION POINT

Convergent thinking, by definition, is thinking among people who have developed mutual understanding. Thanks to good communication they can make significant progress with merely the type of support described on the previous page. But communication is not the only variable that plays a critical role in the success of a participatory process. Two others are just as important: the creativity and inclusiveness of the general approach, and the logical and practical strength of the idea as it develops into an action plan.

Most groups need the boost of one or more structured activities to stretch and reach for an *inclusive solution*. Chapter 16 describes and demonstrates how case studies can be utilized in just that way. Likewise, Chapter 17 provides many structured activities that employ *creative reframing* to support convergent thinking to be more innovative and more inspired.

As for logical and practical effectiveness, a valuable collection of structured tools for strengthening good ideas are provided on the following pages.

# DEFINING STEPS AND MILESTONES

## WHY

Thinking into the future is one of the hardest challenges for any group. We don't have good points of reference to distinguish between a large-scale goal and a small-scale goal. Yet every complex project contains many levels of goals-within-goals.

For example, consider a project with the overall goal of restoring the vitality of an impoverished neighborhood. That goal would no doubt contain many stages and milestones (such as attracting new business to the area). Furthermore, each stage would contain various steps that must be taken before the milestones at the end of that stage could be attained.

Since we lack good points of reference to make the distinctions described above, most groups find it difficult to engage in a planning process that requires them to set overall goals and define stages and milestones.

## HOW

1. Hang a long sheet of paper across the front of the room. At the far right-hand end of the paper, write the group's goal – for example, "Goal: Open a new office in Denver."

2. Ask the group to generate four or five milestones that must be completed in order to reach the goal – for example, "Complete our financial projections."

3. Write the milestones from left to right across the long sheet of paper. Leave as much space as possible between milestones.

4. Break into small groups, and assign one milestone to each group. Each group identifies and lists each step it would take to attain that milestone. Have them write each step on a sticky note.

5. Have someone from each group put the sticky notes on the wall, left to right, in the space provided for their milestone. Others can read what's being posted, and add any missing steps.

# CLARIFYING SELECTION CRITERIA

## WHY

How should a group choose one proposal over another? One way is to agree on the criteria to use in evaluating each proposal. For example, suppose a group agreed that its most important criteria were "easy to do" and "inexpensive." These criteria could help them reject a proposal that would be expensive or difficult, even if the project seemed interesting.

This activity helps groups discuss and agree on a list of five or fewer criteria, by defining them *before* specific proposals are considered.

## HOW

1. Have the group brainstorm a list of answers to this question: "By doing this project (or solving this problem, or developing this plan, for example), what are we trying to accomplish?"

2. Start a new chart titled "Selection Criteria." Facilitate the group to reword each item on the first list as a possible selection criterion. For example, if an item from the brainstorm list is, "We're trying to get two opposing factions to work together," the rewording might be, "It lets both factions work together" or "It appeals to both factions."

3. Explain that the list will soon be reduced to no more than five items. To prepare members for that judgment, have people break into small groups and discuss which criteria seem most important, and why.

4. Reconvene the large group. Have people select items from the list of criteria, and ask them to advocate for retaining those items on a final list of five or fewer criteria.

5. Give everyone five votes. Tally the results, and eliminate all but the top five vote-getters. This may not be a final decision on criteria. It will provide the membership with a sense of what people value most.

## SCAN MAGAZINES AND NEWSPAPERS

Brief anecdotes and well-written stories can both point you toward people with helpful experience.

## WHAT HAVE WE DONE BEFORE?

Has your organization faced similar challenges in the past? Can you learn by talking to key players?

## GOOGLE IT!

Searching the Internet is by far the fastest, easiest way to find information about circumstances that are similar to yours.

## SEEK OUT A SPECIALIST

Whether external to your organization or within it, there are HR generalists, project managers, and others with the experience to understand your ideas.

# HUNTING FOR EXAMPLES

## WHAT HAVE OTHERS DONE BEFORE?

Do you know of another organization that may have faced similar challenges? Who might speak with you?

## CASE STUDIES

Credible, peer-reviewed case studies can be found in professional-academic journals like the Stanford Social Innovation Review (SSIR). Many full-length professional books also contain case studies. Contact information for the authors of these books and articles is usually easy to obtain.

## PROFESSIONAL ASSOCIATIONS

No matter what your situation, it's likely that one or more associations cater to kindred spirits. Go to a conference or search the archives of a members-only library.

## PEER-TO-PEER INTEREST GROUPS

Join a group of like-minded colleagues, and learn from their war stories. Popular options include LinkedIn, meetup.com and many online discussion boards.

There is often a wide gap between the discovery of a great idea and the successful implementation of that idea. One effective way to mitigate risk and tilt the odds toward positive outcomes is to study and learn from other people's experiences of success or failure in similar circumstances. Examples are abundantly available, as noted above, to anyone willing to make a modest effort to seek them out.

# PAYOFFS AND RISKS

## WHY

This activity improves the viability of a proposal by reducing the costs and risks that are associated with it.

For example, a big city mayor recently received several million dollars to improve public transportation. The public favored spending the money on new bus routes. But the mayor was committed to a previously announced hiring freeze: no new city employees could be hired until the budget was balanced. On one hand, without new bus drivers, no routes could be added. On the other hand, if new bus drivers were hired, other government agencies would lobby for exemptions for *their* programs.

*Payoffs And Risks* helped the mayor's planning staff explore in detail the risks they would face if they went ahead with a route expansion. Through the analysis, they discovered a way to reduce their risk. They enlisted the local newspapers in an editorial campaign to build political support for this exception to the hiring freeze. It was successful, and they were able to add three new bus routes without opposition.

## HOW

1. Hang three sheets of flipchart paper. Title the first page "Payoffs" and the second page "Risks." Leave the third page untitled.

2. On page one, list the payoffs associated with the proposal.

3. On page two, list the risks associated with the same proposal.

4. Now title page three "Ways to Reduce Risk." For each risk listed on the "Risks" page, discuss options for reducing the costs and the extent of the risk. Record the discussion on page three.

5. After the options for cost-reduction are better understood, ask for new proposals that retain the payoffs of the original proposal, while incorporating the insights gained through this activity.

# WORK-FLOW PLANNING TOOLS

## PERT Chart

This tool analyzes and maps a project's deadlines and other time requirements by representing them visually.

Milosevic, Dragan Z.
*Project Management ToolBox:*
*Tools and Techniques*
*for the Practicing Project Manager.*
Wiley, 2003.

## Flow Chart

This tool uses everyday symbols – like circles, squares and arrows – to analyze the logic of a sequence of goals and the steps needed to reach each one. *Go / no-go* decision points can also be mapped.

Damelio, R.
*The Basics of Process Mapping, 2nd Ed.*
Productivity Press, 2012.

## Gantt Chart

This tool keeps track of the progress toward completion of various sub-tasks within one or more stages of work in a complex project.

Kerzner, H.R.
*Project Management.*
Wiley, 2013.

## Critical Path Method

This tool organizes and illustrates dependencies among different elements of a complex project. It shows which tasks must be finished before others can be started.

Klastorin, T.
*Project Management:*
*Tools and Trade-offs, 3rd Ed.*
Wiley, 2003.

## WBS Chart

A *Work Breakdown Structure (WBS)* chart is a tool for dividing a project into manageable chunks of work. Assigning responsibility for handling each chunk is also done by the *WBS*.

Haugan, G.T.
*Effective Work Breakdown Structures,*
Management Concepts, 2001.

Implementing any great idea requires quite a bit of planning. Elements like time, money, roles and communication are among many variables that must be defined, monitored and controlled. The tools on this page help planners think through the logic of the tasks to be done, in what order, by whom, and by when. The citations will lead you to write-ups that offer practical guidance for using each related tool.

# RESOURCE ANALYSIS: CAN WE REALLY MAKE THIS WORK?

## WHY

Sometimes groups agree to proposals that sound good but have not been thought through. This is usually not a problem, because issues dealt with in this way are usually insignificant. But occasionally, a group will agree to a huge undertaking with absolutely no sense of what they're in for.

For example, eight nurses decided to organize a major conference that would bring together representatives from over one hundred agencies. Their aim was to build a coalition that could influence state and county funding policies. The organizers did not have the slightest grasp of the effort it would take them, yet they publicized the conference and kept taking on new responsibilities as they came up. Eventually one person lost her job, and another got very sick. The conference itself was poorly attended, disorganized and ultimately inconsequential. In hindsight the nurses said, "We should have been more realistic to begin with."

## HOW

1. Ask the group to list the major tasks that must be achieved if the proposal under consideration is to be implemented.

2. Assign two or three people to think about each task. Have them choose a record keeper and a spokesperson.

3. Say to each group: "For 10 minutes, think about the steps necessary to complete your assigned task. Break it down to doable action steps."

4. When time is up, reconvene the large group and ask the spokesperson from each group to report on his or her group's work.

5. After all committees have reported, ask everyone to discuss whether the overall proposal is adequate or requires modification.

# WHO DOES WHAT BY WHEN?

## WHY

Group decision-making is often viewed as an exercise in futility. In the experience of many, agreements reached during meetings are likely to be implemented poorly, if at all.

The odds of successful implementation increase when a group takes the time to spell out specifically what needs to be done, who will do it, by when, and with what resources. But often this step does not occur. Instead, people act as if they assumed that once an agreement has been reached, the follow-through will happen magically. "Someone else" will tend to the details later.

When a group stays fuzzy about the specifics of implementing an agreement, two or three people will probably wind up with all of the tasks – often without adequate resources. Alternatively, no one takes responsibility, and nothing happens.

This activity supports a group to consider in advance who will do each task, and when. As a consequence, responsibilities are often distributed more evenly, and more effectively.

## HOW

1. Draw a matrix with four vertical columns. Title the columns: "Tasks," "Who," "By When," and "Resources Needed."

2. Under the first heading, "Tasks," list all tasks that need to be done. If additional tasks are identified later, add them to the list.

3. Number each task listed. Then discuss: *"Who will do this? By when? What resources are needed?"* This thinking can done in open discussion format, with no prescribed sequence for answering the questions.

4. As specific agreements are made, write them on the chart.

# WHO ELSE NEEDS TO EVALUATE THIS PROPOSAL?

## WHY

Most decisions do not just affect the people who make them. Obviously, not everyone who will be affected can participate in making a decision and planning its implementation. Nonetheless, it can be very, very costly to overlook the perspectives of those who did not participate in developing the reasoning that led to the decision.

This activity helps a group to think proactively about the question, "Who else needs to be consulted?" *It usually takes a group two or three hours – sometimes longer – to go through the steps.* Taking this time at the start of a planning process might be the difference between success and disaster.

## HOW

1.  Have group members generate lists of people who:

    - Will be directly affected by this decision.
    - Have final sign-off authority.
    - Have to implement the decision.
    - Could sabotage the process.

2.  Take a few moments to examine the list. Discuss the following questions: "What's the likelihood that any of these stakeholders would disagree with our ultimate decision? If any of them did not support the decision, how might that affect our ability to implement?"

3.  Next consider each person or group on the list. Who needs to be consulted before the final decision is made?

4.  For each person or group who will be consulted, choose a consultation method. Some options are interviews, focus groups, questionnaires, and an invitation to a core group meeting.

# FACILITATING IN THE CONVERGENT ZONE

SUMMARY

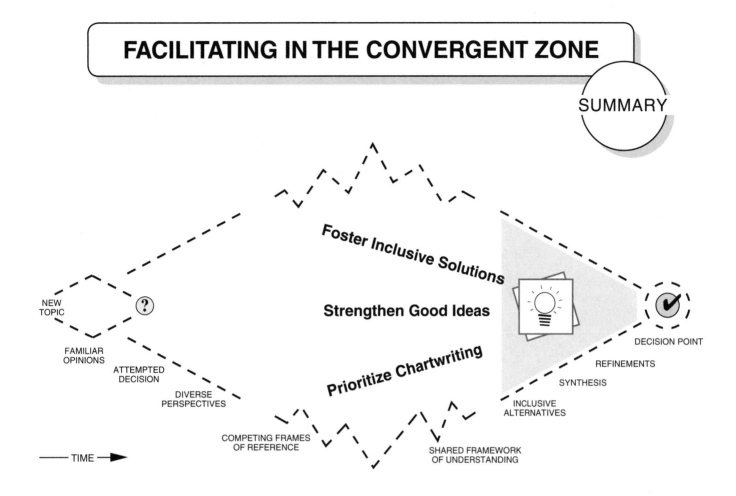

NEW TOPIC

FAMILIAR OPINIONS

ATTEMPTED DECISION

DIVERSE PERSPECTIVES

COMPETING FRAMES OF REFERENCE

TIME ➡

Foster Inclusive Solutions

Strengthen Good Ideas

Prioritize Chartwriting

SHARED FRAMEWORK OF UNDERSTANDING

INCLUSIVE ALTERNATIVES

SYNTHESIS

REFINEMENTS

DECISION POINT

Sustainable agreements require well-thought-out ideas that incorporate everyone's needs and goals. If the struggle of the *Groan Zone* is the heart of a sustainable agreement, the ingenuity of the *Convergent Zone* is the brain.

Structured thinking activities can be quite useful when a group seems trapped in an *either/or* mentality. Groups in this condition need inspiration and stimulation – which members are unlikely to provide to one another, when they're focused on their own positions. Chapter 16 *(Inclusive Solutions)* and chapter 17 *(Creative Reframing)* are helpful for this purpose.

Structured activities will also support groups to be more disciplined at refining the logic of their ideas, and at planning the nitty-gritty work that will enable their ideas to be implemented.

But it would be misleading to imply that groups in the *Convergent Zone* spend much time engaged in structured thinking. The truth is the opposite. Convergent discussions are largely self-managing. For many facilitators, the hardest part of working in the *Convergent Zone* is learning to pick up the markers, face the flipchart, and otherwise stay out of the group's way!

# 21

# TEACHING A GROUP ABOUT GROUP DYNAMICS

IMPARTING WISDOM FROM THE DIAMOND
OF PARTICIPATORY DECISION-MAKING

- ▶ Setting the Frame for Learning

- ▶ How to Introduce Divergent Thinking

- ▶ How to Introduce Convergent Thinking

- ▶ How to Introduce the Groan Zone

- ▶ How to Integrate the Parts into a Whole

- ▶ Real Life Applications and Implications

- ▶ More Tips for Teaching The Diamond
  of Participatory Decision-Making

## TEACHING A GROUP ABOUT GROUP DYNAMICS

# 1.

## *Set the Frame.*

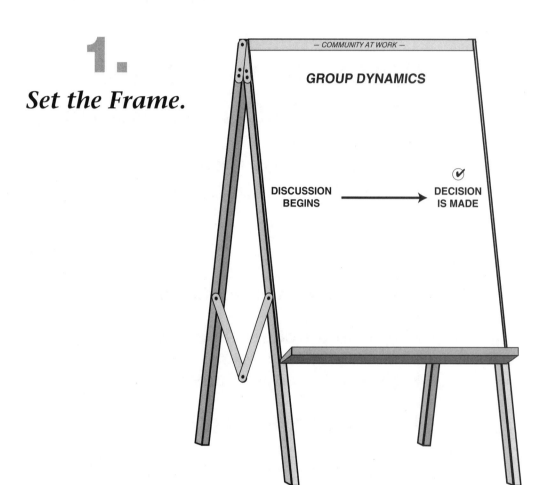

Unveil a flipchart titled *GROUP DYNAMICS*.

The chart should be blank except for:

- *DISCUSSION BEGINS* near the left margin.
- *DECISION IS MADE* near the right margin.
- An arrow that connects them.

Explain to your group that you are now going to present a model that shows why meetings can be so frustrating and unproductive.

## TEACHING A GROUP ABOUT GROUP DYNAMICS

**2.**

*Introduce Divergent Thinking.*

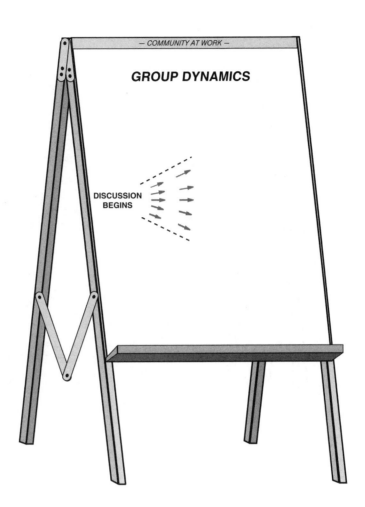

On the left side of the flipchart, draw five arrows as shown.

Say, "Here's a way to see group dynamics at a meeting.
    Imagine people starting to discuss a difficult problem."

Point to each arrow, one at a time, saying (in a humorous voice),
- "The first person says, 'I think we should do ABC.'"
- "The second person says, 'I disagree. That's a bad idea.'"
- "Then the third person says, 'I think XYZ is better.'"
- "The fourth says, 'I don't even think this is a problem.'"
- "The fifth says, 'Shouldn't Joe be here for this topic?'"

## TEACHING A GROUP ABOUT GROUP DYNAMICS

**3.**

*Show
Two Types
of Thinking.*

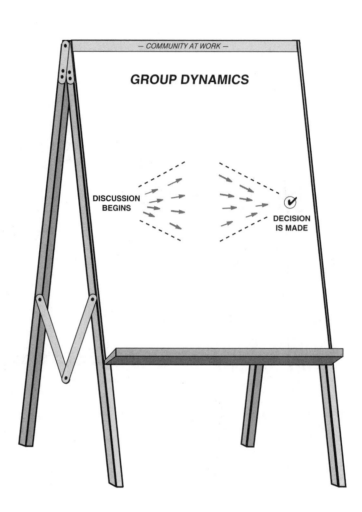

On the right side of the flipchart, draw the convergent arrows.

Say,

> "Later in the meeting, it's not uncommon to see *the very
> same people* behaving quite differently."

Wave your hand across the whole right side of the chart, and say,

> "For example, this group agreed to spend the next ten
> minutes just focusing on the pros and cons of idea ABC.
> After that they spent 10 more minutes shifting their
> attention to the pros and cons of idea XYZ."

## TEACHING A GROUP ABOUT GROUP DYNAMICS

**4.**

*Introduce
the Model.*

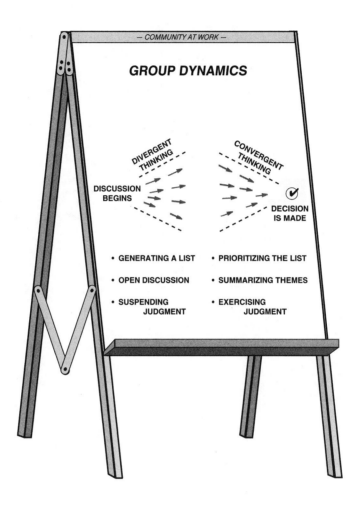

Flip to a new page, made in advance, on which you have
written,

- *DIVERGENT THINKING*

- *CONVERGENT THINKING*

Under the diagram, your chart should list examples of each type
of thinking, as shown above.  As a starting point for creating
this chart, you can refer to the examples on page 6 of this book.

# TEACHING A GROUP ABOUT GROUP DYNAMICS

## 5.
### *Break into Pairs.*

Have everyone partner up with someone sitting nearby. When they have found their partners, ask them to share their thoughts and questions in response to the model they have just learned.

## TEACHING A GROUP ABOUT GROUP DYNAMICS

**6.**

*Reconvene and Debrief.*

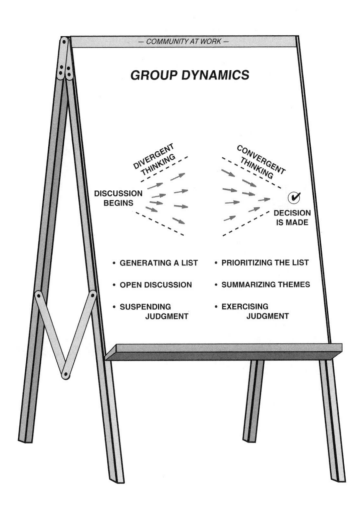

After 3-5 minutes, call everyone back to the whole group. Ask,

"Does anyone have comments? Questions?"

Take all responses. Someone will point out that real life is messier than what you have drawn. That's your cue to introduce the *Groan Zone*.

Point to the gap in the middle of the chart (still unlabeled), saying "this period of time is a stressful one for groups." Use examples (such as, "people repeat themselves" or "people interrupt") to show how grueling it is to communicate across the gap of diverse points of view.

## TEACHING A GROUP ABOUT GROUP DYNAMICS

**7.**

*Introduce the Groan Zone.*

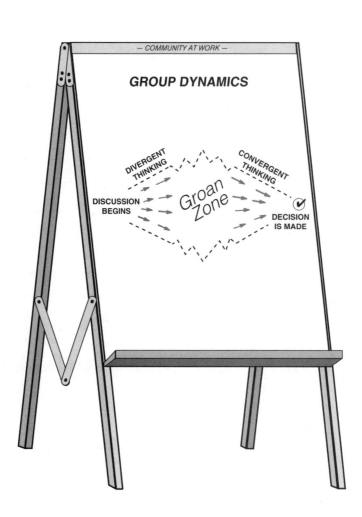

Ask how many people can recognize that period of frustration and misunderstanding from their own personal experience. Possibly ask for an example.

Now point out that even though this period is very common aspect of life in groups, there is no word in the English language that labels or describes it.

With a flourish, write GROAN ZONE in the center of the chart.

Before showing the next page, wait until the laughter subsides.

# TEACHING A GROUP ABOUT GROUP DYNAMICS

## 8.

### *Show the Whole Framework.*

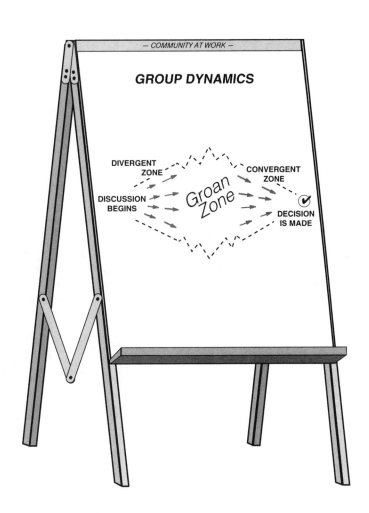

Unveil another flipchart titled
*The DIAMOND of PARTICIPATORY DECISION-MAKING*

The chart should be the same as previous ones, except:
- *DIVERGENT THINKING* is now replaced by *DIVERGENT ZONE*.
- *CONVERGENT THINKING* is now replaced by *CONVERGENT ZONE*.

Please give credit to Sam Kaner and the co-authors, Lenny Lind,
Cathy Toldi, Sarah Fisk and Duane Berger,
and to the *Facilitator's Guide to Participatory Decision-Making*.

Without further comment, send everyone into groups of three or four.

## TEACHING A GROUP ABOUT GROUP DYNAMICS

**9.**

*Apply to Real Life Experiences.*

Ask everyone to partner up with two or three other members. Once everyone has settled down, explain that you would now like them to spend the next 10 minutes testing out this model.

1. Ask each person to silently think of a decision-making group in which they have participated.

2. Now, ask someone in each group to go first, describing their group's communication and problem-solving style. The others in each small group should comment and ask questions. The objective is to explore any opportunities for THE DIAMOND to offer insight into this group's dynamics.

3. Ask groups to change speakers at will, every few minutes.

## TEACHING A GROUP ABOUT GROUP DYNAMICS

# 10.

### *Discuss Implications*

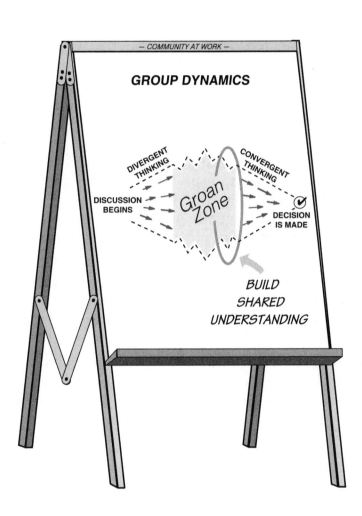

Bring the whole group back together to debrief the small group discussions. Ask for questions and comments.

As you facilitate the discussion, support the group to clarify the principle that if the group really truly wants to achieve sustainable agreement, then spending time in the *Groan Zone* is critical. The resolution of a *Groan Zone* will occur when a shared framework of understanding has been built.

To illustrate this concept, write the words BUILD SHARED UNDERSTANDING below the diagram; then draw a vertical ellipse, as shown above. Explain that this is a "turning point" in any collaboration.

## TIPS FOR TEACHING YOUR GROUP
## THE DIAMOND OF PARTICIPATORY DECISION-MAKING

☐    **1.** To follow this chapter's approach, allow 45 minutes to one hour.

☐    **2.** Best times to use this approach are either at the start of a session or right after the group returns from a break.

☐    **3.** After the first round of small groups, take comments from everyone who wants to speak. Don't respond immediately to the person who points out that real life is messier than the diagram implies. Acknowledge the point and return to it later, when you can put ample time into introducing the *Groan Zone*.

☐    **4.** When taking comments from the group, let people make their own discoveries rather than react to everything that is confusing or uncomfortable for them. Ask "who else has a thought about that?"

☐    **5.** Have your charts ready, even if you don't plan to use them. The best opportunity to raise awareness can arise when you least expect it. If *The Diamond* is a model you enjoy using, a set of these charts should be a standard part of your facilitator's tool-kit.

☐    **6.** Use humor throughout. An exaggerated tone of voice works well. Being funny models playfulness, which in turn will support people to share the angst they feel in the *groan zones* in their own settings.

☐    **7.** Throughout both debriefs (as well as in follow-up sessions), keep reminding your group, "It's painful; it's normal."

☐    **8.** Sometimes it's tempting to teach *The Diamond* when your group is in the moment of a demoralizing *groan zone*. To follow this strategy, use an abbreviated approach. First, call a quick break. Next, show the whole model *on one page*. Explain the basics of each zone, with quick examples. Then shift to pairs, so people can digest what they heard. In the debrief, ask how this fits with their current meeting experience.

Part Five

# REACHING
# CLOSURE

# 22

# THE SIGNIFICANCE OF CLEAR DECISION RULES

CLARIFYING THE SINGLE MOST
IMPORTANT STRUCTURAL ELEMENT
OF GROUP DECISION-MAKING

- ▶ **The Benefits of Having a Clear Decision Rule**

- ▶ **Common Decision Rules**

- ▶ **Decision-Making Without a Decision Rule**

- ▶ **Uses and Implications of Major Decision Rules**

- ▶ **How Different Decision Rules Affect Participation**

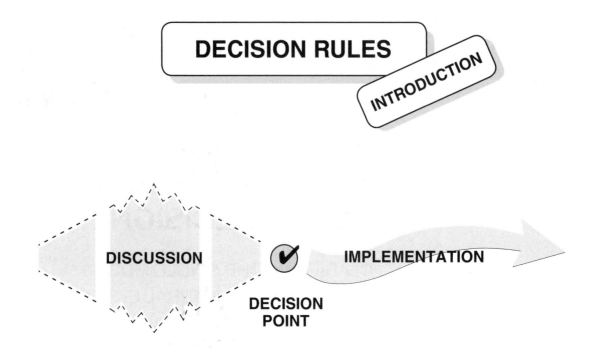

**DECISION RULES** INTRODUCTION

DISCUSSION ✓ IMPLEMENTATION

DECISION POINT

This diagram depicts two entirely different domains of group behavior: the period of discussion and the period of implementation. During a discussion, people think. They discuss. They consider their options. During the implementation, people act on what they've decided. Thus, for example, during a discussion, participants might *figure out the budget* for a project; in the implementation of that project, *people spend the money.*

During the discussion, in other words, a group operates in *the world of ideas;* after the decision has been made, that group shifts into *the world of action.*

In the world of ideas, people explore possibilities; they develop models and try them on in their imagination. They hypothesize. They extrapolate. They evaluate alternatives and develop plans. In the world of action, the group has made a commitment to make a chosen idea come true. Contracts are signed. People are hired. Departments are restructured, and offices are relocated.

*The Decision Point is the point that separates thinking from action.* It is the point of authorization for the actions that follow. Discussion occurs *before* the point of decision; implementation happens *after* the point of decision.

# DECISION RULES

**THE CLASSIC PROBLEM**

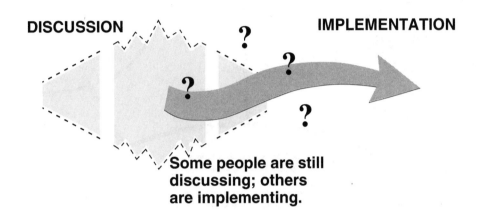

**DISCUSSION**

**IMPLEMENTATION**

**Some people are still discussing; others are implementing.**

Many groups try to problem-solve without first clarifying their decision rules. This can produce a great deal of confusion.

For example, if someone thinks a decision has been made, s/he will feel empowered to take action in line with that decision. Meanwhile, if others think no decision has yet been made, they will view the person who took the action as "impulsive" or "having their own agenda" or "not a team player." It often happens in such cases that the person accused of acting prematurely will justify the action by saying, "But I thought we all agreed . . ."

The same is true in reverse. Inaction after the point of decision is often perceived as "insubordinate" or "passive-aggressive" or "disloyal." In such cases, it is common to hear people defend themselves by saying, "I don't recall us making an actual decision about that" or "I never agreed to this!"

These examples remind us that people need a clear, explicit indicator that a decision has been made. For instance, groups that make decisions by majority rule do know they are still in the discussion phase until they vote and tally the results. But many groups are fuzzy – *they lack clear rules for bringing their discussion to closure.*

This chapter describes the six most common decision rules and explores the implications of each one.

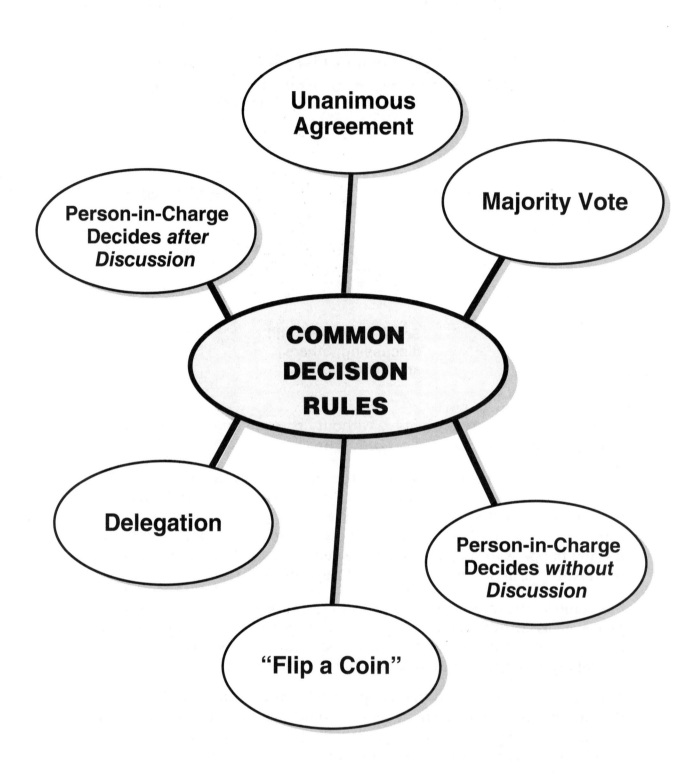

A decision rule answers the question, "How do we know when we've made a decision?" Each of the six rules shown above performs this basic function.

Individual members act on their own idiosyncratic perspectives. Soon, the left hand doesn't know what the right hand is doing.

Those who whine or raise their voice get what they want.

Someone says, "Let's put this on next month's agenda and pick up where we left off." But at the next meeting, the item is superseded by urgent new business.

Just as time runs out, someone makes a new suggestion. This becomes "the decision."

## DECISION-MAKING WITHOUT A DECISION RULE

People assume that since the issue was discussed, a decision was made.

After the meeting ends without agreement, a few people meet behind closed doors and make the real decisions.

Someone's name gets vaguely attached to a poorly defined task (as in, "Duane, why don't you check into that?") Later, that person gets blamed for poor follow-through.

The person who has the most at stake makes an independent decision; later, people resent him or her for taking actions that did not meet other people's needs.

Certain people *always* get their way.

When a quick decision has to be made or an opportunity will be lost, conservative members exercise a pocket veto by stalling the discussion. Thus, "no decision" becomes a decision not to act.

The person-in-charge says, "Is everyone okay with this idea?" After a few seconds of silence, the person-in-charge moves to the next topic, believing that every member's silence meant "yes," rather than "no" or "I'm still thinking."

The meeting goes overtime; the discussion drags on and on. . .

# MAJOR DECISION RULES: USES AND IMPLICATIONS

## » UNANIMOUS AGREEMENT

### High-Stakes Decisions

In groups that decide by *unanimous agreement,* members must keep working to understand others' perspectives until they integrate those perspectives into a shared framework of understanding. Once people are sufficiently familiar with each other's views, they become able to advance innovative proposals that are acceptable to everyone. It takes a lot of effort, but this is precisely why the unanimous agreement decision rule has the best chance of producing sustainable agreements when the stakes are high.

The difficulty with using unanimous agreement as the decision rule is that most people don't know how to search for Both/And solutions. Instead, people pressure each other to live with decisions that they don't truly support. And the group often ends up with a watered-down compromise.

This problem arises from the general tendency of groups to push for a fast decision: "We need unanimity because we want everyone's buy-in, but we also want to move forward as fast as possible." This mentality undermines the whole point of using unanimous agreement: to channel the tension of diversity, in service of creative thinking – to invent brand-new ideas that really do work for everyone. This takes time. In order to realize the potentials of unanimous agreement, members should be encouraged to keep working toward mutual understanding until they develop a proposal that will receive enthusiastic support from a broad base of participants.

### Low-Stakes Decisions

With low-stakes issues, unanimous agreements are usually comparable in quality to decisions reached by other decision rules. Participants learn to go along with proposals they can tolerate, rather than hold out for an innovative solution that would take a lot of time and effort to develop.

One benefit of requiring unanimous agreement for low-stakes decisions is the prevention of decisions that are abhorrent to a small minority. Other decision rules can lead to outcomes that are intolerable to one or two members, but are adopted because they are popular with a majority. By definition, such a decision will not be made by unanimous agreement.

# MAJOR DECISION RULES: USES AND IMPLICATIONS

## » MAJORITY VOTE

### High-Stakes Decisions

Majority vote produces a win/lose solution through an adversarial process. The traditional justification for using this rule when stakes are high is that the competition of ideas creates pressure. Thus, the quality of everyone's reasoning theoretically gets better and better as the debate ensues.

The problem with this reasoning is that people don't always vote based on the logic of the arguments. People often "horse-trade" their votes or vote against opponents for political reasons. To increase the odds that people vote on a proposal's merits, the use of secret ballots is worth considering.

### Low-Stakes Decisions

When expedience is more important than quality, majority vote strikes a useful balance between the lengthy discussion that is a characteristic of unanimous agreement, and the lack of deliberation that is a danger of the other extreme. Group members can be encouraged to call for a quick round of pros and cons and get on with the vote.

## » "FLIP A COIN"

### High-Stakes Decisions

"Flip a coin" refers to any arbitrary, random method of making a decision, including common practices like drawing straws, picking numbers from a hat or "eeny-meeny-miney-moe." Who in their right mind would consider using this decision rule to make a high-stakes decision?

### Low-Stakes Decisions

Upon realizing that the decision will be made arbitrarily, most people stop participating in the discussion. Why bother to keep yakking when your comments won't have any impact on the actual result?

## MAJOR DECISION RULES: USES AND IMPLICATIONS

### » PERSON-IN-CHARGE DECIDES *AFTER DISCUSSION*

**High-Stakes Decisions**

There is strong justification for using this decision rule when the stakes are high. On one hand, the person-in-charge is the one with the access, resources, authority, and credibility to act on what s/he decides. Yet on the other hand, obtaining input allows the person-in-charge to expand his or her understanding of the issues, and form a wiser opinion on the best course of action. This decision rule, in other words, strikes a balance between the compelling reasons for a person-in-charge to make certain decisions, and the benefits that are gained from seeking the group's counsel.

Unfortunately, some group members give false advice and say what they think their boss wants to hear rather than express their true opinions.

There are several ways to overcome this problem. Some groups require "devil's advocate" thinking, thus eliminating the pressure to concur "lest time be wasted." Other groups schedule time to meet without the person-in-charge, who then returns to the room for a joint discussion once any controversial opinions have been surfaced.*

**Low-Stakes Decisions**

There are three decision rules that encourage group discussion: unanimous agreement, majority rule, and person-in-charge decides after discussion. With low-stakes issues, all three decision rules produce results that are roughly equivalent in quality.

Low-stakes issues provide an opportunity to practice giving advice to the person-in-charge. When the stakes are low, the person-in-charge feels less pressured to get it right, and is thus less defensive and more open-minded. Similarly, group members are less afraid of being punished for taking risks.

* Irving Janis, in his groundbreaking classic on the group dynamics of conformity, *Victims of Groupthink* (Boston: Houghton Mifflin, 1972), describes many case studies demonstrating this problem. For suggestions on ways to overcome the problem of *groupthink,* see pages 207-224.

# MAJOR DECISION RULES: USES AND IMPLICATIONS

## » PERSON-IN-CHARGE DECIDES *WITHOUT DISCUSSION*

### High-Stakes Decisions

When a person-in-charge decides without discussion, s/he assumes full responsibility for analyzing the situation and coming up with a course of action. Proponents argue that this decision rule firmly clarifies the link between authority, responsibility, and accountability. Detractors argue that this decision rule creates a high potential for blind spots and irrationality.

The most appropriate time for a person-in-charge to make high-stakes decisions without discussion is in the midst of a crisis, when the absence of a clear decision would be catastrophic. In general, though, the higher the stakes, the riskier it is to make decisions without group discussion.

How will group members behave in the face of this decision rule? The answer depends on one's values. Some people believe that good team players are loyal, disciplined subordinates who have the duty to play their roles and carry out orders. Other people argue that group members who must contend with this decision rule should develop a formal mechanism, like a union, for making sure their points of view are taken into account.

The fundamental point is that whenever one person is solely responsible for analyzing a problem and solving it, the decision-maker may lack essential information. Or those responsible for implementation might sabotage the decision because they disagree with it or because they don't understand it. The more the person-in-charge understands the dangers of deciding without group discussion, the more capable s/he is of evaluating in each situation whether the stakes are too high to take the risks.

### Low-Stakes Decisions

Not all decisions made this way turn out badly. In fact, many turn out just fine. And when the stakes are low, even bad decisions can usually be undone or compensated for.

# THE EFFECTS OF DIFFERENT DECISION RULES ON PARTICIPATION

### Person-in-Charge Decides *Without* Group Discussion

This decision rule gets group members in the habit of "doing what they are told."

At meetings, they listen passively to the person-in-charge. They assume s/he expects to talk without being challenged – and they comply.

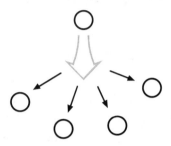

### Person-in-Charge Decides *After* Group Discussion

When the person-in-charge is the final decision-maker, s/he is the main person who needs to be convinced. Everyone tends to direct their comments to the person-in-charge.

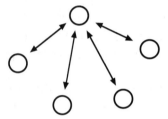

### Majority Vote

Since the goal is to obtain 51% agreement, the influence process is a battle for the undecided center. Once a majority is established, the opinions of the minority can be disregarded.

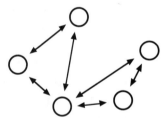

### Unanimous Agreement

When everyone has the power to block a decision, each participant has the right to expect his or her perspective to be taken into account. This puts pressure on members to work toward mutual understanding.

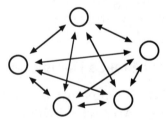

Each decision rule has a different effect on group behavior. Individual group members adjust the quantity and quality of their participation depending on how they think their behavior will influence the decision.

# 23

# STRIVING
# FOR UNANIMITY

WORKING WITH
GRADIENTS OF AGREEMENT

- ▶ **Unanimity and Consensus**

- ▶ **Intro to the Gradients of Agreement Scale**

- ▶ **Gradients of Agreement Scale In Real Life**

- ▶ **Using the Gradients of Agreement Scale**

- ▶ **Gradients of Agreement in Action:**
  - **Enthusiastic Support**
  - **Lukewarm Support**

- ▶ **When to Seek Enthusiastic Support**

- ▶ **What Level of Support is Optimal?**

- ▶ **Gradients of Agreement in Action:**
  - **Ambiguous Support**
  - **Majority Support with Outliers**

- ▶ **Adapting the Gradients of Agreement Scale**

- ▶ **Methods of Polling the Group**

## THE POWER OF UNANIMOUS AGREEMENT

The word *unanimous* comes from two Latin words: *unus*, meaning "one," and *animus*, meaning "spirit." A group that reaches unanimous agreement is a group that acts from one spirit. By this understanding, a unanimous agreement can be expected to contain wisdom and soundness of judgment, because it expresses an idea that is felt by each person to be true. As the Quakers say, the decision speaks for everyone.

To reach unanimity, everyone must agree. This means each person has a veto. Thus, anyone can keep the discussion alive for as many hours or weeks or months as it takes to find a solution s/he can believe in. This veto capacity is the crux of the power of unanimous agreement. When a group is committed to reaching unanimous agreement, the members are in effect making a commitment to remain in discussion until they develop an inclusive solution – one that takes everyone's needs into account.

## UNANIMITY AND CONSENSUS

*Consensus* also has Latin origins. Its root word is *consentire,* which is a combination of two Latin words: *con,* meaning "with" or "together with," and *sentire,* meaning "to think and feel." *Consentire* thus translates as "to think and feel together."

Consensus is *the process*: a participatory process by which a group thinks and feels together, *en route to* their decision. Unanimity, by contrast, is the point at which the group *reaches closure.*

Many groups that practice consensus decision-making *do not use unanimity* as their decision rule for reaching closure. For example, Seva Foundation uses "unanimity minus one." Some chapters of the Green Party use 80% as the acceptable level of agreement. Yet all such groups see themselves as sincere practitioners of consensus decision-making. While no single member has personal veto power, individual voices wield significant influence – enough to ensure that the group will engage in a genuine process of thinking and feeling together.

# STRIVING FOR UNANIMITY

*IDEALISM vs REALITY*

## A SILENCE IS NOT AN AGREEMENT

Many managers want their teams to be strongly aligned on the high-stake, high-impact issues that most affect their work. When tackling such issues, these managers come to meetings with statements like, "I need everyone's buy-in today." Clearly, these managers *want* their groups to find unanimity.

Yet if we look at how such meetings play out, what actually happens? The discussion may go well for a time, but once the group becomes mired in the *Groan Zone,* the person-in-charge often feels pressure to bring the discussion to closure and make a decision.

To close discussion, it's common for a person-in-charge to summarize a key line of thought and say something like, "It sounds like people want to do such-and-such." Then s/he will follow with, "Does everyone agree with this proposal?" Typically, after a few seconds of silence, this person will say, "All right, we're agreed. That's what we'll do. Now let's move on."

Is this actually a unanimous agreement? Not really. The manager has no idea, really, what the people who didn't respond were thinking.

## THE PROBLEM WITH YES AND NO

*Unanimity* means that every person has said "yes." But "yes" does not necessarily mean, "Yes, this is a great idea." It could also mean, "Yes... well... I have reservations, but I guess I can work them out when we implement it," or even, "Yes, though actually I don't much care for this idea, but I'll go along with the majority. I want to be seen as a team player."

Moreover, someone who says "no" is saying, in effect, "I require the group to spend more time on this discussion." Most group members are reluctant to be that person. Who wants to be the one dragging things out?

Thus, the "yes-no" language is a fundamental problem. To strive for unanimity, group members need a way to accurately and authentically convey the extent of their support (or non-support) for a proposal.

# GRADIENTS OF AGREEMENT

**BETTER VOCABULARY**

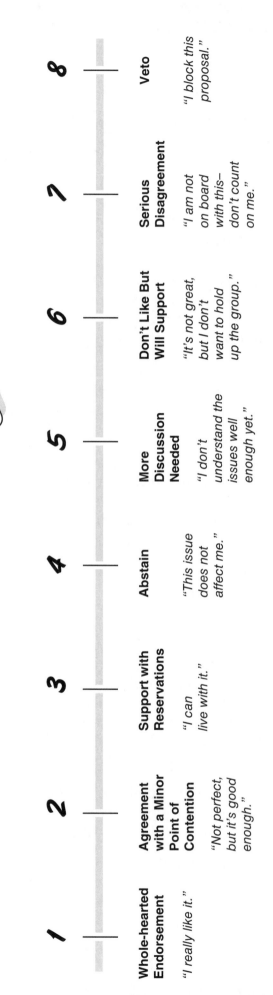

| 1 | 2 | 3 | 4 | 5 | 6 | 7 | 8 |
|---|---|---|---|---|---|---|---|
| Whole-hearted Endorsement | Agreement with a Minor Point of Contention | Support with Reservations | Abstain | More Discussion Needed | Don't Like But Will Support | Serious Disagreement | Veto |
| "I really like it." | "Not perfect, but it's good enough." | "I can live with it." | "This issue does not affect me." | "I don't understand the issues well enough yet." | "It's not great, but I don't want to hold up the group." | "I am not on board with this– don't count on me." | "I block this proposal." |

This is the *Gradients of Agreement Scale*. It eliminates the arbitrary confinement of "yes" and "no." Instead, it allows for many possible nuances of meaning, enabling individuals to express support for a proposal in degrees, along a continuum – in line with the way many people actually think.

The *Gradients of Agreement Scale* was developed in 1987 by Sam Kaner, Duane Berger, and the staff of *Community At Work*. With the passing of time this tool has been translated into numerous languages, and it has been adapted for use in organizations large and small throughout the world.

*Community At Work* ©2014

Aloha Sam,

Thank you for your "gradients of agreement" work. Introducing this in the context of a faculty retreat enabled the group to make a major breakthrough regarding an issue critical to the program's future. Extreme polarization moved to enthusiastic support as a result of the description and use of the tool. I've always appreciated the efficacy of the tool, but have seldom seen as dramatic a breakthrough in a relatively short period of time.

January, 2014
Linda Colburn, President
Where Talk Works, Inc.
Honolulu, Hawaii

## AS TOLD BY LINDA COLBURN, ACCLAIMED CONSULTANT *

A university faculty member asked for facilitation support to resolve an impasse associated with scenarios for future program development. Results from interviews with individual team members surfaced promising conceptual alignment but also a degradation of trust and an increase in tensions between the parties. The chair invoked involvement of a facilitator to reach an accord the entire team could support.

A *gradients of agreement* template was drawn on a whiteboard along with a preliminary statement describing the most critical issue in dispute. The group modified the statement to better reflect the issue at hand. Each member selected the number on the continuum that best described his / her current thinking about the revised proposition.

Faculty members were permitted to further elaborate on their aspirations, assumptions, and fears regarding the issue at hand. This dialogue afforded them a number of opportunities to seek clarification on key points, supply relevant data, and dispel misunderstandings that had deepened over time.

The faculty were asked to state their position number a second time. Their new positions reflected near unanimous agreement to move forward with the proposed initiative. They volunteered to work on collectively determined tasks, and they mapped out an implementation timetable.

There was a discernible improvement in their interactions as evidenced by a marked reduction in interruptions and challenging

behavior. The engagement level balanced out as group members offered to take on various tasks to move the effort forward.

This process helped the group:

- better understand their colleagues' actual motivations and concerns;

- arrive at shared definitions of key terms;

- realize they were actually more aligned in their thinking than their earlier, polarized positions suggested; and

- move forward collectively as a team with less concern about passive-aggressive resistance or sabotage.

The *Gradients of Agreement* tool provided a face-saving and systematic framework for clarifying a collectively crafted path forward.

* Linda Colburn has long been regarded as one of Hawaii's leading collaboration specialists. A chapter of *When Talk Works* by Deborah Kolb, (Jossey-Bass 1997) described Linda's practice as a mediator. The book profiles 12 accomplished mediators including Jimmy Carter.

# HOW TO USE
# THE GRADIENTS OF AGREEMENT SCALE

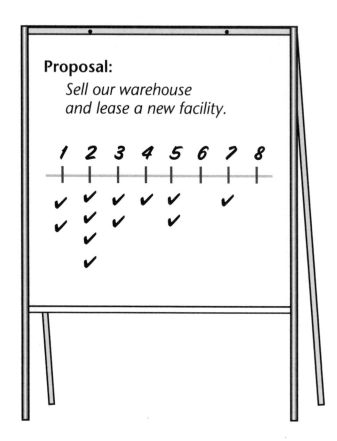

If you prefer, you can show the *Gradients of Agreement* early in a meeting, offering it as a tool that requires endorsement from the group. Or you can wait and introduce it when the time arrives to make a substantive decision.

When using the scale to take a poll, follow these steps:

*Step 1:* Record the proposal being discussed on a flipchart.

*Step 2:* Check to see that everyone understands the proposal.

*Step 3:* Ask for final revisions in the wording of the proposal.

*Step 4:* Draw a "scorecard" below the proposal, as shown on this page.

*Step 5:* Define the gradients. (For example, "#1" means "I really like it.")

*Step 6:* Ask the group, "On this proposal, where do each of you stand?"

*Step 7:* Take the poll. Capture everyone's positions on the scorecard.

Be sure the group understands that this process is not a vote; it's just a poll. The results show *level of support* for a proposal; no decision has been made.

## GRADIENTS OF AGREEMENT IN ACTION: ENTHUSIASTIC SUPPORT

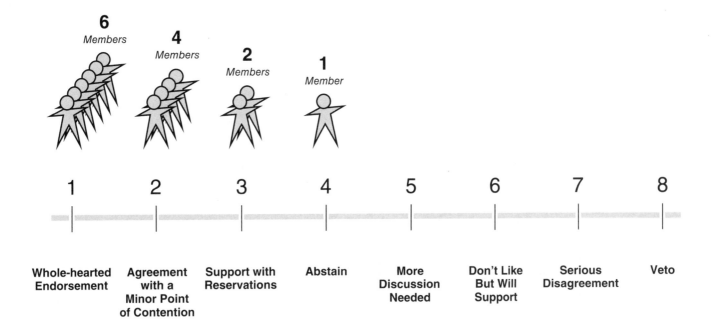

This diagram portrays the result of a hypothetical poll, taken in a group of 13 members. The pattern of responses – also known as "the spread" – indicates a high level of enthusiastic support for the proposal.

An agreement based on this much support will usually produce a successful implementation. After all, six members of the group are whole-hearted in their endorsement, and the others are not too far behind. One could reasonably expect that these participants would care about the results they produce.

Words like *buy-in* and *ownership* carry the same connotation as *enthusiastic support* – they express the depth of enthusiasm and commitment groups experience when they engage in a high-quality thinking process.

## GRADIENTS OF AGREEMENT IN ACTION: LUKEWARM SUPPORT

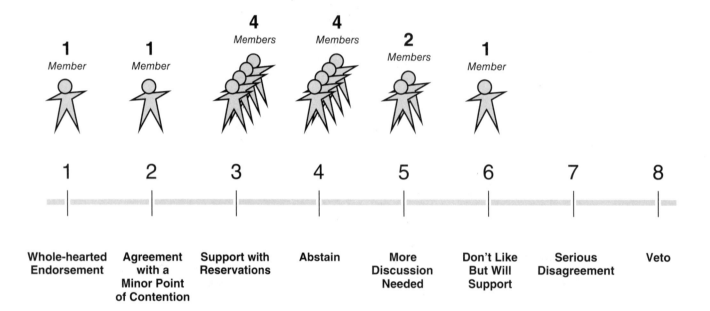

This diagram portrays a different result. Here, the spread indicates significantly less enthusiasm for the proposal. Nonetheless, this spread also indicates unanimous agreement. Not one person would veto this proposal and block it from going forward. In fact, there is no serious disagreement here whatsoever.

For many purposes, lukewarm support is perfectly adequate. For example, when the stakes are low, it is usually not worth pushing for a higher level of support. But in other cases, when achieving a goal will require high motivation and sustained effort, lukewarm support won't get the job done.

# WHEN TO SEEK ENTHUSIASTIC SUPPORT

Enthusiastic support is desirable whenever the stakes are so high that the consequences of failure would be severe. By contrast, when the stakes are lower, a group may not wish to invest the time and energy it takes to develop enthusiastic support.

Some decisions are not easily reversible – for example, the decision to relocate headquarters to a new city. Decisions like these are worth spending whatever time it takes to get them right. But other decisions – such as the question of how to staff a project during an employee's two-week vacation – have a short life-span. To get such a decision perfectly right might take longer than the entire lifetime of the decision.

The chief factors that make problems hard to solve are complexity, ambiguity, and the severity of conflict.* The tougher the problem is, the more time and effort a group should expect to expend. Routine problems, by contrast, don't require long-drawn-out discussions.

When many people have a stake in the outcome of the decision, it is more likely to be worth the effort to include everyone's thinking in the development of that decision. When the decision affects only a few people, the process need not be as inclusive.

The more likely it is that members will be expected to use their own judgment and creativity to implement a decision, the more they will need to understand the reasoning behind that decision. The process of seeking enthusiastic support pushes people to think through the logic of the issues at hand.

*Source: Paul C. Nutt, *Solving Tough Problems* (San Francisco: Jossey-Bass, 1989).

## WHAT LEVEL OF SUPPORT IS OPTIMAL?

**Enthusiastic Support**
is necessary
when the issue
involves:

**Lukewarm Support**
is good enough
when the issue
involves:

| HIGH STAKES | ← OVERALL IMPORTANCE → | LOW STAKES |

| LONG-TERM IMPACT | ← DURATION OF IMPACT → | SHORT-TERM ONLY |

| TOUGH PROBLEM | ← DIFFICULTY OF THE PROBLEM → | SIMPLE PROBLEM |

| HIGH INVESTMENT | ← STAKEHOLDER BUY-IN → | LOW INVESTMENT |

| HIGH AUTONOMY | ← EMPOWERMENT OF GROUP MEMBERS → | LOW AUTONOMY |

## GRADIENTS OF AGREEMENT IN ACTION: AMBIGUOUS SUPPORT

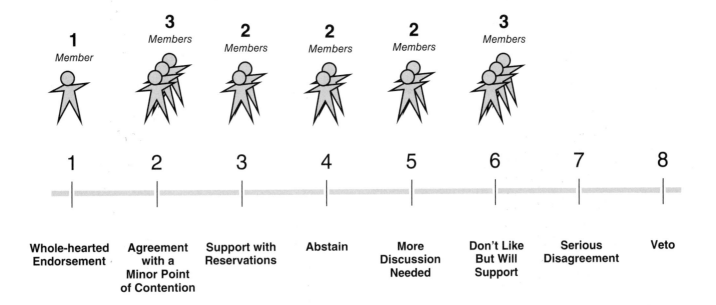

| 1<br>Member | 3<br>Members | 2<br>Members | 2<br>Members | 2<br>Members | 3<br>Members |

| 1 | 2 | 3 | 4 | 5 | 6 | 7 | 8 |

| Whole-hearted Endorsement | Agreement with a Minor Point of Contention | Support with Reservations | Abstain | More Discussion Needed | Don't Like But Will Support | Serious Disagreement | Veto |

This diagram portrays a group of people who are all over the map in their response to the proposal. The group would surely benefit from more discussion.

Ambiguous results frequently indicate that the original problem has not been defined effectively. As Michael Doyle and David Straus have stated, "You can't agree on the solution if you don't agree on the problem."*

* Source: M. Doyle and D. Straus, *Making Meetings Work* (New York: Berkeley Books, 1993).

# GRADIENTS OF AGREEMENT IN ACTION: MAJORITY SUPPORT WITH OUTLIERS

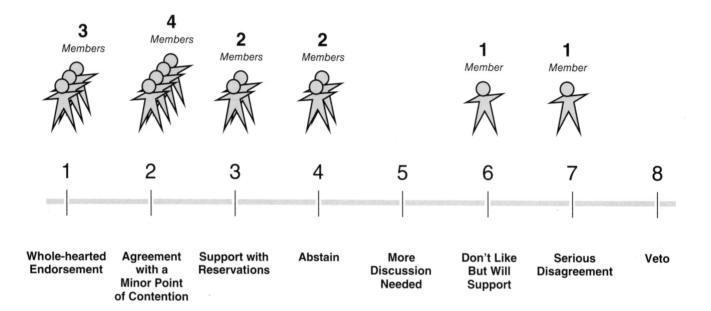

| 3 Members | 4 Members | 2 Members | 2 Members | | 1 Member | 1 Member | |
|---|---|---|---|---|---|---|---|
| 1 | 2 | 3 | 4 | 5 | 6 | 7 | 8 |
| Whole-hearted Endorsement | Agreement with a Minor Point of Contention | Support with Reservations | Abstain | More Discussion Needed | Don't Like But Will Support | Serious Disagreement | Veto |

This spread is surprisingly common. When it occurs, the question arises as to whether the group should disregard the objections of the outliers or whether the group should keep making efforts to resolve those objections.

Often the person-in-charge of the group will try for a compromise, asking those with objections if they can suggest remedies that would increase their level of support. Sometimes this works.

But not always. It depends on whether or not there is a benefit in obtaining enthusiastic support for the eventual decision. When everyone's strong support is needed, lukewarm compromises will not do. In those cases, the group must continue searching for a genuinely inclusive solution.

## ADAPTING THE GRADIENTS OF AGREEMENT SCALE

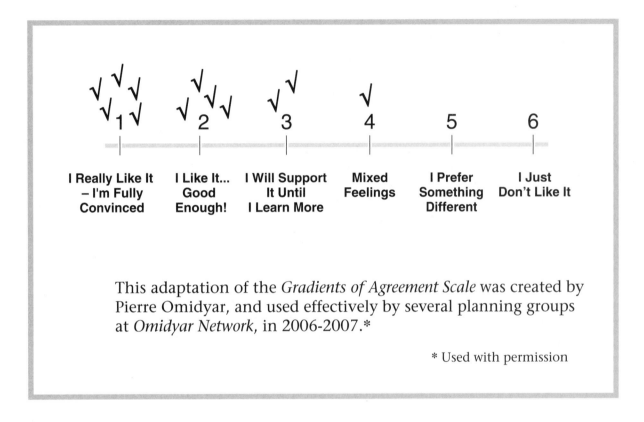

This adaptation of the *Gradients of Agreement Scale* was created by Pierre Omidyar, and used effectively by several planning groups at *Omidyar Network*, in 2006-2007.*

\* Used with permission

Many group leaders prefer to create their own set of gradients, whether to suit their leadership style or to fit the group's culture. To assist in this effort:

1. Explain the benefits of using *Gradients of Agreement.*

2. Show the "generic scale" – the one used throughout this chapter.

3. Ask whether s/he would like to customize the scale.

4. Once the person-in-charge has revised the scale, have him or her present the scale to the group, soliciting further revisions if desired.

Even when a group uses the generic scale for the first few decisions, it is entirely fine for the leader (or the participants) to propose modifications at a later time.

## METHODS OF POLLING THE GROUP

Say, "Please raise your hands if you are a '1'." Record the data on a flipchart. Now say, "Please raise your hands if you are a '2'." Repeat for all gradients.

Go around the room and ask each person to state which gradient s/he prefers and why. No discussion is allowed. Record each preference on a flipchart.

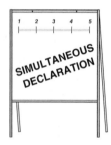

Have each person write his or her preference on a sheet of paper. On cue, have everyone hold up his or her card. Record the totals on a flipchart.

Have each person write his or her preference on a slip of paper. When everyone is done, collect the ballots and tally results. Post totals on a flipchart.

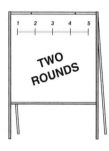

Before beginning, explain that there will be a preliminary poll followed by a brief discussion and then a final poll. Gather the first poll's data in any of the ways listed above. After a brief, time-limited discussion, poll again. This method lets people see where others stand before stating final preferences.

# 24

# REACHING CLOSURE
# STEP BY STEP

WORKING WITH THE COMMUNITY AT WORK
PROCEDURE FOR REACHING CLOSURE

# REACHING CLOSURE

FLEXIBILITY
vs. CLARITY

## DECISION RULES: A BASIC DILEMMA

Many work groups have difficulty establishing a clear *decision rule.* Frequently, the problem is that the person-in-charge does not feel obligated to use a single decision rule. "Sometimes," said a division manager, "I want everyone in my group to agree to a plan before we act on it. At other times I don't want to waste time, so I make the decision myself."

From the point of view of the person-in-charge, it does not make sense to be tied down to a particular rule. But from the perspective of the group members, the inconsistency can be enormously confusing.

For example, a software publishing company held monthly meetings chaired by the chief operating officer and attended by all department managers. The managers complained that the meetings were very frustrating. "Sometimes the boss cuts off discussion after five minutes," they grumbled. "At other times he lets it run on and on. Sometimes it seems like he wants us to buy into a decision he's already made; other times he couldn't care less what we think; and then there are times when he wants us to figure out every little detail. It's driving us crazy!"

This is an intriguing story. From the perspective of the person-in-charge, his behavior was perfectly logical! In each particular case he made a judgment call to determine how much discussion the issue warranted. At times – when the stakes were low or when a solution seemed obvious – he decided it was fine to make a quick decision with very little discussion. At other times, when he wanted everyone to take ownership of the outcome, he kept the discussion going in search of better ideas.

The problem was that he did not share this reasoning out loud. The group members had no idea that there was a method to his messiness. To explain his apparent inconsistency, they made up stories: he was manipulating them. He was fearful of corporate politics. He was incompetent as a leader.

This illustrates the classic tension between the need for a flexible procedure and the need for a clarified procedure. The person-in-charge felt that having a clear, consistent decision rule would hamper his judgment to allocate time wisely. But leaving the decision rule vague didn't work, either. It left group members unsure of when to participate robustly, and when to be passive.

# REACHING CLOSURE

THE META-DECISION *

## The Discussion Reaches a Stopping Point

OPTION A

OPTION B

The person-in-charge decides that the discussion has been adequate. S/he feels ready to bring the issue to closure by making a final decision.

The person-in-charge decides that important issues still need to be thought through. S/he wants the group to continue the discussion.

This diagram portrays a situation that comes up all the time in groups: at a certain point in practically every discussion, the person-in-charge has to decide whether to end the discussion and make a decision.

To most people who play the role of person-in-charge, this fact is intuitively obvious. They recognize the situation because they deal with it every day. But it is *not* so obvious to the other participants at a meeting. They often don't know *how* to interpret what's going on. As a result of such confusion, people can become frustrated, angry, and passive – exactly as happened in the case described on the previous page.

Fortunately, it is easy to reduce the disparity. *The solution is to show everyone what the person-in-charge is doing.* For example, you can present a simple diagram like the one drawn above, and explain the options. When the choice point is made explicit, the confusion is removed.

---

* The word *meta* is Greek and means "above" or "about." Making a decision about whether to make a decision is thus called *making a meta-decision.*

# THREE META-DECISIONS

## THE DOYLE AND STRAUS *FALLBACK*

One of the most well-known meta-decision procedures is the Doyle and Straus *fallback*.*  Here's how it works.

When a new topic is introduced, the person-in-charge sets a time limit to reach a unanimous agreement.  If time expires, the person-in-charge makes the meta-decision:  either s/he will close the discussion and make a final decision, or s/he will set a new time limit and reopen the discussion.

## CAROLINE ESTES' *VOTE TO VOTE*

Meta-decisions also occur in groups that have no person-in-charge.  For example, the U.S. Green Party, which uses unanimous agreement as its decision rule, has a meta-decision that allows it to switch from unanimity to majority vote.  This meta-decision, called *vote to vote,* was popularized by Caroline Estes, one of the nation's leading experts in the field of large-group consensus decision-making.**

The Greens have adapted this procedure:  any group member can call for an immediate vote to close discussion and switch from unanimity to majority.  If 80% of the voters opt to switch, the discussion ends, and the group shifts to majority rule for the proposal at hand; if fewer than 80% want to switch, the unanimity rule remains in effect and discussion continues.

## SAM KANER'S *META-DECISION*

This procedure is shown on the next page.  Its central premise is that *polling helps a group obtain maximum benefit from the use of a meta-decision.*

In groups with a person-in-charge, it is highly advantageous for that person to use a *Gradients of Agreement scale* to take a poll before making a decision.  If s/he sees adequate support from the group, s/he can make a decision with confidence that it will be implemented.  However, if s/he sees that the proposal lacks adequate support, s/he can reopen the discussion instead.

---

  * M. Doyle and D. Strauss, *How to Make Meetings Work* (New York:  Berkeley Books, 1993)
 ** Personal observation by Sam Kaner, while co-facilitating the founding conference of the Green Party of the United States of America, Eugene, Oregon, 1989.

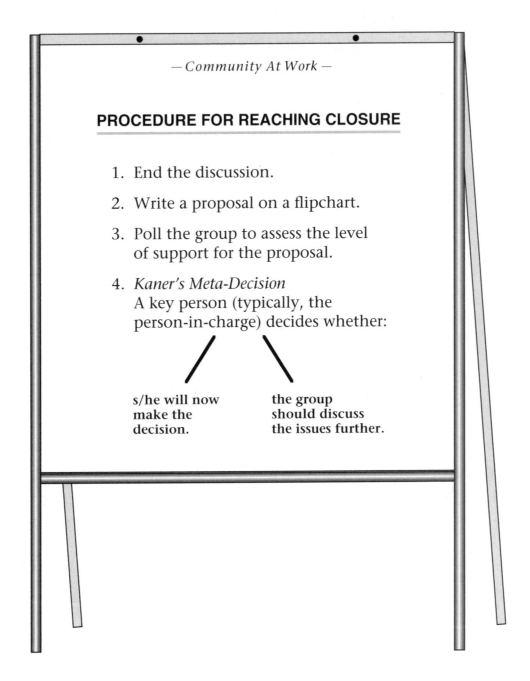

— *Community At Work* —

**PROCEDURE FOR REACHING CLOSURE**

1. End the discussion.

2. Write a proposal on a flipchart.

3. Poll the group to assess the level of support for the proposal.

4. *Kaner's Meta-Decision*
   A key person (typically, the person-in-charge) decides whether:

   s/he will now make the decision.

   the group should discuss the issues further.

This is the *Community At Work* procedure for reaching closure. It helps groups make simple decisions quickly, and it also supports them to take as much time as necessary when the stakes are high. It provides groups with the benefits of participatory decision-making whether or not their organizations are hierarchically structured.

All groups that use this procedure are encouraged to customize it to fit their own circumstances.

# KANER'S META-DECISION
## REAL-LIFE EXAMPLES

### VISA International
#### Global Access Technologies

1. Anyone can move to close discussion. The group is then polled. In case of disagreement, the person-in-charge decides whether to end discussion.

2. Clarify the proposal by writing it down.

3. Poll, using gradients of agreement.

4. If no one vetoes the proposal, the person-in-charge decides:

|  |  |
|---|---|
| there is enough agreement to formalize a decision. | the group should discuss the issues further. |

Used with permission from Paul Weintraub, vice president.

### Alameda County, California
#### Behavioral Health Care Services
#### A.C.S.C. Managers Meeting

1. Anyone can end the discussion with group agreement.

2. Clarify a proposal in writing, using "clarifying questions" and "friendly amendments."

3. Poll the group with gradients of agreement to assess the level of support.

4. Michael or the "person-in-charge" (TBD) makes the meta-decision:

|  |  |
|---|---|
| s/he will now make the decision. | the group should discuss the issues further. |

Used with permission from Michael Lisman, director.

### Charles Schwab & Co.
#### Retail Employee Performance Support

1. Clarify the decision rule to be used. If using the meta-decision process, *identify the meta-decision maker* and proceed as follows:

2. Anyone can close the discussion.

3. Anyone can offer a proposal. If someone is not clear, clarify the proposal.

4. Poll the group. Anyone can block.

5. The meta-decision maker decides:

|  |  |
|---|---|
| s/he will now make the decision. | the group should continue to discuss the issues. |

Used with permission from Janet Manchester, vice president.

# KANER'S META-DECISION
## MORE REAL-LIFE EXAMPLES

### Marshall Medical Center

1. Anyone may call for closure. The chair decides whether to close.

2. A proposal is made by anyone in the group and written down.

3. Clarify the proposal with questions and "friendly amendments."

4. Poll, using gradients of agreement.

5. The chair decides whether:

to move forward on the proposal.        topic needs more discussion.        the proposal will be dropped.

Used with permission from James Whipple, CEO.

### Hospitality Valuation Financial Services

1. Identify issues as *group issues* or *person-in-charge decisions*. For group issues, proceed as follows:

2. Clarify the proposal.

3. Poll the group.

4. The person-in-charge decides:

s/he will now make the decision.        the group should continue to discuss the issues.

5. Proceed as specified in Step 4.

6. After the person-in-charge has made the decision, feedback is welcome.

Used with permission from Harvey Christensen, vice president.

### Watsonville Healthy Families Collaborative

1. Select a *Poll Assessor* at each meeting.

2. Anyone can call to close the discussion.

3. Clarify the proposal and write it down.

4. Poll the group using the polling scale. Everyone in attendance (individual or agency representative) can participate.

5. If no one vetoes, the *Poll Assessor* decides:

The poll result is good enough to be our final decision.        We need more discussion.

6. If no decision has been made after three rounds of discussion, a majority vote will take place, with one vote per agency.

Used with permission from Defensa de Mujeres for the Watsonville Healthy Families Collaborative.

## KANER'S META-DECISION
### EVEN MORE REAL-LIFE EXAMPLES

### San Lorenzo School District Facilities Planning Group

1. Anyone can call for closure to end discussion.

2. Clarify proposal.

3. Poll for preferences by holding up cards that show gradients of agreement.

4. Person-in-charge assesses: Is this enough agreement to be considered a final decision?

If yes, the decision is considered final.

If no, return to discussion. Members identify areas of nonsupport and suggest alternatives.

Used with permission from Janis Duran, superintendent.

### Hollister School District Strategic Planning Team

1. Call for closure to end discussion.

2. Clarify proposal.

3. Poll for preferences.

4. Ask group, "Is this enough agreement?"

If No
Return to discussion, with purpose of revising the proposal to get higher support. (Up to 3 rounds of discussion, then it is final.)

If Yes
Decision is final. A "5" is a veto and the proposal doesn't pass.

Used with permission of full membership of the Strategic Planning Team, Hollister School District.

### Santa Cruz Gardens School

1. Close discussion.
   • Anyone can call for closure.
   • Needs a second and a third.
   • Make time for anyone who hasn't spoken yet to speak if they want.

2. Create or clarify the proposal.

3. Poll the group.

4. Meta-decision: The person-in-charge decides whether:

S/he will now make the decision.

The group should discuss the issue further.

Used with permission from Carl Pearson, principal.

# KANER'S META-DECISION
## STILL MORE REAL-LIFE EXAMPLES

### Urban Strategies Council
### Leadership Technical Team

1. *Call for closure,* to end discussion.

2. Clarify the proposal.

3. Check for consensus by polling.

4. The *meta-decision maker*, a role that rotates each meeting, decides:

| there is enough agreement to formalize the decision. | there is not enough agreement to make a decision. Reopen the discussion. |

Used with permission from Maria Campbell Casey, president.

### Youth Advocates
### Of Marin County

1. Close discussion by unanimity.

2. Collect proposals.

3. Poll for preferences among options.

4. The person-in-charge decides:

| s/he will now make the decision. | the *Procedure Person,* a rotating role, will now make the decision. |

the group should continue discussing the issues.

5. Proceed as specified in step 4.

Used with permission from David Barkan, program director.

### Larkin Street
### Youth Services

1. Collect proposals.

2. Poll for preferences among alternatives.

3. Time-limited attempt to reach unanimity:
   • set time limit,
   • proceed until time expires.

4. The person-in-charge decides:

| she will now make the final decision. | the group should continue to discuss the issues. |

Used with permission from Diane Flannery, executive director.

# KANER'S META-DECISION
## YET MORE REAL-LIFE EXAMPLES

## Independent Natural Food Retailers Cooperative

1. A proposal is made. A second is solicited.

2. Check for further questions, clarification, and discussion.

3. Consider friendly amendments.

4. Test for agreement, using a 5-point gradient scale.

| If there are no 4s or 5s and the average is under 2, go to step 6. | If there are any 4s or 5s, or the average is 2 or higher, return to discussion. |

5. If more discussion is required, repeat the first four steps.

| If the average is under 2, go to step 6. | If the average is 2 or higher, check for the final comment with those who polled 3, 4 or 5. Go to step 6. |

6. Take a formal yes / no vote.

Used with permission from Corinne Shindelar, chief executive officer and Alex Beamer, board chairperson.

## Santa Cruz Zen Center Board of Trustees

1. Call for closure to end discussion.

2. Clarify proposal.

3. Poll for preferences using gradients of agreement.

4. The president decides:

| There is enough agreement to make a decision. | The group should discuss the issue further. |

5. If there is no agreement after three rounds of discussion over three meetings, and if 2/3 of the trustees in attendance want to vote, a vote will be taken.

6. To pass a vote, a 2/3 majority is needed. Those who vote need to have attended all three meetings.

Used with permission from Edie Brown, board president.

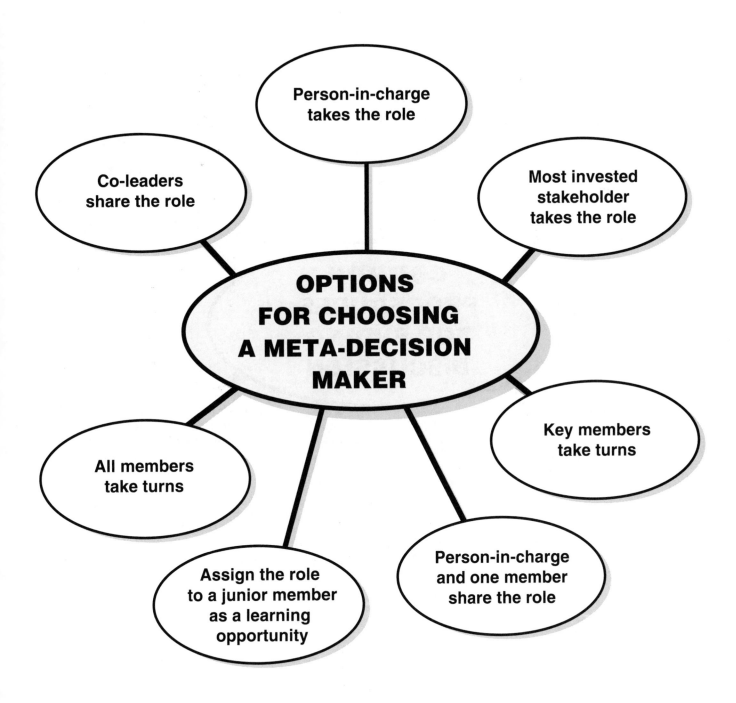

The *meta-decision maker* is the person who decides whether an issue needs further discussion. The role of the *meta-decision maker* can be assigned using any of the options shown above.

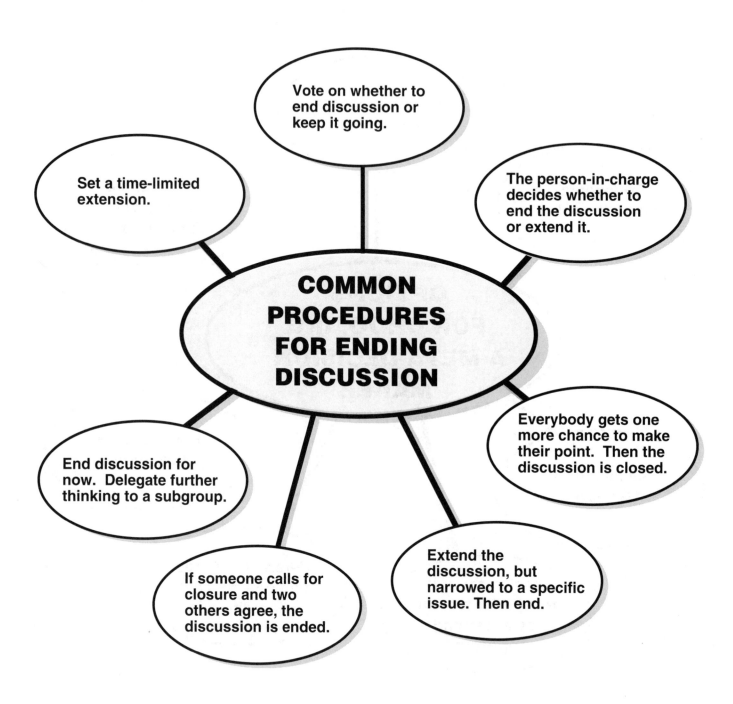

COMMON PROCEDURES FOR ENDING DISCUSSION

- Vote on whether to end discussion or keep it going.
- Set a time-limited extension.
- The person-in-charge decides whether to end the discussion or extend it.
- End discussion for now. Delegate further thinking to a subgroup.
- Everybody gets one more chance to make their point. Then the discussion is closed.
- If someone calls for closure and two others agree, the discussion is ended.
- Extend the discussion, but narrowed to a specific issue. Then end.

A group can use any of these procedures to end discussion. The preferred procedure should be followed consistently, so that everyone knows how to manage the timing of their participation most effectively.

# HELPING THE PERSON-IN-CHARGE DESIGN A DECISION PROCEDURE

**1.** *Show the person-in-charge a flipchart of "Procedure for Reaching Closure."* Read the text out loud. State that you will now explain the mechanics and rationale for each step, starting with Step 4: *Kaner's Meta-Decision.*

**2.** *Describe the use of the Meta-Decision.* Describe the differences between enthusiastic support and lukewarm support. Ask the person-in-charge, "Under what circumstances would you be comfortable proceeding with lukewarm support? And under what circumstances would you want to build more support, even if it meant reopening the discussion?"

**3.** *Show the Gradients of Agreement.* Describe how the polling process works, and demonstrate a result by placing dots on the scale. Explain that there is nothing sacred about the labels or the number of points on the scale and that most groups customize the scale to fit their own group culture.

**4.** *Briefly explain the need for a rule to end discussion.* Give examples of different ways a group can close discussion. See "Common Procedures for Ending Discussion."

**5.** *Briefly explain the benefit of writing a proposal on a flipchart.* Emphasize that the first draft does not have to be perfect. People may wish to tweak it before a poll is taken.

**6.** *Invite and encourage the client to customize any or all steps.* Make sure the person-in-charge is 100 percent comfortable with his/her adaptation of the *Meta-Decision.*

**7.** *Make a plan for bringing the revised procedure to the whole group.* Encourage the person-in-charge to expect — and even hope — that the group will revise the procedure further to make it their own.

## INSTALLING THE DECISION PROCEDURE

**1.**

**SET THE FRAME**

*Person-In-Charge:* Tell the group that you are about to show them a proposal for a decision-making procedure. Explain that you want them to revise this proposal as needed, until it suits the group. Then overview the ratification process (Step 4.)

**2.**

**SHOW YOUR PROPOSAL**

*Person-In-Charge:* Show the group your proposed decision-making procedure in its entirety. Use a flipchart so you can make changes easily.

**3.**

**DISCUSS EACH STEP**

*Facilitator:* Describe the *gradients of agreement* and explain how the polling process will work. Then explain the *meta-decision.* Facilitate a group discussion of each step. Record all suggested revisions on the flipchart.

**4.**

**REVISE AND RATIFY**

*Facilitator:* Have the group use the proposed procedure to end discussion. Then poll to ascertain level of support for each suggested revision. Have the person-in-charge make meta-decisions as needed. There are usually several suggestions to consider. Take them one at a time, repeating the sequence until all revisions are ratified or rejected. Finish by polling for support of the entire final product.

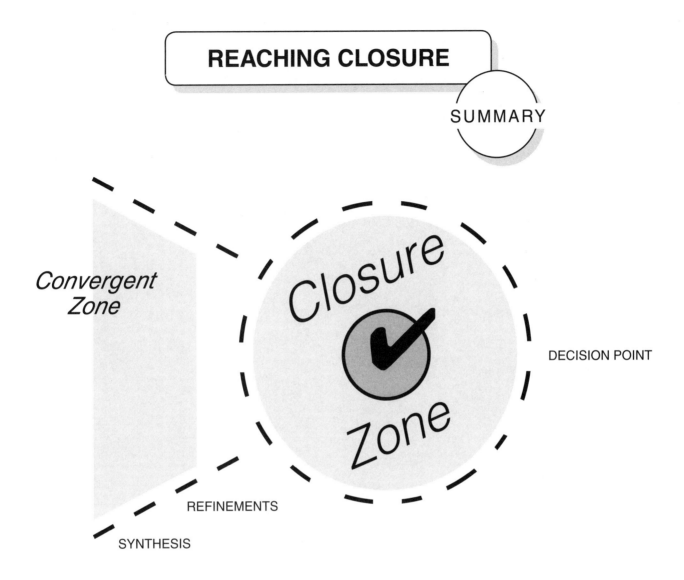

The *Closure Zone* can be viewed as the final phase of decision-making. It consists of four distinct steps:

1. End the discussion.
2. Write a proposal on a flipchart.
3. Poll the group members.
4. Use the group's decision rule to reach a final decision.

Sometimes these steps can be navigated quickly and informally, without the help of explicit procedures – for example, when someone proposes a compelling solution that everyone likes. But in the long run, for all the reasons discussed in this chapter, groups will benefit from an explicit, formal decision rule – even if they use it only occasionally. Facilitators are advised to study well the principles of this chapter. Understanding how to reach closure is essential for anyone who wants to help a group build sustainable agreements.

# 25

# FACILITATING SUSTAINABLE AGREEMENTS

A SUMMARY AND INTEGRATION
OF THE MAIN POINTS OF THIS BOOK

▶ Overview

▶ The Divergent Zone

▶ The Groan Zone

▶ The Convergent Zone

▶ The Closure Zone

▶ One Last Look at the Role
   of Facilitator

## FACILITATING SUSTAINABLE AGREEMENTS

INTRODUCTION

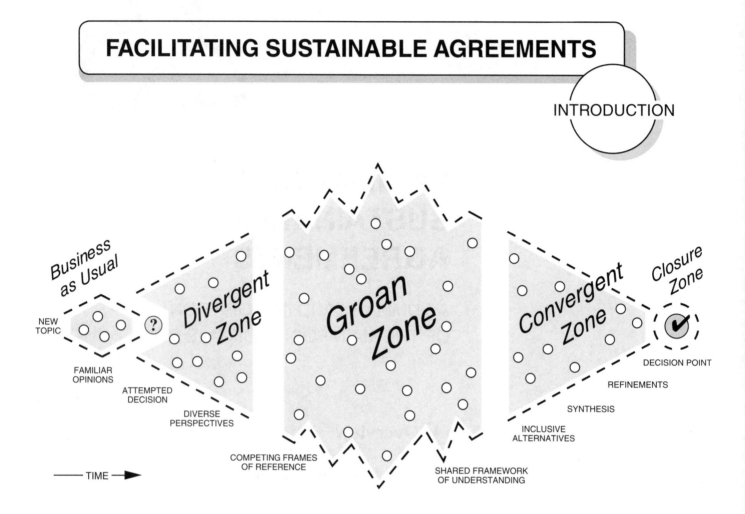

Sustainable agreements don't happen in a burst of inspiration; they develop slowly. It takes time and effort for people to build a shared framework of understanding, and groups need different types of support at different points in the process. Facilitators who understand this will vary their technique to match the group's current dynamics.

The following pages review the theory and practice of working with *the Diamond of Participatory Decision-Making.* Each page summarizes the significance of one zone of *the Diamond,* with emphasis on issues that hold particular interest for facilitators.

# FACILITATING SUSTAINABLE AGREEMENTS

BUSINESS AS USUAL

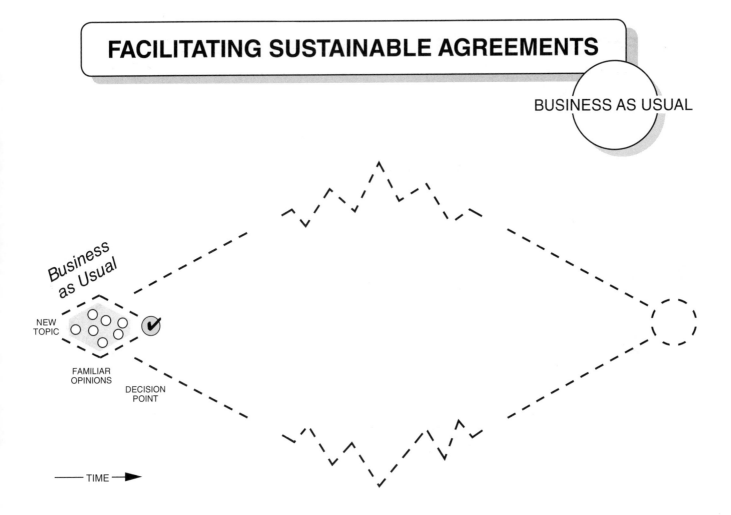

*Business as Usual*

NEW
TOPIC

FAMILIAR
OPINIONS

DECISION
POINT

TIME ➡

When a new topic comes up for discussion, people normally begin the conversation by proposing obvious solutions to obvious problems. The emotional atmosphere is usually congenial but superficial. People refrain from taking risks that would put them in vulnerable positions. If an idea seems workable, it usually leads to quick agreement. "Sounds good to me," people say. The facilitator's main task here is to pay attention to the quality and quantity of each person's participation. Is everyone engaged? Does everyone seem at ease with the thinking? If so, great! The facilitator then summarizes the ideas and helps the group reach agreement quickly.

But suppose some people hesitate. "I do still have questions, but I don't want to stand in the group's way." A facilitator should support the group to see the implication of such comments – namely, that more thinking might be very useful. Then, the facilitator can help them break out of the narrow band of familiar opinions and move their discussion into the *Divergent Zone*.

# FACILITATING SUSTAINABLE AGREEMENTS

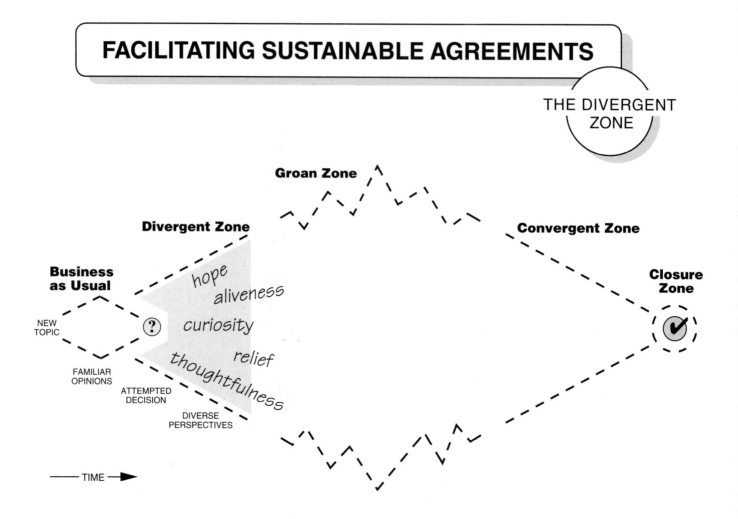

THE DIVERGENT ZONE

When a facilitator shifts a group from *Business as Usual* to the *Divergent Zone,* the mood changes dramatically. *Business as Usual* discussions are tedious and stiff; people censor themselves rather than risk being embarrassed by criticism. In contrast, laughter and playfulness are common in the *Divergent Zone.* So are feelings of curiosity and discovery. ("Whoa," said one group member to another. "You mean *that's* your point of view? I had no idea!")

What creates such a difference between the two zones? To a large extent, the answer is simple: *the attitude of suspended judgment.*

Suspended judgment is one of the most important *thinking skills* facilitators can teach their groups. Facilitators can provide groups with opportunities to *experience* suspended judgment through formats like brainstorming and go-arounds. By teaching suspended judgment and by modeling it whenever possible, a respectful, supportive facilitator can create a relaxed, open atmosphere that gives people permission to speak freely – the very essence of divergent thinking.

# FACILITATING SUSTAINABLE AGREEMENTS

THE AGONY OF
THE GROAN ZONE

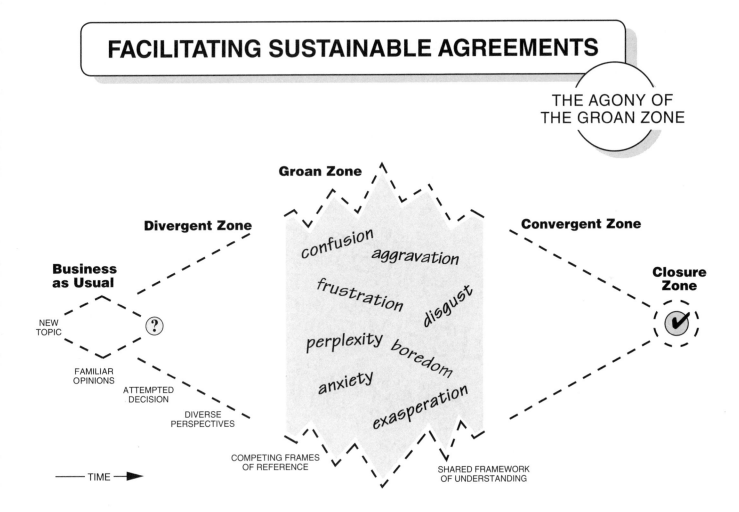

Once a group has expressed several diverging points of view, the members face a quandary. They often don't understand each other's perspectives very well, yet they may not be able to resolve the issue until they *do* understand one other. *This is one of the fundamental difficulties of working in groups.*

Even in groups whose members get along reasonably well, the *Groan Zone* is agonizing. People have to wrestle with foreign concepts and unfamiliar biases. They have to try to understand other people's reasoning – even when that reasoning leads to a conclusion they don't agree with.

The difficulties are compounded by the fact that many people respond awkwardly to this kind of stress. Under pressure, some people lose their focus and start rambling. Others become short-tempered and rude. Some people feel misunderstood and repeat themselves endlessly. Others get so impatient they'll agree to anything: "Let's just get this over with! Now!"

## FACILITATING SUSTAINABLE AGREEMENTS

THE COMMITMENT TO STRUGGLE

Many facilitators, especially beginners, think their task is to prevent people from experiencing the pain and frustration groups face in the *Groan Zone*. *This is a mistake.* The only way to insulate a group from the *Groan Zone* is to block them from doing the stressful, clumsy, necessary hard work of building a shared framework of understanding.

What, then, *is* the facilitator's task in the *Groan Zone?* Essentially, the job is to hang in there – hang in and support people while they struggle to understand each other. Support *them* to hang in there with *each other;* support them not to give up and mentally check out.

The facilitator's tenacity is grounded in a *client-centered attitude* – a faith that the wisdom to solve the problems at hand *will* emerge from the group, as long as people don't give up trying. It is this attitude that allows a facilitator to tolerate the labor pains of authentic collaboration.

# FACILITATING SUSTAINABLE AGREEMENTS

THE CONVERGENT ZONE

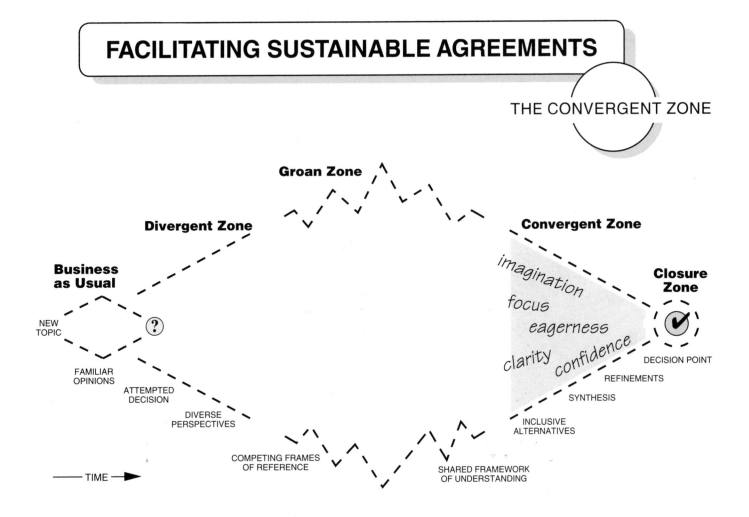

Once a group has developed a shared framework of understanding, thinking feels faster, smoother, easier. The pace of discussion accelerates. People say, "Finally, we're getting something done!" Confidence runs high during this period. People show up on time and stay until the end of the meeting.

The experience of searching for an inclusive solution is stimulating and invigorating. People are surprised to discover how well they seem to understand one another. Members now perceive the group as a team. Years later, many people can still remember the *joyful intensity* of this phase.

Facilitators play a double role during this period of a group's work: sometimes teaching and sometimes getting out of the way. It may be crucial for a facilitator to teach participants how to turn an *Either/Or problem* into a *Both/And solution*. Often the facilitator is the only one who recognizes that *Both/And thinking* is even possible. But for much of the time, a facilitator might be reduced to chartwriting and keeping track of time. When this happens, be happy! It means the facilitation is succeeding.

# FACILITATING SUSTAINABLE AGREEMENTS

THE EXPERIENCE OF
REACHING CLOSURE

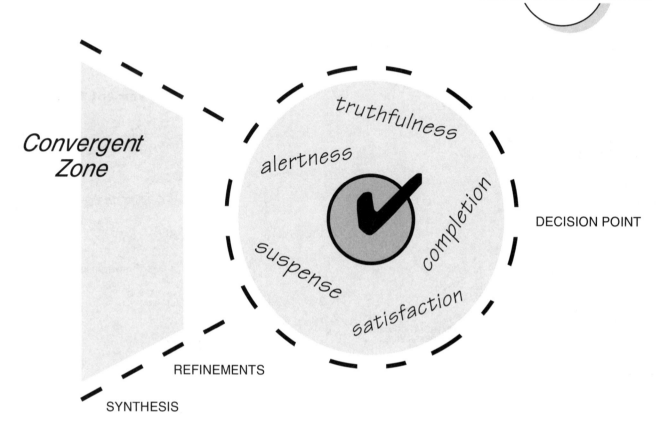

*Convergent
Zone*

truthfulness

alertness

completion

suspense

satisfaction

DECISION POINT

REFINEMENTS

SYNTHESIS

In the *Closure Zone* most people are *focused*. They pay attention to nearly every comment – and most comments are brief and to the point.

These experiences occur, of course, only when the group knows *how the decision will be made*. When a group *does not* have a clear understanding of how they are going to reach closure, the facilitator must look for the earliest opportunity to help the members clarify their decision rules.

Tools for reaching closure are among the most important skills a group can learn. The *Gradients of Agreement Scale* helps members discern the *actual* degree of support for a proposal. Furthermore, a meta-decision procedure allows a group to use different decision rules for different circumstances.

Overall, when group members grasp the principles and mechanics of reaching closure, their group's capacity strengthens dramatically.

# FACILITATING SUSTAINABLE AGREEMENTS

FACILITATOR'S
FOUR FUNCTIONS

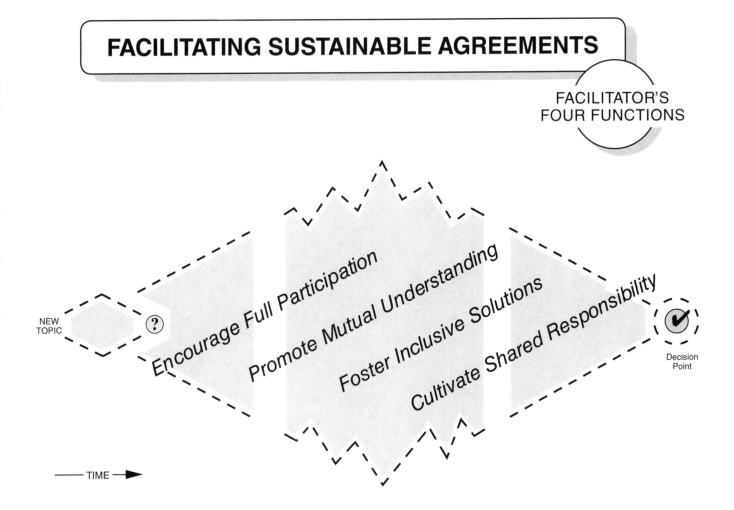

NEW
TOPIC

Encourage Full Participation

Promote Mutual Understanding

Foster Inclusive Solutions

Cultivate Shared Responsibility

Decision
Point

TIME

*The facilitator's mission is to support people to do their best thinking.* The four functions shown above are the guiding principles for enacting that mission.

Embedded in the four functions are the core values of participatory decision-making. They ground the work of group facilitation. They strengthen individuals. They strengthen the whole group. And they enable groups to tap the deep collective wisdom of their membership to develop intelligent, sane, sustainable agreements.

When we facilitate, we are the "delivery system" for participatory values. We embody them, we express them, and we enact them. As such, we are keepers of the flame – we're the advocates, the teachers, and the midwives – for the emergence of inclusive solutions to the world's toughest problems.

# PHOTOCOPYING POLICY

**YES:** Photocopying portions of this book is encouraged for the purpose of supporting a group you are facilitating.

If a group has retained you as a facilitator to help them solve problems and make decisions, and you feel that your group needs to use one or more of the tools presented in this book, feel free to photocopy and distribute the relevant page(s). We want you to be able to use this book to become as effective as possible at facilitating group decision-making.

**NO:** Photocopying portions of this book to conduct fee-for-service training requires our written permission.

If a group has retained you specifically to train them in the process of group facilitation, group decision-making, or a related topic, and your primary role is to serve as their trainer, you may not photocopy these pages without express written permission from *Community At Work*. Our policies are fair and supportive, but please ask first. If you are making money from our work, we will ask you to make a reasonable contribution.

# BIBLIOGRAPHY

Adams, James. *Conceptual Blockbusting* (4th ed.). Cambridge, MA: Perseus Publishing, 2001.

Atlee, Tom. *The Tao of Democracy: Using Co-Intelligence to Create a World That Works for All.* Eugene, OR: Writers Collective, 2003.

Auvine, Brian et al. *A Manual for Group Facilitators.* Madison, WI: Center for Conflict Resolution, 1978.

Avery, Michel et al. *Building United Judgment.* Madison, WI: Center for Conflict Resolution, 1999.

Beer, Jennifer. *The Mediator's Handbook* (4th ed.). Gabriola Island, BC, Canada: New Society Publishers, 2012.

Bens, Ingrid. *Facilitating with Ease! Core Skills for Facilitators, Team Leaders and Members, Managers, Consultants, and Trainers* (3rd ed.). San Francisco: Jossey-Bass, 2012.

Bens, Ingrid. *Facilitation at a Glance.* San Francisco: Jossey-Bass, 2008.

Block, Peter. *Flawless Consulting: A Guide to Getting Your Expertise Used* (3rd ed.). San Francisco: Jossey-Bass/Pfeiffer, 2011.

Block, Peter. *Community: The Structure of Belonging.* San Francisco. Berrett-Koehler, 2009.

Bray, John, Joyce Lee, Linda L. Smith, and Lyle Yorks. *Collaborative Inquiry in Practice: Action Reflection and Making Meaning.* Thousand Oaks, CA: Sage Publications, 2000.

Brown, Juanita and David Isaacs. *World Café: Shaping Our Futures Though Conversations That Matter.* San Francisco: Berrett-Koehler Publishers, 2005.

Bunker, Barbara and Billie T. Alban. *The Handbook of Large Group Methods: Creating Systemic Change in Organizations and Communities.* San Francisco: Jossey-Bass, 2007.

Butler, C.T. Lawrence and Amy Rothstein. *On Conflict and Consensus.* Cambridge, MA: Food Not Bombs Publishing, 1991.

Cameron, Esther. *Facilitation Made Easy.* London, UK: Kogan Page Limited, 2005.

Carpenter, Susan and W.J.D. Kennedy. *Managing Public Disputes.* San Francisco: Jossey-Bass, 2001.

Chambers, Robert. *Participatory Workshops: A Sourcebook of 21 Sets of Ideas & Activities.* London, UK: Earthscan, 2012.

Chrislip, David and Carl E. Larsen. *Collaborative Leadership: How Citizens and Civic Leaders Can Make a Difference.* San Francisco: Jossey-Bass, 1994.

Chrislip, David. *The Collaborative Leadership Fieldbook.* San Francisco: Jossey-Bass, 2002.

Cochran, Alice Collier. *Roberta's Rules of Order: Sail Through Meetings for Stellar Results Without the Gavel.* San Francisco: Jossey-Bass, 2004.

Conklin, Jeff. *Dialogue Mapping: Building Shared Understanding of Wicked Problems.* West Sussex, UK: John Wiley & Sons, Ltd., 2006.

Crutchfield, Leslie and Heather Mcleod Grant. *Forces for Good: The Six Practices of High Impact Non-profits.* San Francisco: Jossey-Bass, 2008.

Danskin, Karl and Lenny Lind. *Technology + Design for High Engagement in Large Groups.* San Francisco, CA: Jossey-Bass, 2014.

de Bono, Edward. *Lateral Thinking.* New York: Harper and Row, 2009.

de Bono, Edward. *Serious Creativity.* New York: Harper Collins, 1993.

Doyle, Michael and David Straus. *How to Make Meetings Work.* New York: Berkeley Books, 1993.

Dressler, Larry. *Consensus Through Conversation.* San Francisco: Berrett-Koehler, 2006.

Dressler, Larry. *Standing in the Fire.* San Francisco: Berrett-Koehler, 2010.

Earl, Sarah, Fred Carden, Michael Quinn Patten, and Terry Smutylo. *Outcome Mapping: Building, Learning and Reflection into Development Programs.* Ottawa, ON, Canada: International Development Research Center, 2001.

Estes, Caroline. "Consensus." *In Context* (Autumn 1984): 19-22.

Fisher, Roger, William Ury, and Bruce Patton. *Getting to Yes* (2nd ed.). New York: Penguin Books, 2011.

Fisk, Sarah. *Psychological Effects of Involvement in Ecological Restoration.* Ann Arbor, MI: University Microfilms International, 1995.

Gastil, John. *Democracy in Small Groups.* Gabriola Island, B.C.: New Society Publishers, 1998.

Gastil, John and Peter Levine. *Deliberative Democracy Handbook: Strategies for Effective Civic Engagement in the Twenty-First Century.* San Francisco: Jossey-Bass, 2005.

Gesell, Izzy. *Playing Along: 37 Group Learning Activities Borrowed from Improvisational Theater.* Northhampton, MA: Whole Person Associates, 1997.

Gray, Barbara. *Collaborating.* San Francisco: Jossey-Bass, 1989.

Hansen, Morton. *Collaboration.* Cambridge, MA: Harvard Business Press, 2009.

Harwood, Richard. *The Work of Hope.* Dayton, OH. The Kettering Foundation, 2012.

Hogan, Christine. *Understanding Facilitation: Theory & Principles.* London, UK: Kogan Page Limited, 2005.

Hogan, Christine. *Practical Facilitation.* London, UK: Kogan Page Limited, 2003.

Howard, V.A. and J.H. Barton. *Thinking Together*. New York: William Morrow and Company, 1992.

Howell, Johnna L. *Tools for Facilitating Team Meetings*. Seattle, WA: Integrity Publishing, 1995.

Hunt, Dale. *The Art of Facilitation: The Essentials for Leading Great Meetings and Creating Group Synergy*. San Francisco: Jossey-Bass, 2009.

Iacofano, Daniel. *Meeting of the Minds: A Guide to Successful Meeting Facilitation*. Berkeley, CA: MIG Communications, 2001.

Janis, Irving. *Victims of Groupthink* (2nd ed.). Boston: Houghton-Mifflin, 1972.

Janis, Irving and Leon Mann. *Decision Making*. New York: The Free Press, 1977.

Johnson, David W. and Frank P. Johnson. *Joining Together*. Englewood Cliffs, NJ: Prentice-Hall, 1975.

Justice, Tom and David Jamieson. *The Facilitator's Fieldbook* (3rd ed.). N.Y: Anacom, 2012.

Kaner, Sam. "Working Effectively in Groups: Developing Your Collaborative Mindset." In *Discover Your Inner Strength*. Sevierville, TN: Insight Publishing, 2009.

Kaner, Sam. "Promoting Mutual Understanding for Effective Collaboration in Cross-Functional Groups with Multiple Stakeholders." In Schuman, Sandy, ed. *The IAF Handbook of Group Facilitation: Best Practices from the Leading Organization in Facilitation*. San Francisco: Jossey-Bass, 2005.

Kaner, Sam. "Five Transformational Leaders Discuss What They've Learned." In Schuman, Sandy, ed. *Creating a Culture of Collaboration: The International Association of Facilitators Handbook*. San Francisco: Jossey-Bass, 2006.

Kaner, Sam, Eileen Palmer, and Duane Berger. "What Can O.D. Professionals Learn From Grassroots Peace Activists?" *Vision/Action*, 9 (1989): 8-12.

Kania, John and Mark Kramer. "Embracing Emergence: How Collective Impact Addresses Complexity." Stanford Social Innovation Review, 63, Winter 2011.

Kearny, Lynn. *The Facilitator's Toolkit*. Amherst, MA: HRD Press, 1995.

Kepner, C.H. and B.B. Tregoe. *The New Rational Manager*. Princeton, NJ: Kepner-Tregoe, 1997.

Kolb, Deborah M. and Associates, *When Talk Works: Profiles of Mediators*. San Francisco: Jossey-Bass, 1997.

Lakey, George, Berit Lakey, Rod Napier, and Janice M. Robinson. *Grassroots and Nonprofit Leadership: A Guide for Organizations in Changing Times*. Gabriola Island, B.C.: New Society Publishers, 1996.

Lind, Lenny with Karl Danskin and Todd Erickson. "Interactive Meeting Technologies." In Bunker, Barbara, and Billie T. Alban. *The Handbook of Large Group Methods: Creating Systemic Change in Organizations and Communities*. San Francisco: Jossey-Bass, 2006.

Means, Janet A. and Tammy Adams. *Facilitating the Project Lifecycle: The Skills & Tools to Accelerate Progress for Project Managers, Facilitators, and Six Sigma Project Teams.* San Francisco: Jossey-Bass, 2005

Michalko, Michael. *Thinkertoys.* Berkeley, CA: Ten Speed Press, 2012.

Nelson, Jo. *The Art of Focused Conversation for Schools.* Gabriola Island, BC, Canada: New Society Publishers, 2013.

Nutt, Paul C. *Making Tough Decisions.* San Francisco: Jossey-Bass, 1989.

Osborne, Alex. *Applied Imagination: Principles and Procedures of Creative Problem-Solving* (3rd ed.). Hadley, MA.: Creative Education Foundation, 1993.

Owen, Harrison. *Open Space Technology: A User's Guide.* San Francisco: Berrett-Koehler Publishers, 2008.

Parker, Marjorie. *Creating Shared Vision.* Clarendon Hills, IL: Dialog International, Ltd., 1991.

Patterson, Kerry, Joseph Grenny, Ron McMillan, Al Switzler, and Stephen R. Covey. *Crucial Conversations: Tools for Talking When Stakes are High.* New York: McGraw-Hill, 2002.

Phillips, Gerald M. and Julia T. Wood. *Emergent Issues in Human Decision Making.* Carbondale, IL: Southern Illinois University Press, 1984.

Roberts, Joan M. *Alliances, Coalitions and Partnerships: Building Collaborative Organizations.* Gabriola Island, BC, Canada: New Society Publishers, 2004.

Rogers, Carl R. *The Carl Rogers Reader.* Edited by Howard Kirschenbaum and Valerie Land Henderson. Boston: Houghton Mifflin, 1989.

Russo, J. Edward and Paul J.H. Shoemaker. *Decision Traps.* New York: Simon and Schuster, 1990.

Schein, Edgar. *Humble Inquiry: The Gentle Art of Asking Instead of Telling.* San Francisco: Berrett-Koehler, 2013.

Schrage, Michael. *Shared Minds: The New Technologies of Collaboration.* New York: Random House, 1990.

Schuman, Sandy. *The IAF Handbook of Group Facilitation: Best Practices from the Leading Organization in Facilitation.* San Francisco: Jossey-Bass, 2007.

Schuman, Sandy. *Creating a Culture of Collaboration: The International Association of Facilitators Handbook.* San Francisco: Jossey-Bass, 2006.

Schwarz, Roger. *The Skilled Facilitator.* San Francisco: Jossey-Bass, 2002.

Senge, Peter M., Art Kleiner, Charlotte Roberts, Rick Ross and Bryan Smith. *The Fifth Discipline Fieldbook.* New York: Currency, 1994.

Sheeran, Michael J. *Beyond Majority Rule.* Philadelphia: Philadelphia Yearly Meeting of the Religious Society of Friends, Book Services Committee, 1983.

Shields, Katrina. *In the Tiger's Mouth: An Empowerment Guide for Social Action.* Philadelphia and Gabriola Island, B.C.: New Society Publishers, 1994.

Sibbet, David. *Visual Meetings: How Graphics, Sticky Notes and Idea Mapping Can Transform Group Productivity.* Hoboken, NJ: John Wiley & Sons, 2010.

Sibbet, David. *Visual Teams: Graphic Tools for Commitment, Innovation and High Performance.* Hoboken, NJ: John Wiley & Sons, 2011.

Sibbet, David. *Visual Leaders: New Tools for Visioning, Management and Organization Change.* Hoboken, NJ: John Wiley & Sons, 2012.

Spencer, Laura J. *Winning through Participation.* Dubuque, IA: Kendall/Hunt Publishing Co., 1989.

Stanfield, R. Brian. *The Workshop Book: From Individual Creativity to Group Action.* Gabriola Isalnd, BC, Canada: New Society Publishers, 2002.

Stone, Douglas, Bruce Patton, Sheila Heen, and Roger Fisher. *Difficult Conversations: How to Discuss What Matters Most.* New York: Penguin Books, 2000.

Strachan, Dorothy. *Making Questions Work: A Guide to How and What to Ask for Facilitators, Consultants, Managers, Coaches, and Educators.* San Francisco: Jossey-Bass, 2006.

Straker, David. *Rapid Problem-Solving with Post-It Notes.* Cambridge: De Capo Press, 1997.

Straus, David. *How to Make Collaboration Work: Powerful Ways to Build Consensus, Solve Problems, and Make Decisions.* San Francisco: Berrett-Koehler Publishers, 2010.

Tabaka, Jean. *Collaboration Explained: Facilitiation Skills for Software Project Leaders.* NJ: Addison-Wesley Professional, 2006.

Toldi, Catherine. *Collaborative Thinking: Becoming a Community That Learns.* Ann Arbor, MI: University Microfilms International, 1993.

Troxel, James P. *Participation Works: Business Cases from Around the World.* Alexandra, VA: Miles River Press, 1993.

VanGundy, Jr., Arthur B. *Techniques of Structured Problem-Solving* (2nd ed.). New York: John Wiley & Sons,1998.

Weisbord, Marvin. *Productive Workplaces, Revisited: Organizing and Managing for Dignity, Meaning and Community in the 21st Century* (3rd ed.). San Francisco: Jossey-Bass/Pfeiffer, 2012.

Williams, R. Bruce. *More Than Fifty Ways to Build Team Consensus.* Palatine, IL: IRI/Skylight Publishing, 2006.

Wilkinson, Michael. *The Secrets of Facilitation: The Smart Guide to Getting Results with Groups.* San Francisco: Jossey-Bass, 2012.

Wilson, Priscilla H. *The Facilitative Way: Leadership That Makes the Difference.* Shawnee Mission, KS: Team Tech Press, 2003.

# ACKNOWLEDGMENTS

The first and most important acknowledgment goes to our N.S.P. editor, Barbara Hirshkowitz, whose vision and commitment to this project is the reason this book exists. In early 1988 Barbara took Sam and Duane on a retreat and convinced us to write a serious theoretical book on participatory decision-making. Over the next four years, with help from an ever-changing team of co-thinkers, we wrote countless drafts and felt dissatisfied with them all. Barbara patiently encouraged us to keep going. In late 1993, Barbara saw that we had produced about a hundred pages of facilitation tools, and she persuaded us to publish the book you are now reading. So Barbara shepherded us through two years more of revising and adding and reorganizing and ambivalating . . . And finally, thanks to Barbara's unwavering faith and persistence, you have in hand the results of her labor.

Second acknowledgment goes to Kathe Sweeney, our Jossey-Bass editor. Kathe was instrumental in bringing both the second and third editions into existence. Without Kathe's perseverance and patience, we would not have even contemplated either of these editions, much less written them. Beyond our editorial relationship, we are also deeply grateful to Kathe for her vision and stewardship in the world of group facilitation. She has been midwife to many important books on collaboration, facilitation, and participatory values – books that may never have been written without her support and gentle guidance. In the true sense of the word, Kathe Sweeney is a leader in our field.

We also want to acknowledge and thank Mark Karmendy, production wizard at Jossey-Bass. In this edition, like the prior two, the authors drew and formatted the entire manuscript. The complexities of publishing this way in the digital era are huge, and we were ready to throw in the towel more than once. With a less seasoned and less flexible production manager than Mark there might well not have been a third edition. Thank you Mark, for your patience and good humor and your can-do support.

We also want to express our enduring gratitude to Shelley Woodman, our *Community At Work* colleague. Shelley engaged with us on the third edition from its inception. We endlessly drew on her wisdom, her penetrating intellect and her unflappable goodwill. She was a sounding board, a graphic artist, a literary critic, an editor, an archivist, a logistics savant and she has been a generous, gracious host and tireless support for the entire edition, start to finish.

Nelli Noakes was a major contributor to the success of the third edition, working evenings and weekends from the moment she joined *Community At Work* in 2013. She was in effect the second or third author for several chapters, notably chapter 14 (*Classic Facilitator Dilemmas*) and chapter 21 (*Teaching A Group About Group Dynamics*). She was clearly a co-author for the new pages in chapters 4, 5, 8, 9, 11, 17, 18, 19, and 20. Every page touched by Nelli benefited from her commitment to excellence. She was determined to keep wrestling with the challenge of that page until we found a resolution that would help and satisfy the reader. The book is smarter and more useful thanks to Nelli's involvement.

Many other colleagues contributed to the development and production of the third edition. We discovered that Liz Flynn, our fabulous, hard-working logistics coordinator, is also an incredibly talented copy editor and proof-reader. Liz spotted more mistakes in punctuation, spelling and grammar than all the rest of us put together. Francesco Kaner wrote vivid outlines and sharply focused drafts of more than 30 pages, and he edited at least a hundred more. His editorial suggestions were insightful and succinct. Both Liz and Francesco also spent many hours on the tedious production details of translating our manuscript from *Illustrator* to *Word* and back again. Without all the heavy lifting by Liz and Francesco, we would still be copying and pasting to this very day!

We also are grateful to Wade Shows for his sage advice and his many astute suggestions, and for his generous production assistance at crunch time. Thanks also to Anna Hastings and Katie Kopacz for their help with typesetting, and to Natacha Sagalovsky for her help with project management.

For new cases that appear in this edition, we are grateful for the professional generosity of Leah Hall, Junious Williams, Edie Brown, Corinne Shindelar, Alex Beamer, Michael Lisman and Linda Colburn. We also thank Sandy Heierbacher and Nancy White for sharing insights for a chapter we ultimately decided not to write, on facilitating in virtual environments.

Many colleagues and friends contributed to the development of the second edition. We are particularly indebted to Libby Bachhuber, who joined the staff of *Community At Work* in 1999, and who worked diligently for the next six years to help us improve the logic of our most frequently used pages. Libby's insights into the application of those tools led to numerous upgrades. She was the person who kept track of all revisions that found their way into this edition. Her determination to get the details right inspired us to keep working to clarify our reasoning and strengthen our writing.

Susan Lubeck and Sunny Sabbini also joined the staff of *Community At Work* in 1999, and both contributed in many ways to the development of material for the second edition. Susan, during her time at *Community At Work*, put much effort into strengthening our tools for reaching closure. Many of the revisions in our chapters on decision-making were occasioned by her suggestions. Also, she drew from her broad experience to give us many ideas for other improvements. Sunny, in her role as client relations coordinator, collected feedback from countless readers on the book's strengths and improvables. She thus provided us with a steady stream of suggestions for making the book more useful to our audience.

Many other people deserve to be mentioned for their suggestions or their help in preparing the manuscript for the second edition. Evi Kahle was a constant source of assistance and advice in 1995-2000. Diane Dohm assisted with the editing of our materials in 2002-03. Buffy Balderston assisted with editing and production in 2004-06. Karen Jovin gave us many useful ideas for improving Chapter 3. Roxane White provided incredibly helpful editorial assistance during the final stage of editing. Thanks to each of you for the many ways your support made this book a better product.

Several people pointed us to books and articles for the bibliography. Thanks to Miriam Abrams, Carmen Acton, Muriel Adcock, Teresa Archaga, Kate Armstrong, Emmanuel Asomba, Susan Auerbach, Vicky Baugh, Candee Basford, Lisa Behrendt, Leslie Boies, Tree Bressen, Trish Cypher, Shoshanna Cogan, Lisa DeGroot, Stacey Duccini, Anne Forbes, Scott Gassman, Gayle Gifford, Michael Hailu, Gloria Hargrove, Doug Horton, Cynthia Josayma, Julie King, Eliska Meyers, Jady Dederich Montgomery, Kathryn Moran, Cookie Murphy/Pettee, Wayne Nelson, Evan Paul, Laura Peck, Jim Roscoe, Cathy Stones, Mady Shumofsky, and Odin Zackman. Thank you each for your thoughtfulness and your generosity.

Many colleagues and friends influenced the development of the first edition of this book. Herman Gyr and Eileen Palmer deserve to be singled out for first honors. Each made deeply significant contributions over several years time. We hold them both in gratitude and high esteem. Marianne Laruffa gave her wholehearted support and encouragement to this project in its earliest forms, from 1988–1990. Rick Peterson helped refine the organization and logic of early drafts in 1990–91. David Barkan in 1990 was the first "road-tester" of the meta-decision-making procedures in Chapter 19. Pat Morris in 1990-91 co-authored the second draft of our collection of structured thinking activities. Gene Bush, who since 1992 has given us countless hours of perceptive editorial advice, also provided the insightful critique which led us to discover the Groan Zone. Jim MacQueen co-authored a 1992 draft of the decision-making chapters. David Kirkpatrick co-authored early drafts of two structured thinking activities. Amaran Tarnoff co-authored early drafts of many pages for Chapter 7. Nancy Feinstein drafted an introduction to Chapter 7. Julie King copyedited a draft of the full manuscript. Ritch Davidson co-authored two structured thinking activities. Michael Tertes co-authored drafts of six case studies for Chapter 16. He also co-authored early drafts of four structured thinking activities. Ritch Davidson, Rob Lawrence, Mitch Glanz, Nancy Feinstein, and Melanie Burnett were readers for the final draft. Sam Fisk was the behind-the-scenes maestro who kept everything running smoothly. Evi Kahle edited and contributed to the logic of Chapters 6, 14, 15, 16 and 20, and her dedication and enthusiasm sustained us through our last year of writing.

We would like to extend our appreciation to the proprietors of the cafes where much of this book was actually written. In San Francisco thanks to *Farley's, Cup O' Blues, The Daily Scoop, Thinker's Cafe, La Boheme, Radio Valencia,* and *Sally's.* In Aptos, a nod to the *Red Apple Cafe.* Also, a special thank you to a special host. Desideriamo ringraziare i proprietari della Nave in Sperlonga, per le affabili ed affettuose attenzioni elargite a Sam mentre scriveva le revisioni di questo libro. Il calore umano ed un illimitato senso di ospitalità di tutta la famiglia hanno lasciato un profondo segno che può ancora essere sentito tra le righe di ogni pagina. We want to express our gratitude to the proprietors of *La Nave* in Sperlonga, Italy, who treated Sam so graciously while he wrote the first revisions of this book. The whole family's warmth and their boundless hospitality left an afterglow that can still be felt between the lines on every page.

Last, our deep appreciation goes to Gene Bush, Monika Steger and Paul Blakely. You opened your homes and your hearts to us, and loaned us your partners – often at personal sacrifice. You share our success as your own.

# THE AUTHORS

**SAM KANER, Ph.D.**

Sam Kaner is the founder of *Community At Work*. His first full-time job as a facilitator was in 1978. In the decades since, he has dedicated his career to studying and teaching collaborative processes, and to consulting with innovative organizations that seek sustainable solutions to the world's toughest problems.

**LENNY LIND**

Lenny Lind is the founder and chairman of the organization development firm Covision. He is a pioneer in the field of technology-assisted meetings – utilizing high-speed connectivity to facilitate high engagement and alignment in large groups. Lenny co-created the original design of this book.

**CATHERINE TOLDI, M.A.**

Catherine Toldi is a collaboration specialist and Zen Buddhist priest. She specializes in working with non-profit managers, educators, and community organizations. For 37 years, she has supported her clients and students to bring both structure and heart to their planning and problem-solving efforts.

**SARAH FISK, Ph.D.**

Sarah Fisk is an organization development consultant and psychologist specializing in multi-stakeholder collaboration and systems change. As a senior associate at *Community At Work,* she devotes her career to supporting groups and individuals to develop sustainable solutions to complex situations.

**DUANE BERGER, M.A.**

Duane Berger has been associated with *Community At Work* since its founding in 1987. As director of *Insights and Applications*, he has studied group dynamics for decades, and he has been a co-thinker / co-developer of all *Community At Work* models and methods for putting participatory values into practice.

# INDEX

public, 202; irresistible distraction happens outside of meeting room, 225; key influencer has to arrive late or leave early, 224; low participation by the entire group, 216; lunch arrives early, 218; many people interrupting one another, 217; minimal participation by members who don't feel invested in topic, 219; not enough wall space to hang flipcharts, 218; one or two silent members, 220; out-of-context distractions, 205; overcoming tendency to defer to person-in-charge, 208; participant shares view with facilitator in private but not in meeting, 225; people keep checking their smartphones, 225; people overwhelmed by the range of open threads, 222; people treating one another disrespectfully, 217; poor follow-through on assignments, 219; quibbling about trivial procedures, 226; rambling discussion, 222; several different topics being discussed at once, 217; side conversations and whispered chuckles, 220; someone becomes strident and repetitive, 226; someone discovers a completely new problem, 226; someone makes a comment someone else finds offensive, 224; something happened earlier and now meeting is going badly, 223; stepping out of the content and talking about process, 212; strengthening relationships, 209; supporting diverse communication styles, 200; supportive attitude in action, 203; two people locking horns, 220; whole group interventions for difficult communication styles, 201

Difficult people, 198

Divergent thinking, 6–19; managing divergent perspectives, 106

Divergent Zone, 266; facilitating in, 267–268, 277; how has this affected me, 274; mind mapping, 272; speaking from your own perspective, 269; specifying requirements, 271; starting positions, 273; three complaints, 275; unrepresented perspectives, 276; who, what, when, where and how, 270

Doyle and Straus fallback, 350

Drawing people out, 45, 105; acknowledging feelings, 54; and linking, 58; listening for the logic, 59

**E**

Early discussion, 8

Either/Or mind-set, 236

Empathizing, 56

Encouraging, 50, 102; and linking, 58

Enter the center, 140

The Enterprise case study, 245

# CoVISION

Covision is an organization development firm that supports clients with design and production capabilities for gaining alignment and convergence in large, important meetings.

Covision's primary approach uses customized software running on a network of tablet computers distributed to participants in small groups across a meeting. This groupware system makes it possible for participants to actually *participate* – having short discussions and giving ideas in response to presentations and other inquiries. The large volume of input is distilled into themes and then responded to by presenters or persons-in-charge. In this way, even very large groups are able to build shared understanding and alignment in time frames commonly spent on *presenting and reporting* only.

Over 20 years, Covision has supported hundreds of facilitators and consultants with this participant-centered approach. In many of their cases, an upcoming meeting was seen as critical to their client's organization. So extra resources were provided to ensure the best outcomes. This is where Covision adds the most value – supporting facilitators as they provide fast-feedback capabilities to their clients. Covision provides expertise on, for example, planning the agenda, selecting various fast-feedback processes, making transitions, managing difficult dynamics, or coaching the persons-in-charge. We consult from the side.

This methodology has proven effective in groups of 25 to 5,000 participants. In the first Clinton Global Initiative conference in New York, 800 world leaders spent two days in interactive panel discussions enabled by Covision. The mayor of Washington, DC, held four Citizen Summits, each engaging 3,000 citizens with fast-feedback processes. Covision has supported the World Economic Forum, multi-stakeholder summits, and scores of Fortune 500 companies in executive-level alignment meetings.

For further information, call Lenny Lind at +1(415) 810-8194.

# COMMUNITY AT WORK

Since its founding in 1987, *Community At Work* has been both a think tank and a consulting firm. Our motto is "building models of collaboration and putting them into practice."

**AS A THINK TANK**  Our purpose is to study the actual dynamics of collaboration and group decision-making – and to build more accurate models – in order to support people to find sustainable solutions to the world's toughest problems.

We take pride in combining insights from psychology and the other human sciences with the practical ingenuity of the business community, grounded in a philosophy of social responsibility.

**AS A CONSULTING FIRM**  We are organization development professionals. We specialize in providing collaborative approaches that enable our clients to address their most perplexing, system-level challenges.

Our services have been put to good use in many different work settings, from high tech to health care. Over time we have developed content-expertise in social entrepreneurship, community-based planning, and social enterprise. We also have numerous clients in education, human services, environmental health and international development.

To support our clients in their work we employ a variety of consulting competencies: we assess and diagnose; we facilitate; we coach; we create, test and produce relevant models; we project-manage; we advise; we conduct training to build capacity – all this and more, as dictated by the needs at hand.

A distinctive feature of our work is a determination to support our clients to think *intelligently* about the challenges they face. We are committed to helping people learn skills for putting participatory values into practice. To this end we provide clients with training in the concepts and skills of collaboration.

During the past 25 years, thousands of people have strengthened their facilitation skills at workshops offered by *Community At Work*.

## GROUP FACILITATION SKILLS
### PUTTING PARTICIPATORY VALUES INTO PRACTICE

This acclaimed 3-day workshop provides experiential training in the methods from *Facilitator's Guide to Participatory Decision-Making*. The program gives participants numerous opportunities to practice new skills and receive feedback. Internationally recognized for its effectiveness at building capacity in the essentials of collaboration, it has been provided to hundreds of organizations and communities around the world, under the sponsorship of organizations as diverse as United Nations, Kaiser Permanente, CGIAR, Burning Man, VISA, Wikimedia Foundation, University of California, World Bank, and a broad range of foundations, CBOs, businesses, schools, NGOs, and federal, state, provincial and local government agencies.

## LEADER AS FACILITATOR
### GROUP FACILITATION SKILLS FOR MANAGERS

This workshop is specifically tailored for project managers, unit supervisors, and others who are responsible for heading up work teams. The course emphasizes methods for balancing the responsibilities of leadership with the goal of reaching decisions that everyone owns and supports. Participants have ample opportunity to practice and receive feedback. At the request of our clients, this program has often been customized to meet specialized objectives. Variations of this workshop have been delivered at many large organizations, including Applied Materials, Symantec, Hewlett-Packard, PricewaterhouseCoopers, Charles Schwab, Mercer, SanDisk, Prudential and a variety of other Fortune 1000 companies.

### For more information

*Community At Work*
1 Tubbs Street
San Francisco, CA 94107

Phone: (415) 282-9876
www.CommunityAtWork.com
Email: Kaner@CommunityAtWork.com